OUT OF THE BLUE

DEPRESSION

AND

HUMAN

NATURE

David B. Cohen

W.W. NORTON & COMPANY

NEW YORK / LONDON

Printed in the United States of America

First Edition

The text of this book is composed in Palatino
with the display set in Gill Sans Condensed.
Composition and manufacturing by The Maple-Vail
Book Manufacturing Group.
Book design by Jo Anne Metsch.

Library of Congress Cataloging-in-Publication Data

Cohen, David B., 1941–
Out of the Blue : depression and human nature / David B. Cohen.
p.   cm.
Includes bibliographical references and index.
1. Depression, Mental.   I. Title.
RC537.C633   1994
616.85'27—dc20   93-36566

ISBN 0-393-03632-4

W. W. Norton & Company, Inc., 500 Fifth Avenue, New York, N.Y. 10110
W. W. Norton & Company, Ltd., 10 Coptic Street, London WC1A 1PU

1 2 3 4 5 6 7 8 9 0

CONTENTS

PART 4: IDEOLOGY AND ANTIDOTE

TO THE READER

"Out of the Blue" is a play on words implying that insights into human nature will come from exploring depression. It also implies that the exploration can yield much that is surprising—in the negative sense, for example, depression often strikes without warning and for no obvious reason, but in the positive sense too, for example, liability to depression often goes along with courage, ambition, and creativity. Finally, "out of the blue" implies that out of genetic "blueprints" come core qualities: competencies, personality traits, and vulnerabilities that define not just our species but ourselves. Out of which comes a most curious insight: We individuals are unique but improbable—given the chancy roll of genetic and environmental "dice," how could we ever *be*? Yet, once the roll is made and we are here, everything changes to highly probable—given the demands and constraints of our inner nature, *how could we ever be otherwise?* Despite our feelings of being in control, despite our sense of free will, once the roll is made it would seem that we are shaped by inner forces about which we have little or no awareness or insight. How then like a dream is our life: compelling yet illusory, timeless yet fleeting, with chaotic and creative qualities that make it mysterious, but lawful and mechanical qualities that make it understandable.

Our exploration can be thought of as an odyssey through psychological realms, some ordinary, some extraordinary. We begin in the extraordinary realm of mental illness, with a special look at depression and suicide. By magnifying the natural elements of the psyche—by creating a caricature of the comedic, tragic, and heroic aspects of life—mental illness opens a window on human nature enabling a better understanding of our own experience. Mental life is a balancing act of competing tendencies to be selfish and generous, impulsive and cautious, fanciful and realistic, optimistic and pessimistic. With the loss of inner checks and balances, these tendencies spill out in behavior that is abnormally self-centered, irrational, moody, disorganized, and socially inappropriate—in a word, dysfunctional. This shift toward suffering, delusion, and self-destruction can sometimes produce existential crises involving a life-or-death struggle within the self that can end in suicide.

Answers to questions raised about human nature are further pursued as our odyssey continues in the more ordinary realm of everyday behavior where psychological defensiveness and the instinct for biased, even irrational, thinking commonly impede accurate understanding of ourselves and our origins no less than of mental illness and its causes. Finally, in the extraordinary realm of scientific investigation, we explore a special style of thinking that, in its playful and creative as well as critical and objective elements, can yield definitive answers to pressing questions raised in the other two realms. In each realm, we discover tendencies that might otherwise have escaped our attention—to be habit-bound and defensive, therefore predictable, yet spontaneous and inventive, therefore full of surprises. By odyssey's end, we gain a greater appreciation of who we are and where we come from.

To make good storytelling out of the proposed exploration, I have tried to promote what historians Will and Ariel Durant would recognize as industry, art, and philosophy—industry in ferreting out key facts, art in bringing meaningful order out of the chaos of information, and philosophy in the search for perspective, insight, and enlightenment. To ensure readability and authenticity, I have cast a wide net for diverse opinions—from ivory-tower academics to real-world people, some professional, some not. Whatever their intellectual or political persuasion—and whether or not they agreed with what they were reading—

their contributions made possible a book that turned out far better than I had reason to expect.

I begin with Cathy Wick and Sandy Lifland, my tough yet fair-minded editors, who brought to this project an extraordinary combination of resources: knowledge of psychology, expertise with language, and a sense of fair play—but more, an uncanny ability to recognize and reinforce another's ideas without unduly imposing theirs. I owe a special debt of gratitude to two other people whose invaluable suggestions and take-no-prisoners attitude toward writing ensured a larger measure of plain talk, clear exposition, and helpful examples than my inclinations would otherwise have called up. Special thanks, then, to my wife, Leslie who put up with more than I care to tell, and to my secretary Kirsten Bradbury who put up with less, but still more than her fair share.

I am grateful to many others who surely deserve—but, alas, cannot expect to receive—more than heartfelt thanks. At the risk of being too selective, I acknowledge the special contributions of the following people: first, Paul O'Connell and Mylan Jaixen whose encouragement, good council, and enthusiastic support for the project during its pre-Norton phase will be remembered with a mixture of gratitude and fondness. Thanks too to David Alexander, Jim Camp, Robert Cocke, Claire Crosby, Augustin de la Peña, Alicia Dunn, Steve Finn, Redge Greenberg, Gerry Metalsky, and Stanton Samenow—and to others whose extensive critical contributions helped in even more substantial ways to ensure a felicitous development of the manuscript. Some of these were at the University of Texas (UT) at Austin: Frank Donahue, John Loehlin, and finally, Kathy McIver to whom I am additionally grateful for her help with digging up historical material for Chapter 1. Others include Jason Cohen, Ron Finke, Vicky Rakoff, and Allan Rakoff. Three other people deserve special acknowledgment—University of Texas psychology professors and colleagues Arnold Buss, Joe Horn, and Lee Willerman. This book bears the silent stamp of their influence on my thinking about theory and data, for which, as I'm sure they already know, I am forever in their debt.

Finally, for their enthusiasm and optimism about the project, and for their unwavering encouragement and excellent council right from the outset, my enduring gratitude and admiration go to Betty Sue Flowers (poet, editor, and UT professor of English), Hsi-ling Cheng (professor emeritus of Chinese studies, University of Northern Iowa), and Del Thiessen (sociobiologist and UT professor of psychology). These three extraordinary people, with radically different views on life, have nevertheless left their mark on my work, but more important, on me. From Betty Sue, in particular, I gained a greater appreciation of the poetic element in human nature, and of the excellent psychology discoverable in great literature and in the insights of its teachers. From Hsi-ling, I gained a deeper appreciation (alas, not mastery) of the difficult arts of tempering facts with metaphor, of placing psychological observations in historical and cultural context, and of always striving to balance empiricism and intuition. From Del, I gained a deeper appreciation of the biological foundations of human nature—our place in the evolutionary scheme of things—and of the desirability of looking for the silver lining whatever else might be suggested by the evidence or one's intuition. Finally, from all three, I gained a deeper appreciation of how literature and science can be understood as complementary aspects of the same timeless search for the truth.

August 1993
Austin, Texas

Deep into the snow mountains my search has led me. Now I have it fast. My dream has given it to me, in utter clearness, that I may know it forever.

—THOMAS MANN
The Magic Mountain

PART ONE

A ROLE OF THE DICE

Ay, in the very temple of delight
  Veiled Melancholy has her sovran shrine,
    Though seen of none save him whose strenuous tongue
    Can burst Joy's grape against his palate fine:
His soul shall taste the sadness of her might,
  And be among her cloudy trophies hung.

                              —JOHN KEATS
                              Ode on Melancholy

1

THE GHOST IN
ROBERT FITZROY'S CLOSET

On a Sunday morning in August 1822, Robert Stewart committed suicide by slitting his throat; he was fifty-three years old. His gruesome death cut short the illustrious political and diplomatic career of England's great foreign secretary. Stewart, better known as Viscount Castlereagh (pronounced CASTLE ray), was a key player on the stage of international politics. Perhaps even more than his celebrated Austrian counterpart, Metternich, Castlereagh guided the Grand Alliance that defeated Napoleon and kept the peace. A distinguished national leader and near-indispensable confidant of King George IV, Castlereagh might even have become prime minister. Prior to his tragic descent into the depths of paranoia and despair, Castlereagh seemed reasonably free of any mental illness signaling a self-destructive potential that would culminate in a catastrophic nervous breakdown.

On a Sunday morning in April 1865, Robert Fitzroy committed suicide by slitting his throat; he was fifty-nine years old. Like Castlereagh, Fitzroy (1805–1865) was an extraordinary man, intelligent, ambitious, and accomplished. His work for almost ten years as a ship's captain had culminated in high honor. In 1837, the Royal Geographic Society awarded him their gold medal for what was glowingly described in the House of Commons as a "splendid survey" of South American coasts.

Later he invented a barometer that bore his name, and still later became chief of England's Meteorological Office and responsible for weather forecasting. In 1863, he published a revised edition of his encyclopedic textbook, *The Weather Book: A Manual of Practical Meteorology*, an impressive and still readable work. Unlike the reserved Castlereagh, the temperamental Fitzroy suffered frequent periods of gloom and sadness, making his suicide that much less mysterious. Nevertheless, Fitzroy's story is more than the tale of a man who suffered from a recognizably manic-depressive disorder; it is a key that, unlocking the enigma of Castlereagh's tragedy, illuminates a world of questions about depression and human nature, and about ourselves. What follows can be thought of as an odyssey through that world.

More than just good stories

Why, for every Fitzroy, whose eccentricity and moody temperament suggests a liability to mental illness, is there a Castlereagh whose condition seems to defy explanation? Why, despite all our information and intuition about behavior, do we still come up short explaining what makes some people vulnerable or predicting exactly who will succumb? Is the problem too complex, our theorizing too simple?

We shall see that good answers can be found, not just in the social environment, but in heritable qualities of mental life shaped by personal experience. The power of genetic influence is often unappreciated because it works subtly from the inside. Moreover, it clashes with assumptions about the long-term influence of rearing and family life. And yet, adopted people generally show greater psychological resemblance to biological relatives whom they've never met than to adoptive relatives whom they've known all their lives. In fact, genetically identical twins reared apart are remarkably similar, while adoptees reared together are remarkably unalike. These stunning observations generally hold for intelligence and personality, but also for certain vulnerabilities, including those to depressive illness and suicide. They imply something profoundly important that is all too often misunderstood when not denied: the powerful influence of genes on mental life.

Mental life is an arena of competing tendencies: selfish

impulses opposed by feelings of obligation, wishful fantasies filtered by realistic thinking, anxieties contained by efforts to cope. Normally, conflict is minimized or suppressed, but the breakdown of inner checks and balances ends all that. With mental illness, behavior becomes abnormally selfish, irrational, and socially inappropriate, while suffering can become a life-or-death struggle within the self. Elements of human nature—the rational and the passionate—are thus magnified, bringing into sharper relief the dramatic play of comedic, tragic, and heroic experiences that make our lives meaningful or absurd, adventures or ordeals. In this magnification, we recognize a serious problem to solve, but also an unusual opportunity to learn. In some sense, then, mental illness isn't just a bad thing. We want to understand it, surely to get rid of it, but also to get something out of it. In this view, mental illness—the depressive kind in particular—becomes a vehicle for exploring who we are and where we come from.

Frequently, misconceptions about abnormal behavior may be caused by a lack of information, but this is easily remedied with a few compelling facts and observations, for example:

- *Depressive disorder and suicide run in families, often for genetic reasons.* Therefore, even psychologically normal people can be carriers and transmitters of genes that cause depression or suicide, sometimes seemingly out of the blue.
- *Depressive disorders can be life-threatening.* They bring increased risk for accidents, alcohol abuse, poor nutrition, and eating disorders. They often get worse over the years, with episodes increasing in severity and frequency to the point of psychological dysfunction and demoralization that, especially in older males, can lead to suicide.
- *Depression can be missed or misleading.* For example, when appearing as a modest change in sleep or appetite, a depressed state of mind is easily ignored or denied. And while it may be a harmless reaction to a depressing situation, even manifest depression can be more significant than it seems, for example, signaling a severe illness to come, a hidden intention to commit suicide, an undiagnosed medical disease such as diabetes or Alzheimer's. Because a depressive illness may signify any one of many disorders, it will help clarify things if we

begin with the manic-depressive kind and then broaden our inquiry into others, including less severe kinds that, while seemingly innocuous, can prove to be just as malignant psychologically.

It takes more than facts, however, to answer the really big questions about depressive illness—for example, its connection to normal personality and everyday behavior, and why certain people are especially vulnerable. Facts can illuminate or mislead, depending on how they are interpreted. So, misconceptions come not just from a lack of facts, but also from the temptation to go for a good story whatever the facts. Good stories are hard to beat, even more so when they serve our needs, but here's the problem. Through our stories we discover—but don't we also invent?—"truths" about the world and about ourselves. Put another way, if our stories draw from fact and fancy, how do we know when they are insightful rather than illusory? How do we know when they are more like the objective theories of scientists than the delusional thinking of the mentally ill?

Exploring mental illness, the depressive kind in particular, therefore means subjecting even appealing ideas to serious tests against hard evidence. It is like asking not just what the microscope reveals but if the microscope is any good and if we are looking in the right places. In short, it means keeping an open mind and balancing the desirability of good theories with our desire for good stories. It is in this spirit of inquiry as both scientific and personal, serious and enjoyable, that I return to the stories of Castlereagh and Fitzroy, whose relevance to my exploration of depression and human nature was suggested by one of paleontologist Stephen J. Gould's essays on evolution [140].

The stories are about two men who seem to have it all until, tragically, something goes wrong. With Castlereagh, a great man is brought down without warning by a delusional and suicidal depression that comes seemingly from nowhere. With Fitzroy, a great man is brought down, but not surprisingly, by a manic-depressive form of depression that comes seemingly from temperament. Each story is interesting, but much more so as parts of a larger story wherein enigmatic aspects of mental illness are clarified. There is mystery here, in both stories, but clues enough for a solution that will serve as the foundation for a wider inquiry.

Castlereagh's story

Born to an aristocratic Irish family, Castlereagh received his higher education in England, eventually becoming one of its greatest statesmen. He was tall and handsome, dignified in manner, stately in bearing, and comfortable in social settings. Nevertheless, he was basically a private person, preferring solitude or the company of his family, and generally keeping his feelings to himself, sometimes to the point of seeming aloof. Only his intimates appreciated the sensitive, kind, and witty person who, in the public arena, remained masked behind an outward imperturbability. Although somewhat shy and reserved, he could nonetheless be forceful and persuasive, and more—he could react emotionally to perceived insult with bulldog tenacity, even vengefulness, about matters of honor, peace, and order. Even his opponents had to agree that Castlereagh showed strong will and unflinching courage. Clearly, there was a lot more to him than first met the eye. Perhaps, then, the outward qualities of distance and formality masked not just strong temperament, but an inner vulnerability.

Hidden vulnerabilities sometimes leak out in eccentric behavior or odd experiences that are seemingly inconsistent with a public persona. Consider just one striking example. During four years (1805–1809) as England's secretary of war, Castlereagh was deep in political crisis, conflict, and criticism. In the fall of 1809, his planned naval battle against Napoleon's forces near Antwerp went bust. For one thing, he was an amateur strategist; for another, he had inherited an inept and disorganized war machine. Moreover, the British cabinet was unenthusiastic about sending 40,000 troops to battle Napoleon's forces. With implementation delayed, the situation deteriorated. By September, injuries, poor diet, weakness, and fever had disabled about half the troops holed up on Walcheren Island. The problem was partly the government's indecisiveness regarding the war effort. But more, both cabinet and king had months earlier secretly agreed that Castlereagh was washed up at the war ministry. In other words, they had been stringing him along. One evening at a dinner party, he discovered the truth quite by chance. Believing his archrival, George Canning, to be the key player in a backroom plot, he demanded satisfaction, and in the old-fashioned way—pistols at dawn.

The fact is, Canning *had* been conniving behind the scenes, as was his right as secretary of state and his duty as politician. He was a brash and provocative person. Where Castlereagh was discrete, Canning waved flags and talked tough. Moreover, Canning had made no special effort to conceal his objections to Castlereagh nor was he required by the rules of etiquette to make amends. Nevertheless, he did try to smooth things over. Castlereagh would have none of it. Friends urged reconsideration, also to no avail. Pistols at dawn it would be. The duel took place on Putney Heath at 6:00 A.M. on September 21. Castlereagh won on the second round by wounding Canning. Both men then resigned their positions.

Now here's the peculiar thing: That morning, verily on his way to mortal combat, Castlereagh was oddly chipper, engaged in lively discussion about a popular opera singer, and even humming parts of her songs. Was this merely the innocent self-delight that comes with a bracing sense of righteousness and special mission or nervous denial in the face of mortal danger? In either case, was it clinically significant, the moderately severe euphoria and irritability of what we now call hypomania? That morning, he seemed to be experiencing the pleasure of releasing normally suppressed anger. Later that day, in a long letter to his father, he vented furious indignation over the whole affair. What, then, should we make of the easily overlooked manic qualities of Castlereagh's mood on this fateful day? Were they clues to the mysterious nature of the depressive disorder that would erupt in darkest despair and self-destruction a scant thirteen years later? We shall see.

By the nineteenth century, dueling was no longer considered appropriate for solving mere political conflicts, especially between men of position and responsibility. *The Whig Morning Chronicle* even went so far as to call the incident a disgusting exhibition. To some, the usually unflappable Castlereagh seemed to have become emotionally unbalanced; to others, he seemed calculating, cold-blooded, remorseless. Nevertheless, sympathies generally ran with Castlereagh, and once the Canning threat had passed, he soon regained his footing. Two and a half years later, in 1812, he was appointed foreign secretary, and in May of that year, leader of the House of Commons.

For ten years he managed the vital interests of England, leading his country and the Grand Alliance that triumphed over Napoleon. His cherished idea of a concert of European states in just equilibrium, formally established by the 1815 Congress of Vienna, officially launched the post-Napoleonic era. It was Castlereagh's year in the sun. Then another odd thing happened: At a dinner party, he quizzed one of the guests about the location and anatomy of the jugular vein. The physician answered all questions but cautioned that, given the obvious dangers, it was nothing to experiment with. Another guest observed that Castlereagh had the strangest look and seemed to be in an equally strange mood. Why would someone at the pinnacle of his career admit to such preoccupations?

By the summer of 1822, Castlereagh was under unbearable pressure. There was the constant strain of balancing two demanding jobs—foreign secretary and House leader—either one of which would have sorely challenged a lesser mortal. But more, there were innumerable personal and political problems. A year earlier, he had lost his beloved father on whom he greatly depended. He was suffering from episodes of gout, an excess of urate crystals in body fluids, which can produce arthritic-like pain, especially in the big toe, leaving a person sleepless, irritable, helpless. Moreover, Castlereagh was reviled for supporting a hated tax and other repressive policies and for being conciliatory toward despotic authoritarian regimes on the Continent. He was forced to carry a pistol because of the so-called Cato Street Conspiracy to assassinate the cabinet. The liberals despised him and their poets tortured him with cruel verses such as this one:

> Why is a pump like Viscount Castlereagh?
> Because it is an empty thing of wood,
> That up and down its awkward arm doth sway,
> And coolly spouts, and spouts, and spouts away
> In one weak, washy, everlasting flood.

Moreover, it was painfully evident that while Castlereagh's political fortune was at an all-time low, and ever declining, his archrival Canning's political star was on the rise.

On the verge of attending a critically important international conference, Castlereagh complained about being worn-out and sick of politics. No longer able to count on his courage and intellect, he was painfully conscious of being in over his head. His deteriorating memory affected his ability to keep appointments or to remember what they were about. He had lost his powers of concentration. His normally neat handwriting was increasingly illegible. He seemed to have aged five years in almost no time at all. Delusional suspicions that political enemies were plotting his downfall punctuated unshakable feelings of being ignored or slighted. At times he even hurled accusations at his loving and loyal wife, a clear indication that his depressed condition was becoming increasingly paranoid.

Early in August, he was seen wandering along the Pall Mall seemingly aloof to his surroundings, one boot flopping over his ankle. At a coffee house, his agitated behavior attracted public attention. Later, in Piccadilly, he paid a peddler one shilling for a knife with a white handle that he promptly hid away in his waistcoat pocket. By August 8, seven days before his scheduled departure for the Verona Conference, his self-doubt and low spirits prompted one of his staff to try to cheer him up, but to no avail.

The next day, August 9, was even worse. During sessions with the king and later with his friend, the Duke of Wellington, Castlereagh was wild-eyed, agitated, and delusional. He insisted he must flee to France to escape public humiliation for having done reprehensible, even criminal, things. (About three years earlier, Castlereagh had been tricked into going to a brothel with a "woman" who turned out to be a man. Being caught red-handed in the presence of a naked female impersonator meant that, at any time, he could be blackmailed and subjected to public humiliation. No matter that Wellington's subsequent investigation failed to turn up solid evidence of actual blackmail.) Thinking Castlereagh's frantic behavior was a joke, the king initially responded good-naturedly with an innocent if insensitive: "You must be crazy!" Castlereagh persisted. "I know well that you are my enemy. Everyone hates me and shuns me. When I walk down the street, people take the opposite side to avoid meeting me. I am very unhappy." Finally, recognizing the gravity of the situation, the alarmed monarch became increasingly solicitous. Touched, Castlereagh broke down, sobbing: "I am mad. I know I am mad. I have known it for a long time, but no one has any idea of it."

After witnessing a similar scene, Wellington was moved to write: "To see a man with such a sober mind, who one would think could not be influenced by any illusion, in a state bordering on insanity is not calculated to raise one's opinion of the strength of the human mind." Sadly, the king and duke, his two closest companions, had to leave town just when he needed them most. Alerted, family and friends mobilized their forces. They brought Castlereagh home for the weekend, removing dangerous objects and keeping an apprehensive vigil.

On Saturday, his physician-friend of thirty years, Dr. Bankhead, found him in an incoherent and paranoid state. The next morning, August 12, Castlereagh summoned Bankhead, then grabbed the overlooked white-handled knife and quickly cut his throat. Just as Bankhead entered the drawing room, a bloodied Castlereagh, facing the window and bathed in morning's light, played out his last moments like one of Shakespeare's tragic figures. As the distraught physician rushed to the window, Castlereagh spoke his last: "Bankhead, let me fall on your arms; I have opened my neck; it is all over."

Bankhead would later describe Castlereagh during those last few days as perfectly insane. After this and other testimony, the coroner recorded a suicide from a delusion caused by disease, but what kind? My guess is manic-depression, a disease recognized since ancient times that can produce manic as well as depressive shifts in mood, the manic aspect often subtle or hidden. In the end, the disorder was evident in morbid despair, delusions, and suicide. In the beginning, it was manifest only occasionally in outbursts of bottled-up temper, and in peculiarities of temperament whose significance had gone largely unrecognized. My guess is consistent with the fact that manic-depressive illness can occur, autonomously or in the face of stress, after a lifetime of conventional adjustment or great achievement.

Of course, there are other possibilities, any one of which

might have figured in Castlereagh's undoing, either alone or in concert with the manic-depressive disposition that I am hypothesizing. One possibility is loss of his parents at two crucial stages of his life: his mother at the beginning, when nurturance and affection were most needed, and his father at the end, when support and guidance were most needed. The sense of loss Castlereagh felt can be gauged from the touching fact that, throughout his life, he wore a locket containing the painted portrait and lock of hair of the mother he had really never known. The beautiful Lady Sarah Ann Seymour-Conway had died while giving birth to a stillborn fetus when Castlereagh was only two. Another possibility—demoralizing feelings of guilt and helplessness—could have arisen from multiple failures in his professional life plus a threat that a secret transgression might be exposed. Finally, declining health suggests additional sources of stress, for as we will see, undetected diseases can cause psychiatric symptoms, including severe depression.

Considering everything, we must be sympathetic to the man for managing as well as he did for so long, and with such style and integrity. But sympathy is not enough. We want to understand the nature of his mysterious condition and what it means for us. Toward that end, we continue with one more story.

Fitzroy's story

Robert Fitzroy was an extraordinary man of deeply opposing qualities. He was disciplined yet naturally excitable, charming yet suspicious and mean-spirited. He was grandiose and expansive yet given to periods of melancholy. By 1865, a combination of temperament, job stress, and diminishing personal conditions was pushing him toward a suicide that few could have predicted. Yet, acute personal crisis and suicide were but the most dramatic aspects of a prominent life, the highlight of which had come some thirty-odd years earlier while Fitzroy was commander of the *Beagle*, a ten-gun brig commissioned to survey the coasts of Patagonia, Tierra del Fuego, and the Straits of Magellan. Between 1831 and 1836, it was the *Beagle* that carried Charles Darwin (1809–1882) to South America, back to England, and into history.

By the summer of 1831, the *Beagle* already had a large crew, including a ship's surgeon. Nevertheless, at considerable personal expense, Fitzroy hired the young Darwin to be the ship's naturalist. But why did Fitzroy want someone to be ship's naturalist? The superficial reason was to provide the companionship of a gentleman. The most pressing reason, however, seems to have been Fitzroy's fear that physical confinement and social isolation during a long sea voyage might aggravate his tendency to become irritable, moody, and suspicious. His fears proved to be prescient. In 1834, despite Darwin's presence, Fitzroy developed a severe depression, perhaps brought on by feelings of isolation and a sense of foreboding about the enormous surveying task before him. Moreover, he felt betrayed by an Admiralty unwilling to support him financially in a manner consistent with his high expectations. Fitzroy wrote of unhappiness and despair and the sense of being close to insanity. Fortunately for the voyage, the *Beagle*'s crew helped him rally.

In 1841, Fitzroy came into conflict with a colleague who had challenged the process by which Fitzroy was elevated to the House of Commons. Deeply offended, Fitzroy called for a duel, but the man never showed. The matter ended with both men publishing their accounts, but not before they had got into a physical scuffle. People must have wondered at this tendency toward low-class behavior in a gentleman Tory. Darwin wondered. His autobiography describes Fitzroy as "generous to a fault, bold, indomitably energetic, ardent," but "his temper was a most unfortunate one. . . . He was also somewhat suspicious and occasionally in very low spirits, on one occasion bordering on insanity. He seemed to me often to fail in sound judgment or common sense. He was extremely kind to me, but was a man very difficult to live with. . . ." For example, Fitzroy could blow up over ideas that threatened his fundamentalist religious beliefs. During one heated discussion, an enraged Fitzroy suggested most emphatically that Darwin might as well take his stuff and clear out of the captain's cabin. After cooling down and feeling remorse, however, he proceeded to make amends, once again displaying his magnanimity and nobility.

By the 1850s, the two sometime friends were becoming alienated, mainly over the implications of Darwin's theories for religion. While Darwin's star was rising, Fitzroy's was fading. Growing debts were a painful signal of declining prospects. His fundamentalist devotion to the literal meaning of the Bible was becoming increasingly strident and incompatible with Darwin's evolutionary theory. After 1857, their views irreconcilable, the two saw nothing more of each other—except for one last time.

In June 1860, Darwin went to Oxford to attend a meeting of the British Association. During this meeting, a great debate on evolution was to take place, largely in response to Darwin's controversial book, *On the Origin of Species*, which had just been published (1859). The evolutionists were led by scientist and humanist Thomas Huxley, the religionists by the glib-tongued Bishop of Oxford, Samuel ("Soapy Sam") Wilberforce. At first the debate was civilized, even dull, but it soon heated up with much hooting and hollering on both sides. Then, a strange thing happened: Up stood a gray-haired man waving a Bible overhead. Like some gaunt, agitated Moses with tablets, he angrily pronounced evolution to be a false and pernicious doctrine. Here was old Fitzroy, coincidentally come to the meeting to read a meteorological paper, but drawn to the debate out of a crusader spirit driven by religious—might we speculate, manic-depressive?—zealotry. Shouted down and allowed to withdraw, he must have had a keen sense of inconsequentiality in the glare of Darwin's notoriety. Perhaps he also sensed the irony of having once helped Darwin. Barely five years later, Fitzroy would be dead by his own hand, finally succumbing to adversity and a particularly lethal kind of mental illness.

Darwin described Fitzroy as well-mannered, energetic, courageous, and generous, but also, authoritarian, argumentative, puritanical, and arrogant [50].* His riotous and violent temper was his greatest enemy, always capable of eruption into angry and self-destructive depressions, with his black moods typically worse in the morning. In many ways, then, Fitzroy's personality had the distinctive mark of a manic-depressive temperament. Finally, his not unreasonable fear of slipping into insanity was doubtless reinforced by two related facts of which Fitzroy was

---

*A bracketed number indicates a reference listed in the References at the end of the book; uncited sources are listed in the Additional Sources at the end of the book.

acutely aware [50]. One, a fact of life, is that moodiness and depressive illness have a hereditary basis. The other, a fact of Fitzroy's life, was that his family history included a notorious suicide, Fitzroy's maternal uncle—Lord Castlereagh.

2

HIDDEN IN THE
HUMAN LANDSCAPE

Fitzroy's striking manic-depressive temperament and bouts of melancholy make his suicide mostly understandable. All the more so, given that the severity of manic-depression increases with age, as does the risk of suicide, especially in elderly men. In contrast, Castlereagh's apparent mental health and great accomplishments make his suicide mostly mysterious, that is, until we recognize his connection to Fitzroy. Simply put, an explanation for otherwise ambiguous or mysterious behavior may sometimes come from clear-cut information about the personality or illness of even a distant relative.*

The stories of Castlereagh and Fitzroy make clear that a serious inquiry into the nature of personal experience, behavior, and mental illness must address the continuities of human nature that exist within persons and among family members. That is why exploring mental illness is not enough; we need to inquire about the soil out of which illness grows. We begin by characterizing psychological landscapes that diverge from lowland regions of conventional normalcy through hilly areas of

---

*Six years after the death of Castlereagh's mother, Lady Sarah Ann Seymour-Conway, his father married Lady Frances Pratt who bore him two sons and eight daughters, one of whom—Castlereagh's half-sister—would become Fitzroy's mother.

eccentricity to mountainous regions of mental illness. Each psychological landscape is distinct, yet blends into others to make boundaries uncertain. The schizophrenic, for example, is a peculiar terrain that varies from mild quirkiness to the outright bizarre and disorganized behavior of schizophrenia. The psychopathic is a soulless terrain that varies from mild egocentricity to the cold-blooded disloyalty and cruel exploitiveness of psychopathy (the evil kind of antisocial personality).

Given our special interest in the problem of depression, we will focus on the manic-depressive landscape, a moody terrain that varies from episodic blues to the mania and melancholia that we recognize as manic-depression. Through looking below the surface of the landscape for answers to the deepest questions about diverse expressions of human nature, we can come to an understanding of just how much heredity influences the kind of plains-people or highlanders we are.

The manic-depressive landscape

The striking continuities in the manic-depressive landscape have been noted throughout history. In a widely celebrated and still readable textbook, the great turn-of-the-century psychiatrist Emil Kraepelin described so-called peculiarities of emotional life not only in manic-depressive patients, but also in their depression-free relatives. "We are led to the conclusion that there are certain temperaments which may be regarded as *rudiments of manic-depressive insanity*" such that episodes of manic and depressive disorder would thus "rise like mountain peaks from a structurally similar plain" [190].

Kraepelin described four manic-depressive temperaments that could occur alone or combined with others: the depressive (moody), the manic (excited), the cyclothymic (cyclic), and the irritable (nasty). Depressed types are gloomy, introspective, guilt-ridden; they seem to take life too seriously, experiencing even simple things as burdensome and obligatory. Manics are just the opposite: playful, boastful, reckless, and disputatious, if not clever, versatile, even brilliant. The irritables are hotheaded, irascible, even dangerous, their sometimes cruel and abusive behavior causing violence within the family or on the job. The cyclothymics are familiar with all these states of mind, the depressive and both the euphoric and irritable manic.

Depending on its severity, a manic-depressive temperament can be awful in itself, as with Fitzroy, and when alloyed with other potent traits. Mix a Fitzroy's temperament with suspicious insecurity, for example, and you might get paranoid aggressiveness with a tendency to abuse alcohol or family members. And yet, manic-depressive temperament can also be *positively* awesome. Mix a Fitzroy's temperament with even otherwise unexceptional but healthy qualities of a mature personality and you might get admirable results: drive, ambition, and a willingness to work hard and take chances. Mix it with exceptional qualities, say sensitivity and an exquisite feeling for words, and you might even get the poets Shelley, Blake, Byron, Coleridge, the writers Goethe, Hemingway, Fitzgerald, Melville, O'Neill, and the composers Beethoven, Schumann, Tchaikovsky, Rachmaninoff.

There is new evidence for the age-old belief in the connection between craziness and creativity [15; 134]. Nevertheless, the connection is imperfect. At best, manic-depressive temperament kindles—it doesn't produce—creativity; at worst, it destroys creativity through illness and suicide. A gifted manic-depressive may swing precariously between triumph and disaster, vision and oblivion. In the private hell of novelist Herman Melville, says literary historian V. L. Parrington, "all the powers of darkness fought over him, all the devils plagued him. They drove him down into the gloom of his tormented soul, and if they did not conquer, they left him maimed and stricken . . . an arch romantic, he vainly sought to erect his romantic dreams as a defense against reality, and suffered disaster" [243].

Manic-depressive temperament can make experience and behavior more intense, fluent, and expansive; it can bring a sense of perspicacity and power. As it boosts creative potential, so may elated mood galvanize courageous acts, enabling a person to take risks and endure hardships that would otherwise seem out of the question. And yet, something more subtle than elation may be sufficient—perhaps we should call it force of personality. Just after turning seventeen, Castlereagh witnessed a boating accident during a sudden storm. Without much thought to his own safety, he plunged into a lake to rescue a twelve-year-old boy who could not swim. Despite numbing cold, he managed to keep the boy afloat for hours. Some might have called it intemperate, others, grace under pressure.

Expressed in unique patterns of behavior, personality traits provide a certain stamp of specialness that, along with distinctive physical appearance, is immediately recognizable in both normal and abnormal traits. Furthermore, being conscious of one's traits and their effects on others contributes to a sense of self and self-delight. And this can be true even with undesirable traits. Melancholy Jacques, Shakespeare's memorable character from *As You Like It*, savors being the disillusioned malcontent, for it wraps him in "a most humorous sadness." No malevolence here, however, nothing misanthropic. The man who can "suck melancholy out of a song, as a weasel sucks eggs" still cares, and may love again, notwithstanding his gloomy posturing. His is the philosophical melancholy of world-weariness, not the tragic melancholy of self-weariness that alienates a Hamlet. In the melancholy of Jacques, there is more muse than intellect, more vain self-indulgence than demonic self-preoccupation [238]. Good grief, you might call it. Goethe called it sweetest melancholy, a sensuous alloy of sadness and pleasure. Montaigne described it as "a design, consent, and pleasure in feeding one's melancholy . . . some shadow of daintiness and luxury that smiles on us and flatters us in the very lap of melancholy. *Are there not some natures that feed on it*" [231]?

Like Castlereagh, many people at risk for severe depression are not usually melancholy. Rather, they are excessively self-critical and conscientious. Such traits may seem healthy, since they can enhance achievement, social attractiveness, and a sense of dignity. Yet, they can deepen, intensify, and become burdensome, with even ordinary as well as idiosyncratic traits, such as compulsivity, self-denial, or risk-taking, becoming exaggerated in defending against depressive tendencies. It is as if personality were at war with itself, attempting to contain threatening impulses and compensate for vulnerabilities. The stories of Castlereagh and Fitzroy remind us that the war can be lost by even the bravest and most talented. How can this be?

A matter of time

Imagine a depressive disorder that is highly *heritable*. By heritable we mean that the more genes of a specifiable kind a person has, the more likely that person will display certain behaviors (the symptoms of an illness, for example); we say "more likely" because, even with a strong genetic potential, the manifest behaviors may not show up. So, the more heritable a depressive disorder, the greater the influence of genes in determining the likelihood of succumbing, *other things being equal.* Those other things include talent and temperament that can aggravate or buffer the effects of the culprit genes. To keep it simple, we'll ignore all that. Imagine, then, that a person has inherited enough genes to guarantee that he will become mentally ill. His genetically determined potential is therefore like a time bomb analogous to a young child's potential for puberty.

Many people have just enough of these genes to make them sensitive, moody, or charming, but not enough to make them ill. The person in question, on the other hand, has more than his genetic fair share. His traits are therefore not just the felicitous expression of temperament but rather the insidious symptoms of a genetic abnormality. Still early in the game, however, there is good news as well as bad. The good news is that, like in an early stage of alcoholic intoxication, he is full of energy, optimism, and engaging thoughts. He can handle troublesome symptoms by denying or explaining them away. Maybe he blames others, or adverse circumstances, or bad luck. None of this is frank mental illness, nothing diagnosable. Indeed, his defensiveness has a distinctive stamp of vibrant normalcy! Alas, the bad news is that he is increasingly inattentive, forgetful, and moody. In a year's time, the frequency and severity of his symptoms are evident to even the most casual observer. He has passed, perhaps without even noticing the transition, from the excesses of normalcy to the psychological dysfunctions—the emotional and cognitive breakdowns—of mental illness.

This little scenario makes clear that disorder can mean either of two things. Obviously, it can mean something we see: an illness, or *syndrome* of abnormalities and suffering. However, disorder can also mean something we infer: underlying pathology, or *disease.* Disease need not involve manifest illness. It can mean high *liability,* or risk of succumbing, to an illness. Think of it this way: The biological relatives of manic-depressives have an elevated liability; though most of them turn out fine or even wonderful, a greater-than-normal number will succumb. But even more of them, *including many who may look perfectly normal,* will be close to succumbing. For some of these relatives, it's inevitable, just a matter of time, while for others, it depends on circumstances, maybe just a little bad luck at the wrong moment that pushes them over the edge.

Liability is, in a sense, something waiting to happen. Because we infer it from elevated rates of illness in the relatives of ill people, liability is a statistical concept. Because we speculate about its genetic and environmental sources, liability is also a theoretical concept. But liability is more than just academic; ask any manic-depressive, alcoholic, or diabetic. He knows that whatever his current condition, he is always at risk because something is wrong with him—something physical. And yet, all this liability business may still seem remote until its personal relevance becomes evident, that is, if *our* risk for mental illness is elevated because *we* are related to a person who commits suicide or who succumbs to manic-depressive disease or other mental illness.

Thus it was with Fitzroy, whose appreciation of liability had a special urgency—and for Clifford Beers (1876–1943), a Yale graduate, aspiring businessman, and a founder of the American mental hygiene movement. Like Fitzroy, he couldn't shake the idea of being vulnerable because of a relative's abnormal behavior. Such suspicions are laid out in *A Mind That Found Itself,* a courageous autobiography that describes the horrors of mental breakdown and hospitalization. "Now, if a brother who had enjoyed perfect health all his life could be stricken with epilepsy, what was to prevent my being similarly afflicted. This was the thought that soon possessed my mind. The more I considered it, the more nervous I became; and the more nervous, the more I was convinced that my own breakdown was only a matter of time. Doomed to what I then considered a living death, I thought of epilepsy, I dreamed epilepsy . . ." [33].

A role of the dice

We recognize high liability in people like Fitzroy who wear it on their sleeve. We are far less clever at recognizing it in people like Castlereagh who show little evidence of being at risk until late in life. The imperfect relation between behavior and outcomes—

between personality and subsequent adjustment—makes the exploration of liability all the more challenging. Why is it that, even for people at risk—relatives of manic-depressives, for example—most prosper while only a few come to grief? Saying it is partly genetic and partly environmental doesn't help much, for how could it be otherwise? On average, genetic and environmental influences must add up to 1.0 (which means 100 percent) on a scale that runs from 0.0 to 1.0. If, on average, the genetic influence contributes 0.6 (60 percent), the environmental must contribute 0.4 (40 percent); if the genetic is 0.2, the environmental must be 0.8. Measure the one and you have the other.

Well, not exactly, for strictly speaking, what must add up to 1.0 are genetic and *nongenetic* influences. Calling the nongenetic influence "environmental" is common practice and understandable; after all, "environmental" is surely the nicer word, with its familiar images of parents, family settings, and neighborhoods. Trouble is, those images can obscure the fact that *nonsocial* influences also figure in the development of human potential. Let us therefore illuminate that fact with two kinds of evidence, one regarding the surprisingly *limited* effect of the rearing environment in promoting family resemblances; and the other regarding the surprisingly *strong* effect of the prenatal environment in promoting family differences.

The influence of rearing on personality development can be estimated with unusual clarity by studying people adopted early in life. Unlike the rest of us, adoptees have *two sets* of parents, the biological set representing *genetic* influence, and the adoptive set representing *rearing* influence. Each influence can thus be separately estimated from the resemblance of adoptees to each set of parents.

Adoptees generally show the usual moderate resemblance to their biological parents, but *little or no resemblance to their adoptive parents*—sometimes no greater than to people randomly picked from the population. In contrast, genetically identical twins generally show unusually strong resemblance even if, due to parental misunderstanding, they are raised as "fraternal" twins. And identical twins show unusually strong resemblance *even if they are reared apart from birth.* And consider this: Adoption agencies carefully select people who will be *above-average* parents with above-average means. If quality of rearing were generally important to liability, then the adopted offspring of a severely mentally ill parent should nevertheless have *below-average* rates of mental illness. Actually, their rates are relatively high—sometimes *as high as the rates for offspring reared by their mentally ill parents.* In short, genetic overlap more than common rearing seems to determine the resemblance [45; 202].

Now consider the sometimes powerful influence of the *prenatal* (nonsocial) environment. A pathological example is maternal drug and alcohol consumption during pregnancy, which increases the risk for fetal brain damage and thus the risk for mental retardation, attention deficits, impulsivity, and antisocial behavior. More important, while we have always known that our genetic potential is shaped by prenatal influences, we can now get *measures* of that influence by studying identical twins. Psychological differences between genetically identical twins can only be environmental, but *in what sense?* By asking that not-so-obvious question, we may discover rather surprising answers. But we must be willing to search in not-so-obvious places.

Our unconventional search begins with pairs of identical twins who show a striking difference in their mental condition. Specifically, one twin is manifestly schizophrenic, while the other—the co-twin—is manifestly normal. Such psychological *discordance* between identical twins will sometimes be found even with highly heritable disorders, such as schizophrenia. The reason, as we will see, is that heritability estimates refer to genetic *potential* expressed at best imperfectly in manifest behavior—for example, intelligence expressed in IQ scores, or *liability* expressed in psychological adjustment. Assume, then, that our discordant twins have a *comparably elevated genetic potential*—that schizophrenic illness in one of the twins implies *elevated liability* in the well co-twin. Question: What kind of environmental influence can turn genetic potential (liability) into a manifest illness, but in just one of two identical twins?

Naturally, we are inclined to search for answers in the familiar social environment, for example, blaming mom for a child's vulnerability to schizophrenic illness. Since the relevant evidence flatly contradicts this idea, let's consider an intriguing clue recently discovered in a most unusual place: the hands. The hands of manifestly schizophrenic twins are often abnormal in size, shape, and definition, for example, the fingerprints of the ill twin display an abnormally large or small number of ridges [51; 52]. Such anomalies can originate only during the second trimester of pregnancy when, because of adverse fetal location, abnormal physiological connections, or just bad luck, deleterious conditions (drugs, obstruction of the blood supply, infection) can impact disproportionately on one of the two fetal twins, the one that is thereby destined to become ill [301]. In short, the nonsocial environment may play a powerful role— sometimes, as we will see, more powerful than rearing—to bring out genetic potential.

The evidence we have touched upon here tends to invoke the sense that our personal destiny is determined by a roll of genetic and environmental dice. It's an age-old feeling about human life, hauntingly expressed in the musings of eleventh-century Persian mathematician-turned-poet Omar Khayyám, as translated by Edward FitzGerald:

'Tis all a Chequer-board of Nights and Days
Where Destiny with Men for Pieces plays:
    Hither and thither moves, and mates, and slays,
And one by one back in the Closet lays.

Later, we will take up the question of how this deterministic imagery squares with our sense of free will. For now, the more concrete point is that environmental insults capable of boosting genetic liability may, *but need not*, involve social life. No wonder that mental illness sometimes strikes just one member of an otherwise healthy family. None of this means that parents are off the hook. Rather, it means that parental responsibility is less important for some disorders, or important to fewer disorders, than we may have imagined. No dry academic point, this, when, partly out of misguided professional "help," countless parents have needlessly suffered shame and guilt over their supposed responsibility, say for a child's schizophrenia or suicidal depression.

A big message in the "little" numbers

Just for a moment, imagine that you have located 100 individuals, each an identical twin who is ill with manic-depression. You then discover that in 70 percent of the cases, the co-twin is likewise ill with manic-depression—a concordance (similarity) rate of 70 percent. Question: What about the 30 percent who are not ill, that is, who are discordant? Look more closely, and you will discover that some of them display nervousness, sensitivity, and other illness-like qualities; you could call them the "near ill," or the "almost-concordants." The rest, however, are quite normal, at most mildly eccentric, or even "supernormal" in their creativity, personal charm, and singular achievements. This interesting variety of not-ill (discordant) co-twins can tell us much about mental illness and more generally, about the human landscape. To see how, think once again about the distinction between behavior and potential, specifically, between illness and liability.

Recall that for environmental reasons, genetically identical twins can look sometimes strikingly different in appearance and behavior; one twin might be a gifted scientist or celebrated pianist, the other merely a competent lab technician or piano tuner. Moreover, where *capability* (talent or giftedness) is highly heritable, high achievement in identical twins implies high-level capability in their co-twins; likewise, if *liability* to manic-depression is highly heritable, manic-depressive illness in identical twins implies strong liability in their co-twins. In time, confirmation of the suspected liability comes with increasing rates of illness either in the not-ill *co-twins* or in their *offspring*. Let's take a closer look, starting with a key question about the co-twins themselves.

What does it really mean that identical twins are "only" 70 percent concordant (30 percent discordant) for manic-depressive illness? The answer comes first from an understanding that, like behavior, numbers taken out of context can be misleading. By itself, no concordance rate means much—not a 70, not a 45, *not even a 20*. Example: Identical twins are "only" about 15 percent concordant for suicide. That 15 percent seems small, yet it is at least 15 *times* the near-zero concordance rate for fraternal twins, suggesting that the *liability* for suicide is highly heritable. Second example: Identical twins are "only" 45 percent concordant for schizophrenia—incidentally, a bit less than identical twins *reared apart* [136]. Nevertheless, that seemingly modest rate is 3 to 5 times the rate found for fraternal twins, and 45 *times* the usual (population) rate—all consistent with the high heritability of *liability* to schizophrenic illness.

Now consider the 70 percent concordance for manic-depressive illness in identical twins. This rate turns out to be quite impressive, indicating a high heritability for manic-depressive disease—specifically, for the *liability* to manic-depressive illness. For one thing, this 70 percent concordance is much higher than typically found with psychiatric disorders—even higher than the impressive 45 percent concordance found for schizophrenia. For another, this rate is well matched by identical twins *reared apart*, who are 60 to 70 percent concordant; yet it is poorly matched by fraternal twins *reared together*, who are only 10 to 15 percent concordant [11; 254]. Now we appreciate just how high a concordance of 70 really is. Only the co-twins of ill identicals can have such *relatively* high rates, rearing notwithstanding; no other group even comes close, apparently because no other group is genetically so well connected to an ill group.

The most intriguing part of the story of discordant twins is about their offspring. Manic-depressive illness occurs in roughly 1 percent of the population, but in 10 percent of the offspring of an ill manic-depressive. That same elevated prevalence of 10 percent applies to the offspring of ill identical twins and *apparently also to the offspring of the not-ill (discordant) co-twins* [36]. On average, the not-ill co-twin parents must be carrying and passing to their offspring the same liability genes carried and passed by their ill twins.

Are we not struck by the ironic story of those identical twins? Their discordance (30 percent) suggests environmental influence, yet their offsprings' comparably elevated prevalence (10 percent) suggests genetic influence—specifically a heritable liability. In sum, those percentages may seem "little," but they convey three big messages:

- A heritability estimate is just the beginning of an understanding of genetic *and environmental* influence.
- The environmental influence implied by discordance in the identical twins may, *but need not*, involve rearing or other social factors; nonsocial environmental (as well as genetic) influence is surely implied by *comparably elevated* rates of illness

in the offspring of ill and not-ill (discordant) identical twins.
- Disorders such as manic-depression have *two aspects:* the most obvious (illness), but also the mostly hidden (liability); that is, like the proverbial tip of the iceberg, illness is just a small part of the landscape of human potentialities.

Continuities of human potential are often masked by discontinuities of human behavior. Granted, our efforts to ameliorate suffering and understand liability may be enhanced by dividing abnormal regions of the human landscape into discrete categories of mental illness. Yet, an exclusive focus on those few far-out regions can leave out much of the personality, experience, and human potential that is connected to that liability. We would not really understand a carnival by visiting just the oddest attractions. Amusing and fascinating, they can mislead by diverting attention from the larger domain of games, rides, eateries, and characters, and from the hidden needs that the carnival satisfies. Thus it is with mental illness, one of the more fascinating and edifying, yet potentially diverting, aspects of the human carnival.

PART TWO

IN THE BELLY OF THE WHALE

Now will come the season of depression,
after congestion, suffocation.

—Virginia Woolf

3

WHEN THE BOUGH BREAKS

Despite good sense and self-restraint, Abraham Lincoln was a moody person who suffered mild and severe depressions. After his friend Ann Rutledge died in 1835, his depressive disposition seemed to deepen, making half-hearted his courtship of Mary Owens. By 1841, Lincoln was so depressed that his friends put him in seclusion without knives and other potentially dangerous objects. On his wedding day, he remained secluded in a state of suicidal depression with delusions about failure and unworthiness. According to psychiatrist Karl Menninger, Lincoln said he was the most miserable man living, and that "if what I feel were equally distributed to the whole human family, there would not be one cheerful face on earth. Whether I shall ever be better, I cannot tell; I awfully forebode I shall not." His friends and colleagues were rather gloomy about his dark moods, and his future in-laws considered him insane [227].

Depression has many guises, from melancholy so disabling it is recognized as illness, to moodiness so mild it is taken for a problem of living. Masked by comic or even tragic behavior, it may escape notice; or it may be evident in persistent unhappiness mild enough to be discounted. Either way, it usually escapes psychiatric attention unless it develops into severe illness. Like outrageous crimes, murders for example, severe depressions arrest attention, provoke emotion, and galvanize efforts to learn more. Closer to home are the moodiness, reactivity, and personality problems that make up the more common, less severe depressive illnesses. Like robberies or muggings, they are easier to identify with and, like their spectacular counterparts, prove valuable to our inquiry into the human condition.

Episodes

A surprising amount of low-grade depression exists in the population. In one study, up to 20 percent of so-called normal subjects reported crying spells, sleep disturbance, low mood, fatigue, and feelings of guilt or worthlessness; 5 percent even had death wishes [65]. In another study, lifetime prevalence— the proportion of people ever having succumbed to some kind of mental illness (mostly depression)—appeared to be over 30 percent in women claiming to be healthy and normal [143]. Nevertheless, we can distinguish such common symptomatology from the comparatively uncommon and debilitating full-blown depressive illnesses whose mark is painful sadness, aimless agitation, irrational guilt, delusional self-condemnation, and suicidal inclinations. Depressive illnesses can be elicited by unhappy circumstances; they can develop more spontaneously, erupting episodically or evolving insidiously through a deepening of moody temperament. However formed, they can persist as if having a life of their own, most often for months, but sometimes for years.

The term *depression*, first arising in the seventeenth century, comes from the Latin *deprimere*, a state of being pressed down— *de*, or "down from" + *primere*, or "to press." Current convention says that you are seriously depressed if, for *at least two weeks*, you satisfy five or more diagnostic criteria that we will examine in chapters that follow. The first of these criteria is necessarily present: either unhappy or otherwise depressed mood, or a marked loss of interests and/or ability to experience pleasure. Others include:

- feelings of worthlessness or inappropriate guilt,
- appetite loss/gain and significant weight loss/gain,
- insomnia or excessive sleepiness,

- restlessness or profound sluggishness and inactivity,
- fatigue or lack of energy,
- indecisiveness and deficits in thinking and concentration,
- suicidal tendencies of any kind, whether in thought or deed.

The more numerous these criteria, the more likely you are depressed; the more numerous the criteria involving appetite, energy, and sleep, the more likely the diagnosis will be *melancholia*, an especially severe form of depressive illness that nevertheless responds surprisingly well to medical treatments. This term derives from the Greek words *melaine chole* meaning black bile, one of four bodily humors first hypothesized by the ancients to explain temperament and mental illness marked by delusional thinking.

Some depressions are chronic, with persistent low-grade moodiness and pervasive pessimism. People with these kinds of depression may report feeling blue and having crying spells; they may even have feelings that things will never get better, and fantasies of going to bed and never waking up. Other depressions have a more episodic course, with sharply delineated boundaries between periods of normalcy and dysfunction. For people with both kinds of depression, a condition called *double depression*, depressive episodes represent the deepening of a more chronic pattern, like the panic attacks that punctuate the chronic apprehensiveness of people afflicted with anxiety disorder.

Like any living thing, a depressive episode develops, ripens, and fades. Onset may be acute, taking at most a few days, or, more typically, gradual over weeks or even months. In any event, the typical episode begins long before hospitalization. One study found that depressed patients had begun showing signs of their illness by age sixteen and were diagnosable by age nineteen. By twenty-two, they had begun treatment, and by age twenty-six experienced a first hospitalization [93].

The onset of an episode is described in the harrowing personal imagery of a former patient: "Each part of you dies when depression sets in. You try to remember the tools and the tactics that got you through the last bout, but the amount of energy and will needed to defend against such an ominous beast seem nowhere to be found. Alcohol and drugs cannot take the pain away. I don't care what anyone says; you cannot drink enough, snort enough, or smoke enough to forget about the death inside of you that keeps growing and scarring more tissue. Soon there is no use fighting, and you crawl into your bed or sit in front of a window or a blank TV without emotion—no tears or anger—and you just let the beast take full control."

Without a depressing situation, it is difficult to recognize the early stages of changing mood, or to know what it means. It could signal the onset of a depressive illness, but it could be a sign of something else—a medical condition, such as diabetes, or a psychiatric illness. Up to 50 percent of schizophrenics start out looking tense and nervous before they succumb to their first illness. They eat less, have trouble concentrating and sleeping, feel apathetic, and look "depressed." Nevertheless, they are schizophrenics, not depressives. Depression aggravates all kinds of psychological problems. For example, up to 40 percent of patients with depressive illness suffer from clinically significant anxiety. They have panic attacks, phobias, obsessive-compulsive symptoms, and persistent worrying. Up to 20 percent abuse alcohol, cocaine, or other drugs.

Depending on the person and on the definition of recovery, typical episodes of depression may last from three to nine months. However defined, recovery is often mysterious, yet there are two good bets: One is a time-heals-all-wounds factor, a natural tendency for abnormalities to self-correct. The other is a personal-resources factor, the power of personality, intellect, good will, and optimism too oppose the forces of disintegration. In his autobiography, Clifford Beers describes "a mental civil war, which I fought single-handed on a battlefield that lay within the compass of my skull. An Army of Unreason, composed of the cunning and treacherous thoughts of an unfamiliar foe, attacked my bewildered consciousness with cruel persistency, and would have destroyed me, had not a triumphant Reason finally interposed a superior strategy that saved me from my unnatural self" [33].

In most cases, at least in the short run, some kind of recovery is a good bet. There is even reason to hope that new drugs will not only ameliorate and shorten an episode but, with continued use, delay the next one, perhaps permanently. That's the good news. Unfortunately, there is also much bad news: Genuine,

des become shorter while episode duration changes little.
n a person has his first episode when he is in his early
ties, it might take forty months from the end of the first
de to the beginning of the next. However, it might take
ten months between the end of the fourth episode—
rring, say, when the person is in his mid-forties—to the
nning of the fifth. Apparently, rate of recurrence is a matter
e more than number of prior episodes.

costs

ression disrupts friendships and marriages by its destruc-
effect on trust and communication. It traps its victims in a
-fulfilling pattern of depression that begets depression
ugh its disruptive social effects; depressives may become
reasingly irritable, dependent, hostile, resentful, argumenta-
, spiteful, suspicious, indignant, and sexually unresponsive.
ny people living with a depressed person—40 percent in one
dy—are distressed enough to need psychiatric help. Chil-
n of the severely depressed fare poorly, sometimes showing
ychological disturbances long after their parents have recov-
ed. A worst-case scenario would involve something like the
llowing: A severely depressed woman languishes in a state
spital. She is full of self-contempt and delusions of her sin
d damnation, and mostly unresponsive to signs of support
d reassurance offered by friends and relatives. No longer
pable of functioning as wife, mother, and breadwinner, she is
emotional and financial drain on the family. The constant
reat of suicide keeps loved ones on edge, teetering between
ope and anxiety.

Finding the depressive condition aversive, even well-meaning
iends and loved ones are thrown into a disconcerting ambiva-
nce. Enlightenment philosopher-philanthropist Claude
drien Helvétius confessed that his concern for the miseries of
ome unhappy person corresponded to his fear of being afflicted
ith the same miseries. Thus, he avers, it is common sense to
ithdraw when sympathetic efforts to ameliorate someone's
depression are clearly hopeless. But the observer's reaction to
socially unresponsive depression can reflect more than defensiveness in the most selfish sense; it can reflect a moral senti-

speedy, and permanent recovery from de
be the exception rather than the rule. Even
sodes can last for a year or more, followed b
post-episodic demoralization, and not just
living conditions. Longstanding personality
emotional excess, defensiveness, egocen
dependency can make things worse. Three o
First, neurotic and psychopathic traits indic
personal resources—in psychology's jargon,
strength. Second, such traits promote and p
by their outward effects, for example, creatin
tions, alienating others, and making thing:
Finally, such traits make it more likely that a p
sponsible about taking medication or enga
therapy.

Recovery from an episode of major depressi
degree. In many cases, recovery sufficient to le
doesn't necessarily mean true normalcy; rathe
persistent self-doubt and *dysphoria*, literally h
ings of being unwell or unhappy. A recovered p
normal yet sensitive, sometimes reacting to
thought with weeping that is hard to control. U
of discharged patients may develop chronic de|
others experience residual unhappiness, pessin
self-esteem. A young woman writes anonymous
ing the hospital I slipped into my usual lows. I dr
where we used to go. Every afternoon I sit there
ing into the water or taking long walks. Sometin
go by without eating anything. I don't know whe
snap out of this horrible nightmare. It has been r
year, not one single pleasant thing has happene
afraid I can no longer hold on this way."

Incomplete recovery is bad enough; worse is re
can occur in as many as a quarter of recovered patie
mere eighteen-month period. Greatest risk of rel
cated by certain characteristics. One is early o
younger than twenty years of age at the first episode
factors include chronic moodiness, prior episodes
with psychotic thinking), and a family history of dep
order. In many cases, the comparatively well perioc

ment directed at behavior deemed at least vaguely reprehensible because it seems to imply a kind of irresponsibility. Eighteenth-century writer Pierre Charron describes depression as a "dangerous enemie of our rest, which presently weakeneth and quelleth our soules, if we take not good heed, and taketh from us the use of reason and discourse, and the meanes whereby to provide for our affaires, and with time it rusteth the soule, it corrupteth the whole man, and brings his virtues a sleepe, even then when he hath most need to keep them awaked, to withstand that evill which oppresseth them. . . ." The ancient Roman philosopher-statesman Cicero had an even sterner view of depression as "a rash and outrageous complaint," a sign of ignorance or denial of melancholy facts of life that ought rather to be acknowledged and accepted.

Unremitting depression thus engenders in observers a mixture of compassion for what seems like illness, with defensiveness against what seems personally threatening, and irritation perhaps tinged with righteous indignation over what seems self-indulgent—a moral failing, an inability to come to grips. Unevenly sensitive to such mixed messages, the depressed person will respond to signs that reinforce negative ideas about self and world, and about the hopelessness of changing things for the better. The depressive view, through its effects on the environment, is thus self-fulfilling.

The personal cost of depression is difficult to measure, though an important indicator is the more than 15 percent of depressed people who commit suicide and the more who come close. Excess mortality for people with depressive disorders appears to be more than a matter of suicide. For example, there is evidence of elevated risk of cardiovascular disease, and this might be aggravated, perhaps even caused, by cigarette smoking [126]. The reliable depression-smoking connection is clearly evident, whether we select smokers and look for depression or select depressives and look for smoking. First, consider depressives.

Victims of depressive disorder have elevated rates of smoking, almost as high as for alcoholics, and the relatives of depressives have an elevated rate of smoking. Clearly, *depressive disorder is an indicator of liability to smoking*. Now consider smokers. Smokers are more anxious and depressed than average; the more prominent these symptoms, the harder it is to quit smoking and the easier it is to relapse. Also, smokers have elevated rates of depressive disorder, with the highest rates associated with the greatest smoking problems. Even regardless of being a smoker or nonsmoker, risk for depressive illness depends on the number of smoker relatives. Finally, smokers' relatives have elevated rates of depressive disorder. Clearly, then, *smoking is an indicator of liability to depression.* Smoking and depression can aggravate each other, the one often used to self-medicate against the other. Nevertheless, it is likely that, rather than representing two distinct liabilities, smoking and depression are different expressions of a common liability [177].

The social cost of depressive illness has been variously estimated, and may be as high as $40 billion annually in lost productivity, lost income, and health-care costs. That estimate puts depressive disorder right up there with cancer, schizophrenia, drug abuse, Alzheimer's disease, and other big destroyers of lives. Clearly, depression is but a part, albeit a major part, of a much larger problem. Roughly 20 percent of adult Americans, or 50 million people, struggle with moderate to severe problems involving anxiety, psychosis, addiction, impulse and sexual dysfunction, and brain disease as well as depression. The burden on the afflicted, their families, and society is in some sense incalculable, for how do we measure the personal costs in suffering, conflict, disruption, and demoralization caused by all forms of mental illness? The total cost to the economy in health and treatment expense and diminished productivity is another matter—estimates vary up to $300 billion lost annually [25; 299].

Lies, damned lies, and statistics

Calling depression a *mood disorder* is misleading because much more is involved than just feelings and emotions. Other aspects are *cognitive* (poor memory, negative self-concept, hopelessness, delusions), *behavioral* (social withdrawal or kleptomania), *motivational* (abnormal needs for protection and support), and *vegetative* (lack of energy, insomnia, lost appetites, and hormone abnormalities).

Because a depressed state of mind can have many guises besides depressed mood—in particular, vegetative symptoms— it may be mistreated as a medical problem, at least initially [184;

326]. Sometimes these problems do indeed turn out to be medical diseases such as high blood pressure, diabetes, or irritable bowel syndrome. Such diseases can cause the symptoms of depression directly by altering brain activity, or indirectly by making life miserable. In many cases, however, the problem is more psychological than medical.

In some cases, the depression is identified. For example, complaints of insomnia, lack of appetite, troublesome pain, and boredom—*but no sadness*—are diagnosed as depressionless depression. Now, you might ask: What kind of cheeseless cheeseburger is that? Leaving a fuller answer till later (Chapter 9), we can say that, in some cases, the sadness—really the *potential* to experience sadness—is converted into something else, mostly vegetative. This conversion, in theory at least, is like anxiety converted into muscle tension, alcohol craving converted into militant teetotalism, or scorn converted into craven solicitousness.

In other cases, depression masked by somatic symptoms goes undiagnosed, even when the doctor-patient relationship is well established. In one study, physicians diagnosed a psychological disorder in only 20 percent of the cases of independently diagnosed depressive or anxiety disorder if the patient complained of somatic symptoms while denying emotional problems. On the other hand, the recognition rate was about 50 percent when somatic complaints were associated with a willingness, when asked, to accept the idea of an underlying psychological problem. In any event, physicians were more likely to recognize psychiatric disorder when somatic complaints were medically inexplicable or presented in an anxious, hypochondriacal manner [181]. In the weeks before their final act, perhaps 75 percent of suicides will have consulted a physician who often misses the suicidal potential. Each year, a physician may see six seriously suicidal patients, but identify the problem in only one. Clearly, then, the problem of depression is much more than unhappy mood or even hidden illness. It is also often a problem of hidden liability. Remember those psychologically normal identical twins whose children's high rate of depression, like their co-twin's illness, signaled a hidden liability.

Two clear consequences follow from the fact that we often can't recognize either illness or liability. One is that we will sometimes need a more inclusive term than either mood disorder or depressive disorder. Remember, all depressions involve more than unpleasant mood, and some depressions involve a connection with manic illness that we will consider in Chapter 8. Therefore, to speak generally about the problem of depression—about the illness, about its frequent link to mania, and about underlying causes—we will sometimes want to use the more general term *affective* disorder, that is, a disorder marked by manic and depressive moods and emotions. A good example, discussed in Chapter 5, is the so-called seasonal affective disorder that involves seasonal changes in mood, thinking, and vegetative symptoms, any of which can signal a depression, but also a manic illness.

Another consequence is that we will need to recognize that an affective state can be expressed indirectly, incompletely, or not at all. In other words, the problem of depression will be underestimated to the extent that statistics—including the statistics given shortly—represent manifest illness rather than masked depression or quiet desperation. The problem is more than just a matter of underestimating depression; it is something more personal. Like death, depression touches us more in the singular than in the plural. Rather than so many statistics, we want sensible explanations and practical solutions for concrete problems involving real people, even better, people we know or care about. We want to know why Uncle George is demoralized, acting crazy, threatening suicide, and scaring the hell out of Aunt Martha and the kids. We may wonder if his upbringing and its effect on the way he thinks about himself might explain his troubles and suggest a means to help him get better. No doubt, it is important to ask questions about the unique experience of an individual. However, a second approach is to ask about what people have in common.

Novelist Somerset Maugham, arguing for using the individual case to illustrate the general, once suggested that, if the proper study of mankind is man, it is evidently more sensible to occupy yourself with the coherent, substantial, and significant creatures of fiction than with the irrational and shadowy figures of real life. Well, psychology provides a third way to occupy ourselves, namely with statistical summaries of those irrational and shadowy qualities of living people. Strictly speaking, these abstractions are neither real nor fictional; they are empirically true and, if we are lucky, they will tell us *generally* why people are at risk and what abnormal behavior says about us all.

Admittedly, statistical abstractions can be a problem, and for two good reasons. First, statistics can seem remote and lifeless, as evident in Russian dictator Joseph Stalin's ironic comment that one death is a tragedy, a million merely a statistic. The obvious antidote for this problem is always to keep in mind that the numbers ultimately refer to suffering people whose motives and reasons for behavior get lost in the statistical averages. It is therefore essential that we have examples that illustrate the rules, *but also exceptions that raise questions about the rules.* In this way we can keep a reasonably open mind while we explore human nature for insights into what is true about all people and what is unique to individuals.

Second, statistics can be misleading, as evident in British prime minister Disraeli's sardonic comment that there are lies, damned lies, and statistics. The proper antidote for this problem is a simple truth: While statistics can be tortured to the point of confessing to anything, we can discover the truth, or at least interesting and useful things, by keeping an open mind while we look for meaningful regularities. Just remember that, however defined, rates of disorder can vary dramatically across studies. For example, the percentage of people who have ever been depressed can range from lows of 5 and 9 percent to highs of 10 and 25 percent, for males and females respectively. Here, then, with the proper caution in mind, are a few good statistics on depressive illness.

Who's at risk?

During any *one-month period* in the United States, at least 5 percent of the adult population is suffering from depressive illness. Of these more than 13 million adults, 2 percent are severely afflicted. The other 3 percent have moderate depression, a somewhat less intense but more persistent illness. We are talking about *prevalence rate*, the percentage of people who, *during a given time period*—typically a one- or six-month "window"— were ill either for the first time (new cases) or not for the first time (recurrent cases). For example, prevalence of moderate-to-severe depressive disorder depends on age and sex. Rates for middle-aged people, twenty-five to sixty-four years old, are higher (5 to 6.5 percent) than for young adults (4.4 percent) and for the elderly (2.5 percent).

Across all age groups, however, females outnumber males by up to 3:1. Why? Is it a sense of helplessness that comes from depending too much on others for one's well-being? Maybe women more often are the helpless victims of neglect, abuse, or other depressing conditions. Perhaps they more willingly confront feelings that men either deny or express indirectly in aggressive behavior and drug addictions. Without opportunities for such outlets, perhaps, the sex differences in depression would be less evident or nonexistent. Perhaps that explains why there is no such sex difference in the Old Amish community of southeastern Pennsylvania; this conservative Protestant sect tolerates neither aggressive behavior nor the use of drugs.

With *lifetime prevalence*, we stretch the temporal "window" as far back as possible to get the percentage of people who have *ever* experienced the illness. This means including all those who are currently ill *plus* all those who, even if not ill now, have been ill at least once in their life. For the American population over eighteen years old, our best estimate of lifetime risk for moderate to incapacitating depressive disorder is about 8 percent, though some estimates have been as high as 20 percent. (See the "Taking Stock" Appendix note on prevalence and related measures, and how mental illness is assessed in the community.)

Lifetime risk is especially high in the first-degree relatives—in the parents, siblings, and children—of affected persons. Moreover, that risk is related to the number of relatives affected and the severity of their illness as indicated by early onset, high recurrence, and profound psychological dysfunction, or "mental breakdown." In this, depression is like many medical diseases. For example, risk for breast cancer depends on certain facts regarding a woman's first-degree relatives, in particular, the number affected, age when their tumors first appeared, and whether the cancer exists in both breasts. So, first-degree relatives of depressed patients have lifetime rates of depression as high as 15 to 20 percent, which is at least double—it can be as high as triple—the population rate [324].

Any relative of a severely depressed person is likely to wonder: Exactly *which* relatives are at risk, that is, how can we tell who is one of those "15 to 20 percenters"? For most mental illnesses, this question has not been answered to anyone's satisfaction. There is simply no sure-fire sign—no "smoking gun"—to indicate who among seemingly normal relatives is at greatest risk, let alone who will definitely succumb. Scientists continue their search for liability indicators, or markers, and with highly heritable illnesses, such as depression associated with mania, they naturally search for the *biological* kind.

A biological marker might be something behavioral, perhaps eye movement abnormalities manifested during the tracking of a moving stimulus in some laboratory task; it might be something physiological, such as a distinctive pattern of brain waves (EEG) or body chemistry, some abnormal protein that might reveal the nature and location of the genetic abnormality. Whatever its form, a biological marker is mostly unconscious, involuntary, and culture-free; that is, it is "close" to the mechanisms of a disease rather than merely a feature of an illness. A biological marker of liability must therefore be:

- *disorder-specific*—it must indicate elevated risk for a distinct disorder, for example, manic-depression but not schizophrenia;
- *illness-independent*—it must be found in people not only when they are ill, but also when they are well, for example, after they have recovered from an episode;
- *familial*—it must run in the family, that is, it must have an elevated frequency in not only the ill but also the well relatives.

To date, biological markers satisfying these criteria have not been unquestionably established for depression, though the heritability of depression suggests that they exist, and a couple of candidates will be mentioned later in the book.

Age of Melancholy

The problem of depression involves biological liability, but also social conditions that enhance or trigger that liability. Even without changes in the biological aspect, dramatic changes in social conditions—in the promotion of materialism and egocentricity, for example, or the toleration of incompetent, irresponsible, and antisocial behavior—can produce correspondingly dramatic changes in the rate of depression and other forms of mental illness. This point is well underscored by social criticism and by epidemiology suggesting that increasingly we live in an Age of Melancholy. As Jacques Barzun observes, "our towering civilization is in fact an abyss of degrading misery. . . . Social workers and psychiatrists who cope with the now commonplace event of mental breakdown take for granted the 'lack of meaning' in modern life; and these cries of pain are chronicled in journalism and conversation as 'the crisis of the modern mind,' or even more hopelessly as 'the human condition' " [27].

The sadness of our times can be documented in an increasing prevalence of depressive illness for people born between 1940 and 1959 (younger age group) compared to those born before 1940 (older age group) [124; 182]. Over the last twenty-five years, the average age for experiencing a first episode has decreased from about age thirty to about twenty. That means that the incidence of first episodes is accumulating over the years more *steeply* for the younger age group, with more of them experiencing their first and subsequent episodes at an earlier age. For example, by age twenty-five, 10 percent of the younger age group may have succumbed at least once versus only 2.5 percent of the older age group. This kind of thing—earlier onset and greater prevalence of depression in young people—is happening not just in the United States, but also in other parts of the world such as Germany, Sweden, Canada, and New Zealand; and it is happening not just in the cities, but also in suburban and even rural areas. What's going on?

One possibility is that there's nothing to explain. The apparent differences might be an illusion, perhaps some artifact of not taking account of the poor memory of old people who have trouble remembering their first episode of depression. Don't bet on it, because comparable differences exist between people in younger age groups, and these people presumably don't have poor memories caused by old age. Well, what about this: The differences reflect changes in the way diagnoses are made, or perhaps in the willingness of professionals to diagnose mental illness. Then, why, for example, has there been only a small increase in the rate of mania, and *no* increase in the rate of panic or phobic disorders, and schizophrenia? It looks like the changes are real, but no one knows exactly how to explain them. A presumably environmental effect must be *bringing out* more of the potential for depression—or, in professional lingo, lowering the threshold to the expression of the liability.

Perhaps there is a simple explanation. People of the older generation had to work harder, and with relatively lower expectations for themselves but higher expectations for their children. That combination meant less self-centeredness but greater hopefulness, that is, less reason for depression. This formula has changed, at least in the United States. Increasingly, there is diminished commitment to stable family life and a consequent weakening of moral and religious influence, cultural traditions, standards of civil behavior, and respect for education. The postwar fruits of technology have given young people not only more (or at least the expectation of more) but worse, the sense of entitlement to more. Impatient preoccupation with more means having more to lose, all of which increases liability, especially for people who, increasingly lacking in self-reliance and self-confidence, are likewise increasingly dependent on industries and institutions for which they have much cynicism and little trust. To the extent that this evolution from inner- to outer-directed personality is both enabled by family disintegration and encouraged by social institutions, we have a formula for increasing liability to depression.

Risk for depressive illness increases in people who suffer loss or separation from loved ones, lack of support, failure at work, or disability. Liability is increased especially when such depressing conditions are experienced as unavoidable, insurmountable, and irremediable. People become destructive, even suicidal when, hopeless in the struggle against helplessness, they are demoralized by the unshakable sense that life either lacks meaning or that its meaning is absolutely and ineluctably inimical.

In the belly of the whale

The Book of Jonah tells of the prophet's unwillingness to accept God's mandate to go to Nineveh and rail against the Assyrian people for their notoriously cruel and violent ways. Mysteriously, Jonah attempts to escape to Tarshish, a town in a different direction from Nineveh, and requiring a journey by sea. While at sea, Jonah sleeps during a great tempest that threatens to capsize the ship. Discovering the cause to be divine wrath over Jonah's behavior, the crewmen reluctantly agree to Jonah's request to "take me up, and cast me forth into the sea; so that the sea be calm unto you." Descending to the depths, Jonah is in a state of fear and despair when, almost dead, he is swallowed by "a great fish" sent by God. After three days and nights of praying for forgiveness and giving thanks for asylum, he is vomited onto dry land whereupon he heads for Nineveh to prophesy the city's overthrow in forty days. However, his prophecy is contradicted when, at the end of the forty days, a merciful God spares the suddenly reformed people. Jonah reacts with suicidal anger ("It is better for me to die than to live"), saying that he knew from the beginning that God would show mercy (". . . was not this my saying, when I was yet in my country?")

This comment is clue to Jonah's otherwise mysterious reaction. After all, Jonah's work as prophet is spectacularly successful, that is, in the sense of professing (educating) as opposed to merely predicting. Given their awful reputation, the Ninevites' religious transformation is a stunning achievement; by comparison the failed prediction of their overthrow is surely minor. What, then, explains Jonah's reaction? Biblical scholarship suggests that Jonah has suffered a deeper, more personal insult than mere embarrassment over being contradicted in front of gentiles [3; 315]. Jonah represents a stern school of religious thought regarding the nature of justice. Accordingly, guilt is an almost tangible quality, making a guilt-ridden soul analogous to a disease-ridden body. Like disease, guilt must be treated, sometimes by bloodletting; it must not be waived. Moreover, justice is fundamentally a matter of eye-for-an-eye lawfulness. If great sin requires great punishment, then the merciful treatment of long-sinful Nineveh is as unjust as the cruel treatment of long-upright Job. Such unjust acts of mercy (or cruelty) are, in Jonah's view, emblematic more of a passionate god of the Greeks than the principled God of the Hebrews.

To the extent that justice is derailed by mercy (or cruelty), life becomes capricious, and prophecy cannot work. God's mercy for the Ninevites therefore does more than contradict Jonah's prophecy. It undermines his theology and threatens his very way of being. It is this threat to his sense of justice that made Jonah try to flee to Tarshish. It is this threat that he must now put out of mind if he is to escape the whale and get back to doing God's work. But deep down this suppression puts Jonah in conflict with himself as well as with God. In the end, Jonah's original fear proves correct; God *is* merciful to the Ninevites, which triggers Jonah's final demoralization. But demoralization comes not only for religious but also for psychological reasons. It is a denouement at the end of what can be viewed as a depressive disorder that has been unfolding in five stages.

The first (fleeing to Tarshish) is *resistance*, using denial and avoidance to defend against a depressive state of mind. Denial means suppressing doubt about the value and meaning of one's work, one's way of life, one's very *self*. Avoidance means fleeing from situations that promote depression—evading but also escaping into oneself through social withdrawal and sleep (Jonah in the hold of the ship fast asleep during the storm).

The second stage (drowning in the sea) is *crisis*—in Jonah's case, emotional and spiritual breakdown. With nervous breakdown comes painful feelings and fantasies of sinking, drowning, suffocating ("waters compassed me about, even to the soul"). There is a deep sense of being cut off from people and, through moral inadequacy or sinfulness, from providence and salvation ("cast out of thy sight"). The person may be represented delusionally as inadequate or bad, even as the devil incarnate.

The third stage (in the belly of the whale) is *recovery*, which has two aspects. One is *compensation*, a mobilization of psychological defenses that check further breakdown by facilitating a search for meaning, a coming to terms, and either an acceptance of one's fate or an effort to change one's life in order to reduce future liability. The other aspect is *asylum*—protection from the stressful outside world to enable the healing process.

With recovery comes the fourth stage (at Nineveh), namely *renewal*, an awakening from the nightmarish struggle with suffering and a re-dedication to meaningful relationships and work. Some survivors return to a reasonably normal life while the less successful make joyless accommodations ("dry land") that mask an enduring liability and a nagging sense of vulnerability.

A sometimes fifth stage is *setback*, with its disillusionment (failed prophecy) and even demoralization (outside Nineveh, alone, blown about by the wind). Disillusionment comes from the frustration of being disappointed by people, events, and oneself. Demoralization comes from the sense of hopelessness about loss of power and purpose. It comes from a painful, unshakable insight that, after all, one is not a new person, that there cannot be genuine rebirth. In the end, Jonah can no longer maintain the illusion of being an autonomous agent bearing witness to lawful truth. The man of God has become a mere extension of external forces he no longer understands.

Depression involves questions of personal responsibility that can haunt people long before and after a personal crisis, but personal responsibility is only a part of the story. The rest involves enduring helplessness—being overwhelmed by forces alien to the self, both external (a stressful job, bad luck, or providence) and internal (lack of insight, self-consuming anger, heredity). In this as in other ways we discern parallels between the Jonah and Castlereagh stories. Both these highly principled men experience a personal crisis involving the sea, yet survive to become more effective than ever. Later, both become suicidally demoralized in connection with a required trip to a foreign city where they must confront a threat to their life's great work. Both men avoid the trip by traveling partly into themselves (Jonah asleep at sea, perhaps dreaming of cetacean rebirth after drowning in sin; Castlereagh wandering through London absorbed in a delusion of having sinned homosexually). Ultimately, both men, victims of an incomprehensible ego-alien force, are unable either to change the course of events or to accept them through some sort of adaptive accommodation.

The story of depression is universal; it is told in every part of the world. The story of depression is for all time; it goes back beyond Castlereagh—beyond even our earliest recorded history. The story of depression is compelling; it is about loss and suffering, but more important, it is about the moral, spiritual, and tragic qualities of human life that suffering can illuminate.

4

MOURNING AND
MELANCHOLIA

The face of deep depression—lean, withered, and hollow-eyed—has been recognized since ancient Greek times. That ghastly look comes with a heavy body of symptoms, including painful sadness and anger, delusions of guilt and unworthiness, hopelessness and suicidal thoughts. Here is depression clear for all to see, but how can we understand it? One way is by appreciating the role of mental life.

Behind the humbug

Recall Ebenezer Scrooge. Scarred as a child by his father's neglect and as an adult by the loss of his sister, he labors compulsively with pecuniary preoccupations that mask a depressed spirit. Alone one fateful Christmas Eve, he hallucinates his dead partner Jacob Marley. Initially, Scrooge comes up with the facile explanation that the apparition is merely an undigested bit of beef. Of course, Scrooge's problem is mental, not physiological; he suffers not from undigested beef, but from undigested experience, that is, from repressed memories of being unloved and unloving. This explanation, encouraged by the ghosts of Christmas past, present, and future, is confirmed by Scrooge's eventual redemption through a spectral therapy that promotes self-confrontation.

To understand depression, we must recognize the role of certain qualities of mental life, for example, *responsiveness*. Mental life responds to events outside of itself—external events such as the loss of life, limb, or status, and internal events such as normal hormone fluctuations or diseases that change body chemistry. However—and this is critical to understanding pathological depression—mental life also has an autonomous quality, as in dreams and imagination that seem to have a life of their own. In other words, mental life is self-sustaining; it has a life of its own that is mostly unconscious. It is the *autonomy* of mental life that explains why depression can occur in benign circumstances but also fail to occur in depressing circumstances.

Responsiveness and autonomy explain why molehills can be transformed into mountains, why even innocuous stimuli can set off a sea change in mental life that can move experience in far-off directions. With morbid imagination or self-critical obsessionality, thinking can become irrational and self-defeating. If you believe that sinfulness has caused you to be damned, how can you not be depressed, even hopelessly and suicidally so? If you believe you are unworthy or unlovable, how can you not, like Scrooge, devote yourself to compulsive work or other forms of denial? Irrational or destructive ways of thinking, such as always suspecting the worst, are at the heart of *psychogenic* (mind-caused) depressions. (Psychogenic depressions are called "neurotic" when they are associated with anxiety, emotional reactivity, or immaturity.) But what is the origin of a psychogenic depression?

If it is largely congenital, for example, a heritable brain abnormality, we call the depression *endogenous*—originating inside. However, if the origin lies in the outside world, in the school of hard knocks that distorts personality by abuse or neglect, we call the depression *exogenous*. Charles Dickens rightly embraced the romantic view of normal people turned into neurotics by harsh circumstances and haunting memories. That explanation will surely hold for some cases of depressive illness, yet not for those involving something more endogenous.

For now, it seems best to start with uncomplicated grief over loss of a loved one, a normal depressive reaction that, like the flu, comes from external events, passes relatively quickly, and leaves no pathological residue, no increased vulnerability. From that vantage, we can explore the psychogenic nature of abnormal depressions and where they come from. Our strategy, then, is to move from outside in, from situational to psychogenic, from mourning to melancholia.

Sweet sorrow

Grieving may be good for the soul. Nevertheless, it takes its toll in changes in appetite, energy, emotion, and cognition sometimes as severe as in the pathological depressions. Fatigue, restlessness, poor concentration, memory problems, and increased use of alcohol and nicotine are common. Sleep problems may develop: trouble falling asleep, restless sleep, and early-morning awakening without feeling refreshed. Here is how a scholarly seventeenth-century Anglican clergyman and librarian Robert Burton described grief in *The Anatomy of Melancholy*, a 500,000-word best-seller classic on melancholia. Grief "takes away their appetite, desire of life, extinguisheth all delights . . . causeth deep sighs and groans, tears, exclamations: O mother's sweet child! O my very blood / O tender flower! alas! and art thou gone. . . ."

Grief involves a deep sense of loss, helplessness, and intense preoccupation with the loved one that can even involve suicidal thoughts, perhaps involving the fantasy of reunion. Occasionally, the lost person can be sensed, and even a hallucinated presence, perhaps a voice, is not that rare. Burton described it long ago: "they think they see their dead friends continually in their eyes." Such hallucinatory reminiscence can apply to lost body parts as well as lost love objects. Phantom limbs are experienced by amputees—in 95 percent of cases when the loss is *acute* [167; 225]. Phantoms are more likely to be experienced by older children and adults than by young children, presumably because of greater experience with and emotional attachment to the limb. (That they are experienced by children under two— even by people born without limbs—implies a genetically determined "idea" of body parts built into the brain.) Perhaps, analogously, then, the hallucinatory reminiscences of the bereaved— call them phantom love objects—will be discovered to appear and persist most readily in older children and adults acutely bereaved of someone long depended on. Incidentally, hallucinatory reminiscence can occur in brain disease, such as epilepsy, and need not be unpleasant. On the contrary, it may be deeply satisfying. Neuropsychiatrist Oliver Sacks gives examples of compelling memories of childhood galvanized by epileptic brain activity. One of his patients described these as overwhelming, nostalgic, poignant, joyous, and precious [275].

All of this raises a point: As with all melancholy states, grief may have a somewhat paradoxical, *pleasurable*, aspect whose quality depends on the person. Positive quality—as in good grief or sweet sorrow—involves feelings of appreciation as well as loss. It is a quality of sadness in which a kind of respect is mixed with yearning—a "pleasing woe in which we indulge with a grateful tear," in the words of Homer. Negative quality, on the other hand, is spiteful, even cruel if not outright antisocial. It is a quality of demoralization in which neurotic neediness and self-pity is mixed with psychopathic egocentricity and a "voluptuous pleasure" in being hateful, as Russian novelist Dostoevsky put it.

Grief reactions can vary from the short-lived to the persistent, with many symptoms sometimes still evident twelve months or longer after the loss. Were there no loss of a loved one to explain such extended depressions, about a third of them would be diagnosable as symptoms of a disorder. Within a year, the depression usually subsides, though feelings and memories may linger. Eight hundred years ago, Talmudist and physician, Maimonides, wrote about his grief upon learning that his beloved younger brother drowned while traveling from Egypt to India. "About eight years have since passed but I am still mourning and unable to accept consolation. . . . Whenever I see his handwriting or one of his letters my heart turns upside down and all my grief returns again."

Grief is only one of many depressive reactions to adverse, uncontrollable events. There is also the post-traumatic distress of the abused and the demoralization of victims of incapacitating illness or mutilation. Adverse situations are experienced by victims as unlucky ("It's just not my day."), unfair ("What did I do to deserve this?"), or inconceivable ("This is crazy!"). They are analogous to the effect of stupid commands typed into a computer run by a normal program. The computer performs stupidly, but for reasons entirely external to the hardware or software. Once the input normalizes, the computer's behavior normalizes. Yet what if the input normalizes but the computer's behavior doesn't?

What begins as situational reaction can become permanent vulnerability [313]. Just as grief can evolve into severe depression, distress from parental abuse can evolve into vigilance, sensitivity, and chronic demoralization. Depressing experience can be denied, but often at great cost to personality. This cost comes in the form of incapacity for initiating or sustaining normal interpersonal relationships or a normal sex life. Lack of trust, living only for the moment, and pessimism about the future are emblematic of a depressed spirit. So are deceptive, destructive, and unstable patterns of behavior. Depression and defense against depression are thus inextricably connected.

The resulting behaviors, however, need not be abnormal, at least not in the long run. Depressing circumstances may be overcome. One can keep busy, get back to work, look on the bright side, cultivate a positive outlook, even new patterns of behavior. You can see this with cancer patients who take stock, reassess values, find new meaning, adopt a healthy lifestyle, and build a new life. All this has the effect of promoting self-enhancement. One can go further, galvanized by loss and other kinds of adversity, taking sometimes heroic actions that make a difference on a large scale. For example, parents of a child killed by a drunk driver might become full-time activists in Mothers Against Drunk Drivers (MADD). Such actions point to a natural resiliency of human nature. That resiliency is as much a part of the story as the vulnerability.

From protest to despair

Grief is recognizable cross-culturally and throughout history, in infants as well as adults. It is also evident in our genetically close cousins, the monkeys and chimps [98; 320]. Did the grief reaction to separation or loss, like other adaptive mechanisms, evolve to enhance survivability, by enabling social organisms to exploit opportunities and cope with the twin threats of helplessness and hopelessness?

Look at how grief appears in human and monkey infants separated from their mothers, and in adults during bereavement

[48; 222]. In infants, loss initially produces an outburst of anxious agitation, disconsolate crying, and aimless activity. Sometimes called *protest*, this pattern seems to represent an active struggle against helplessness. The ready responsiveness of caregivers to distressed infants strongly suggests its adaptive value. Moreover, there are marked differences in responsiveness to separation that apparently reflect differences in monkey and human temperament.

Right from early childhood, about 20 percent of monkeys are unusually sensitive to separation, nervous in novel situations, and timid [5]. Apparently, these are inherited qualities of temperament since they appear even in animals reared by calm *adoptive* mothers. Under stable and familiar social conditions, the traits aren't too apparent; the uptight monkeys can grow up to be normal adults, with the females generally making excellent mothers. However, in unstable or conflict-ridden conditions, the outcome is quite different. There, uptight monkeys become excessively nervous around peers, dependent on adults, even abusive to their offspring.

Research on human personality development reveals a similar picture [169]. About 15 percent of children, right from the beginning, are like uptight monkeys: timid, restrained, cautious, and tense. When asked to fall backward onto a mattress, the inhibited children tend to fall into a sitting position or refuse outright. When asked to make facial gestures that simulate different emotions, they are more restrained. When asked to throw a ball into a box whose distance can be adjusted, they have the box placed relatively close to them. Such reactions are in marked contrast to those of the most socially and emotionally outgoing children.

Something reminiscent of protest can erupt in adults threatened by situations that disallow more effective coping strategies. The adult form, however, differs from the infantile in that adults can remember and appreciate a lost person. They can recognize a symbolic loss of status, value, or esteem. They can experience sorrow, sympathy, and guilt. In short, the protest-depression of adults is a distinctive mix of passion, pain, and preoccupation that is alien to infants. So, while the infant cries in distress over lost creature comforts, the adult weeps out of the melancholy apprehension of life and the world. Nevertheless, like its infantile counterpart, adult protest-depression does not merely express distress. It can have powerful self-serving effects, attracting attention, eliciting sympathy, and otherwise manipulating people in ways not possible during periods of emotional sobriety.

Consider a mother whose child is dying of cancer [64]. In the early stages of grief, she is frightened, angry, disconsolate, and a little paranoid, fantasizing about diagnostic errors made or alternative treatments not considered by incompetent or indifferent physicians. A closer look reveals an element of instrumentality, of effective ploy. More than merely the neurotic self-expression of a woman driven to extremes by impossible circumstances, the behavior is instrumental, creating at least an illusion of really doing something about helplessness—something that, for a while anyway, denies hopelessness.

We recognize in this protest against helplessness an awakening of ancient adaptive mechanisms—to lash out and fight back against all odds. Nevertheless, helplessness-protest can arise seemingly out of the blue or as an inordinate, overblown reaction to mildly depressing events. Sometimes it is unusually autonomous, unshakable despite the most positive changes in circumstance. In the weepy, angry, fidgety behaviors of *agitated* depression (the pathological version to be discussed shortly), we recognize both a caricature and the collapse of inherited mechanisms of adaptation.

Typically, things will get better and for at least two reasons: reversal of situations, and the resiliency of organisms. In most cases, it is simply that the situation improves before helplessness-protest turns into hopelessness-despair; bad situations usually get better, either largely on their own or as a result of the protest behavior. A little crying can do a lot to get mom's attention. More important, the capacity to recover from psychological stress, like from other illness, eventually kicks in. With depression, recovery may be a matter of shifting from protest to more effective ways of mastering helplessness. For example, an infant becomes attached to a substitute caregiver, or a bereaved adult shakes off the obsessional preoccupation with a dead spouse and directs more attention to friends and projects.

Alas, mastery of helplessness may *not* occur. Protest seems to wither, along with a deepening feeling that there are no alternatives. Rather than master helplessness, one surrenders to it, as did Jonah at Nineveh. The result is despair, a depressive state of mind marked by behavioral apathy, inactivity, social withdrawal, and demoralization, the most extreme form being so-called *retarded* depression (also described shortly). This, too, will pass, even when the loss of vitality has become something akin to a state of suspended animation, as evoked in Emily Dickinson's haunting poetic imagery:

> After great pain, a formal feeling comes—
> The nerves sit ceremonious, like Tombs . . .
> This is the Hour of Lead—
> Remembered, if outlived,
> As Freezing persons, recollect the Snow—
> First—Chill—then Stupor—then the letting go—

The shift from protest (agitated depression) to despair (retarded depression) has been documented systematically in laboratory animals, and somewhat less so in humans. Few human infants, maybe 15 percent, develop a despair reaction after prolonged maternal loss. These differences in the "15 per-centers," like those observed in the laboratory animals, point to innate and heritable differences in vulnerability. Hopelessness-despair may represent an inherited abnormality of adaptive mechanisms. When functioning normally, they enable organisms to withdraw from social engagement, thereby preserving life and limb and conserving energy. Giving up and disengaging when hopeless is like falling asleep when bored, fainting when horrified, or becoming catatonic when scared. Perhaps it confers an advantage to helpless organisms that cannot attack, withdraw, or secure support in more active ways. Yet this so-called conservation-withdrawal mechanism can get out of hand. The organism may give up the struggle—developing a retarded depression, even dying—despite favorable changes in the environment.

Melancholia

"O God! what a misfortune to be born! Born like a mushroom, doubtless between an evening and a morning; and how true and right I was when in our philosophy-year in college I chewed the cud of bitterness with the pessimists. Yes indeed, there is more pain in life than gladness—it is one long agony until the grave." Thus writes a patient from a French asylum one hundred years ago. It might have been yesterday, or 2,000 years ago, for depressive illness has been observed throughout history.

Severe depressions are marked by striking changes in energy, appetite, thinking, and motility that come in two patterns: agitated and retarded (see "Anatomy of a Syndrome" Appendix note). With the *agitated* form, movement is restless, involuntary, and seemingly without purpose. A person will pace back and forth, stand up and sit down repeatedly or wander through the house for no apparent reason. An inability to relax when effort is not required comes with an inability to act when action is called for. Agitated depression often occurs with high levels of anxiety, that is, nervousness, apprehensiveness about bodily functions (hypochondria), feelings of being unreal, and panic attacks. Not surprisingly, agitated depression typically means diminished and disorganized sleep (insomnia) that is restless and fitful, with frequent movement or incomplete awakenings. After only four or five hours, further sleep is impossible. Moreover, there is a sense of having been awake and thinking rather than asleep, and a feeling of being tired all the time.

Along with insomnia comes a loss of appetite and consequent loss of weight, a condition called *anorexia* if these symptoms become severe enough. We get pleasure from anticipating an ice cream cone or a sexual encounter, and ultimately from consuming the ice cream and consummating the liaison. Severe depression, especially the agitated form, changes all this. With some, the capacity for both anticipatory and consummatory pleasures is lost. Others lose only the anticipatory capacity, remaining indifferent to the idea of eating or having sex, but retaining the consummatory capability [26]. It is *anhedonia* (from *an:* without; *hedonia:* pleasure) that pervades many areas of experience. The smells and taste of good food or the drifting off to sleep in a warm bed no longer have that delicious sensuality. There is no pleasure in seeing a beautiful sunset, walking barefoot on luxurious carpet, being caressed.

In *The Canterbury Tales*, Chaucer describes the effect of appetite loss in Arcite, a melancholy knight caught up in the grips of an agitated depression. "His sleep, his food, his drink were banished from him so that he grew lean and dry as the shaft of a spear. His eyes were hollow and frightening to look at; his complexion was sallow and pale as dead ashes. He was given to solitude and ever alone, and wailing all night as he uttered his complaint." Loss of appetite, reduced eating, and consequential loss of weight, especially in conjunction with poor sleep: all these can give the person a certain pinched appearance of premature age. In more severe cases, anorexia may develop with significant weight loss. The older the patient, the more typical is the anorexia-insomnia pattern of agitated depression.

Agitated depression brings complaints, sometimes to the point of hypochondriasis, about bodily discomfort and dysfunction, for example, about headache, nausea, poor vision, and even physical appearance. Poetic talent can represent the somatic complaints of melancholia in compelling physical metaphors, for example, of poet Gerard Manley Hopkins (from "I Wake and Feel the Fell of Dark"): "I am gall, I am heartburn. God's most deep decree / Bitter would have me taste: my taste was me"—and of the writer Virginia Woolf who, tortured by a sense of the monstrousness of her body, spoke of "a sordid mouth and sordid belly demanding food—repulsive matter which must then be excreted in a disgusting fashion."

Psychic pain, a common complaint in the severest depressions, can be the most painful of experiences. In a candid TV interview, author William Styron made a similar observation: that "the pain, when it attacks, resembles suffocating, being in a monstrously overheated room, immobilized without a breeze stirring, and no way to get out of it." In an equally candid TV interview, Mike Wallace of "60 Minutes" described his depression as involving "physical pain, I mean real knifelike pain. . . ." Complaints of psychic pain, so common in psychiatric patients, are particularly noteworthy because their meaning can be ambiguous. There may even be something vaguely positive in all this. The pain behind the mask proves you're not dead. Alloyed with reproach toward those who have not suffered, it may even provide a saving sense of moral superiority. Yet this is poor recompense at best, and cold comfort against feelings that one's past is a house of cards, one's existence mere will-o'-the-wisp.

Sometimes depressed patients try to conceal or minimize their emotional problems with complaints of physical distress, for example, headache or back pain. Physical distress may be a vehicle by which one kind of pain (dysphoria) turns into another (physical pain). One psychiatrist called chronic pain an expression of a "muted state of agony" [40]. The muted state of strong feelings and judgmental attitudes may sometimes be masked behind a facade of stony silence. Flinty exteriors can defend against psychic pain, but they can also serve to hide rage against a sense of impotence. In this way, the depressed patient is like the concentration-camp inmate who, despite appearances, is anything but apathetic. And measured elevations of stress hormone lend support to the impression that there can be pain and anger behind the mask of studied indifference [216]. (Hormone abnormalities, plus postpartum and premenstrual depressions, are discussed in the "Hormones and Depression" Appendix note.)

In many ways *retarded* depression is the opposite of agitated depression. In what seems like a loss of vitality in every sphere of life, retarded depression is marked by diminished energy, heightened sleepiness with longer time spent sleeping (at least one hour more), and increased appetite with excessive eating and weight gain. The increased appetite of retarded depression may involve binge eating that can end with self-induced vomiting. It can also involve a dramatic eruption of food cravings, for chocolate, of course, but sometimes also for sugar, jam, or candy. Incidentally, carbohydrate craving, either as an isolated symptom or as part of a depressive illness, may be treatable with antidepressant drugs [228]. But what does it mean?

A carbohydrate-rich meal can make most people sleepy. For cravers, however, it can reduce tension, anxiety, or fatigue. Apparently, chocolate in particular not only tastes good, it feels good. For this reason, it can be used as a kind of self-medication. Carbohydrates may normalize brain chemistry by stimulating with amphetamine-like chemicals, and by stimulating the release of the hormone insulin, the effect of which is to elevate levels of the neurotransmitter, *serotonin*. (This neurotransmitter was thus named because it was first isolated in blood *serum* and because it *tones* the size of blood vessels.) A serotonin abnormality may indeed underlie some depressions. That would explain why formerly depressed patients taking various antidepressants relapsed when brain serotonin was reduced by a diet free of tryptophan, the amino acid the brain uses to construct that neurotransmitter [87].

In retarded depression especially, everything seems to slow down and become more strenuous; even routine activities like washing or dressing become a chore. Speech is monotonous and impoverished, movements hesitant and leaden, face expressionless, posture hunched to the point of seeming Parkinsonian. There is a strong sense of being worn out, run down, debilitated by fatigue and lethargy—of being weighed down even in the morning after what ought to have been enough sleep. Psychologist Norman Endler, writing about his bout with depression, describes the fatigue as "extreme to the point of exhaustion. I was too tired to make decisions and felt as if I had a huge weight on my back that wouldn't allow me to achieve anything. . . . No matter how long I stayed in bed and slept I never felt rested and refreshed. . . . I was slow as molasses" [96].

Loss of energy and paralysis of will can affect thinking. Depressed people complain that their thinking has slowed and their memory has become poor. They have trouble concentrating on what others are saying. The more effort required to learn something new, the worse the memory, and the greater the need for reminders. Mike Wallace explained it this way, "I could no more listen to your question and remember what you had in mind, or read my research and keep it in mind beyond thirty seconds—it was a real struggle, and it went on for months, and I did have to fake it."

Deficient memory and slowed thinking can make a severely depressed person appear to be in the early stages of an Alzheimer's type of dementia [106; 253; 276].* Occasional misdiagnosis makes it all the more important to consider the differences between severe depression and early-stage Alzheimer's disease, especially since depressive disorder may kill up to 20 percent of

*Depression and dementia are linked historically. In 1904, a 40-year-old psychiatrist moved to Munich to work with Emil Kraepelin, famous for his research on manic-depression. In 1906, Kraepelin's new colleague, Alois Alzheimer, discovered cortical abnormalities—tissue loss, amyloid plaques, cell tangles—in a 56-year-old demented man, and later in other patients. Kraepelin honored his colleague by naming the disease after him.

its victims, mostly through suicide, while Alzheimer's disease kills *all* of its victims through progressive, irreversible brain deterioration. In depression, memory problems are greatest *early in the day*, gradually lessening with the lightening of mood; in Alzheimer's they are greatest *later in the day* with the deepening of other symptoms involving deficits in language and thinking. Moreover, depressed people readily complain about lost memories and slowed thinking, while people in the early stages of Alzheimer's typically deny such things.

Special methods can be used to distinguish the memory problems of the two disorders [83]. For example, a person is asked to complete a three-letter word-stem, for example, *def* (for *defe*nse), using the first word that comes to mind. Given such partial stimuli, people (including depressives) tend to think of words recently heard. This "priming effect" of recently heard words is weak or absent in patients with Alzheimer's disease. These and other observations indicate that with depression the memory deficit is a matter of energy—a temporary loss of motivation; in contrast, with Alzheimer's, it is a matter of matter—a permanent loss of brain tissue.

The cognitive deficits of severe depression are more than problems of poor memory; they are often matters of *selective* memory boosted by inimical fantasy, whereby the imagery of sin, disease, or persecution can become fantastical, delusional, and frankly psychotic in up to 25 percent of the cases. With the delusions of a psychotic depression, the possibly reasonable but private metaphors of self-evaluation ("I am capable of rotten behavior." "I am indifferent to my fellow man.") become bizarre public diagnoses ("I am rotten to the core." "I am dead.") [278]. Later, in Chapter 6, we will take a closer look at this delusional side of depression. Here we pursue a different aspect of morbid thinking.

Mind matters

"When melancholia descends," says psychologist L. E. Cole, "the springs of life seem to dry up: the pinched expression and drooping posture suggest the weeping willow. Matching this posture, both inner visceral changes and the subjective withdrawal of all tentacles of hope and aspiration complete the picture of despair. Even the sluggish colon participates in this general nonfeasance" [70]. The effect can be dependency, passivity, and in the severest cases, immobility.

Pervading everything is hopelessness, an irrational sense that, regardless of effort, nothing will change or that things will only get worse. Some ability to react positively to positive events may remain; most depressed people can at least smile when offered affection or encouragement, and most will work harder in response to urging. Yet, given the overriding sense of futility that takes on a life of its own, these responses are often evanescent, and even a little thing may come to have exaggerated significance. "It's not the large things that send a man to the madhouse," says writer Charles Bukowski in *The Shoelace*. "No, it's the continuing series of small tragedies that send a man to the madhouse . . . not the death of his love, but a shoelace that snaps, with no time left."

When purpose, meaning, and hope all vanish, the organism may even die—give up the ghost as it were. Our word, courage, comes from *coeur*, the French word that derives from the Latin *cor*, meaning heart. Having courage is having heart, but also a sense of heartiness, vitality, aliveness. Quite the opposite is true of the depressed person—dis-couraged, disheartened, dispirited, and with diminished vitality and diminished self-affirmation, or loss of what theologian Paul Tillich calls "the courage to be."

There is much anecdotal documentation of the power of the depressed mind over bodily matters to the point of threatening survival [286]. An elderly man develops a heart condition and dies, seemingly of grief over the sudden death of his daughter. Another dies during the opening bars of a concert marking the fifth anniversary of the death of his wife, a well-known piano teacher [97]. Psychiatrist Viktor Frankl describes the death of a fellow inmate of a concentration camp. In February 1945, the man dreamed that the camp would be liberated on March 30. By late March the news was not hopeful. On the twenty-ninth, he developed a fever, on the thirtieth became delirious, and on the thirty-first, died. Frankl believes that the loss of hope lowered the capacity to resist a latent typhus infection [113]. Stress researcher Paul Rosch describes a man with advanced cancer whose tumors seemed to vanish after taking the "drug" krebiozen. After newspaper articles appeared exposing krebiozen as bogus, he experienced a resurgence of the cancer. It again faded, however, after the desperate physician pooh-poohed the stories, and gave him what he said was a larger and purer dose but that was just distilled water. The cancer recurred and the man died when the truth of the placebo treatment was undeniable [263].

Intriguing scientific evidence of such mind-over-matter phenomena comes from psychosomatic research showing how unconscious mental life can take over, causing bodily symptoms [47]. Consider the dramatic illustration of psychosomatic influence in the following example of an experimenter using hypnotic suggestion to inhibit allergic reactions in a patient [215]. An asthmatic woman had suffered attacks of wheezing, itching, and runny nose that had made her a chronic invalid over a ten-year period despite treatment. She was given the hypnotic suggestion to become normal. The result was that she no longer had asthmatic attacks. Moreover, she failed to react adversely to an allergen injected into her blood. A stunning story, no doubt, but it gets better. The nonallergic experimenter then injected her serum into his arm and exposed himself to pollen. Incredibly, he showed a hypersensitive allergic skin reaction, the very reaction apparently suppressed by the "hypnosis-virtuoso" patient through some feat of mind over matter.

Extreme psychosomatic determinism also appears in so-called experiments of nature, for example, multiple personality where a deeply depressed state of mind is almost always discoverable. One personality seeks treatment for chronic fatigue, lack of energy, muscle weakness or pain, depression, hallucination—a variety of symptoms suggesting various diagnoses but again, almost always involving depression. Another is more vigorous, healthy, extraverted, even outright antisocial. The personalities may differ, for example, in allergies (only one allergic to cats), food sensitivities (only one hyperreactive to citrus), endocrine abnormality (only one diabetic), even visual acuity (only one requiring glasses) [72; 130].

Exotic examples of psychosomatic phenomena merely illustrate in the extreme a surprisingly mundane process. Most people are capable of some somatic compliance with suggestion and imagination. During an athletic event, for example, word gets out that someone has contracted food poisoning. Soon the stadium is full of people "sick" to their stomachs, retching, fainting, and whatnot. Then word of false alarm gets out, at which point miraculous "cures" take place. Psychosomatic phenomena include not only mass hysteria but also placebo effects and even voodoo deaths. A placebo response, for example, can be powerful. Warts may disappear when painted with a dye the patient believes to be a new drug; even bleeding ulcers may heal with injections of distilled water believed to be medicine. Placebos can work even when the person is told that they are pharmacologically inert. Perhaps the biblical story of Sampson losing his strength after Delilah cut off his hair represents a sort of reverse placebo reaction to losing an imagined source of strength. If so, then voodoo death might be a negative placebo reaction—the ultimate psychosomatic reaction to an anti-therapeutic "treatment."

Psychosomatic phenomena suggest that the body is mentally represented in mostly unconscious imagery and thoughts. This may explain how the hysteric may "lose" a physically existing body part. Perhaps it's no different from forgetting any idea; if you can't remember it—if you can't bring it to (conscious) mind—it doesn't exist. Body knowledge also explains the opposite of a loss, namely the presence of something that seems not to exist. An amputee's experience of a movable phantom limb that itches or hurts implies an idea of limb that is activated. Like a dream, the active idea can be experienced as reality.

We may appreciate, if not entirely understand, the power of mind over matter—really, the power of the mental (cerebral) over the vegetative (subcortical) part of the brain. But what accounts for a state of mind so inimical it may confound even life's very prime directive? One answer is *psychogenesis*—the causal powers of all those habits of thinking, expectations, and needs that comprise the psychological baggage we bring to situations. Negative views of the self and world, for example, can create hopelessness out of anything—from minor frustration to major loss. The obvious question is what is the source of this psychogenesis.

Is the source *exogenous*, that is, rooted in the external facts of early conditioning by the school of hard knocks? Indeed, the term *psychogenesis* has always lent itself to assumptions about

exogeneity—in some theorizing, the two terms seem synony-
mous—but this need not mean external *environ*mental. What
about inner sources? Depression, especially the melancholic
type, seems to involve something deep down—something
endogenous—as evident not only in its often spontaneous onset
and typically autonomous course, but also in the evidence of the
high heritability of depressive disorders. Trying to get to the
bottom of melancholic psychogenesis raises many possibilities,
one of the most intriguing being the biological rhythms that
influence mental life.

5

RHYTHM IN BLUES

"My creative powers have been reduced to a restless indolence. I cannot be idle, yet I cannot seem to do anything either. I have no imagination, no more feeling for nature, and reading has become repugnant to me. When we are robbed of ourselves, we are robbed of everything!" Thus articulated by Werther, Goethe's manic-depressive hero, the state of alienation is without charm, flavor, or purpose, and living no longer seems to make sense. In the absence of obviously depressing circumstances that could explain such a state of mind, we naturally look elsewhere. One of the most intriguing explanations is an abnormality of the inner clockwork that governs our biological rhythms, both daily and seasonal.

'Tis the season

Ever since Hippocrates, the seasonality of mood has been recognized by physicians—poets too. Emily Dickinson speaks of "a certain slant of light, on winter afternoons, that oppresses, like the weight of cathedral tunes. Heavenly hurt it gives us; we can find no scar, but internal difference where the meanings are . . . 'tis the seal, despair,—an imperial affliction sent us of the air." Likewise, novelist Theodore Dreiser speaks of our efforts to keep busy, to make merry, indulge in warm pleasures, and be part of the crowd. Otherwise, he says, "we would quickly discover how firmly the chill hand of winter lays upon the heart; how dispiriting are the days during which the sun withholds a portion of our allowance of light and warmth. We are more dependent on these things than is often thought. We are insects produced by heat, and pass without it." Arctic explorer Frederick Cook noted in his journal: "The winter and the darkness have slowly but steadily settled over us. . . . The curtain of blackness which has fallen over the outer world of icy desolation has also descended upon the inner world of our souls. Around the tables . . . men are sitting about sad and dejected, lost in dreams of melancholy from which, now and then, one arouses with an empty attempt at enthusiasm" [340].

These observers would thus not have been surprised to learn about *seasonal affective disorder*, or *SAD* [241]. Up to one-third of the normal population may experience some seasonal fluctuation in mood, sleep, weight, energy, and social activity. When these fluctuations are severe, SAD may be diagnosed, either fall-winter SAD or spring-summer SAD, depending on when the illness begins. A minority of affective disorders are of the SAD kind; estimates vary from 10 to 40 percent, depending on the study. While we briefly consider the depressive side of SAD, we should acknowledge its manic element. Manic episodes can occur seasonally, either alone or after recovery from seasonal depressions, that is, as temporary "overshoots" beyond normalcy. (The manic element, seen in as many as half of the cases, suggests that SAD is often a variant of manic-depressive disorder, but more on the manic element later.)

The diagnostician will identify seasonal depression if at least two episodes separated by periods of normalcy occur during the same season of successive years. Most cases are of the fall-winter variety whose symptom signature is the retarded pattern described in Chapter 4. Episodes of what is commonly called "winter depression" start anywhere from August through October, but often in September. (In the Southern Hemisphere, all this is reversed, with onset of fall-winter SAD occurring from March to April.) Some cases are of the less frequent spring-summer variety, more commonly known as "summer depression."

With an agitated symptom pattern, it affects about one-half of 1 percent of the population, with onset occurring anywhere from March to June.

Those early Arctic explorers would also not have been surprised to learn that winter depression, more prevalent with increasing distance from the equator, is believed to be an effect of seasonally decreasing light. The inference is consistent with the remarkable effects of *phototherapy*, the therapeutic application of very strong light for a few hours each day. The idea of phototherapy goes back to ancient times when the Roman physician Aretaeus of Cappadocia (first century C.E.) first suggested using strong light to treat depression. Even relatively weak light may be effective if, toward the end of sleep (4:00 to 6:00 A.M.) each morning, it is made to increase gradually, thereby simulating dawn's early light [23]. However done, phototherapy helps in as many as 75 percent of the cases. Morning applications may be preferable—the question of timing remains controversial—but understanding why this might be so requires that we learn more about how seasonal changes in light might affect what are known as "circadian rhythms."

Inner clockwork

Circadian rhythms (from *circa:* around; *diem:* day) evolved to help living things anticipate external events and increase their ability to perform their best at the right time, extending this anticipatory ability to the 24-hour light-dark cycles caused by the earth's rotation. A rhythm is nothing more than an endless repetition of cycles, for example, cycles of breathing in and out and cycles of sleep and wakefulness. Each sleep-wakefulness cycle, for example, might involve a shift from initial awakening (say at 7 A.M.) to peak wakefulness (8 P.M.) to the trough of deepest sleep (3 A.M.) and back to initial awakening. During the same 24-hour period, body temperature shifts about 1.5 degrees. It is at its highest point, or peak, during late afternoon or early evening and its lowest point, or trough, during the middle of sleep.

In animals, circadian rhythms are found for alertness, body temperature, hormone output, protein synthesis, allergic sensitivities—even the timing of birth and death [21;205]. In other words, time of day influences many things. For example, animals who learn to fear a stimulus presented at some point during the day show the greatest fear when that stimulus occurs at the same time of the day. Tolerance of poisons, drugs, pain stimuli, or X-rays is time-dependent. For example, a dose of ethanol or endotoxin *(E. coli)* that kills 60 to 80 of 100 laboratory mice during their rest period (daytime) may kill only 20 during their active period (nighttime). Human performance on laboratory tasks is most efficient during the later afternoon and evening when body temperature peaks. Sensitivity to tooth pain caused by cold is greater in the morning and evening than in the afternoon (which might suggest a good time to plan that dental appointment).

Clocks, noises, artificial lighting, and social interactions vary with the changing light conditions of the solar day. All these external facts of life, being systematic and thus predictable, are time cues, or *zeitgebers*—from the German word for "time giver." Normally, circadian rhythms must comply with zeitgebers, the most powerful one being natural light. Forced compliance, or *entrainment,* produces a daily resetting of a "biological clock," a neural pacemaker located deep in the oldest part of our brain.*

Rhythms continue their cyclic oscillations even when freed from zeitgebers, for example, under conditions of constant lighting or blindness. Under such conditions, we discover that inner rhythms are naturally set to oscillate, not exactly at 24 hours per solar day, but anywhere from 22 to 28 hours, depending on the organism. The biological clock of some plants is set for a 22-hour "day," as expressed in a circadian rhythmicity of their leaf movement or metabolism evident during constant light or constant darkness. For some animals, the preferred setting is 23.5 hours; for humans, it is 24 to 25 hours.

Without entrainment to a 24-hour external clock, endogenous circadian rhythms would slow down or speed up relative to the light-dark cycle of the external world. For example, an inner ten-

*One good bet is the suprachiasmatic nucleus, or *SCN*, of the hypothalamus [21;256]. Isolated cells of the SCN continue to show a spontaneous circadian rhythm. Destroying a rat's SCN eliminates the circadian rhythmicity of nocturnal activity and diurnal quiescence, while transplants of SCN tissue from donor rats can restore circadian rhythm (but now the circadian rhythm displayed is that of the donor rather than the recipient).

dency to cycle roughly once every 25 hours could put blind people completely out of sync with the external light-dark cycle every twelve days, all of which could cause intermittent insomnia and fatigue [54]. Observations such as these suggest that depression might involve out-of-sync or otherwise abnormal circadian rhythms.

Each cycle of a circadian rhythm reaches a maximum and a minimum at roughly the same time of the 24-hour day, but usually at a different time from that of other cycles. Body temperature, for example, may peak in the early evening while the amount of some hormone might peak just before awakening. However, the time difference between any two rhythms tends to remain constant, that is, between the peak or trough of the one, and the peak or trough of the other. With rhythms out of step with each other *to some degree*, measuring their time difference, or "distance," in degrees makes perfect sense. Just think of any cycle as a *circle*, and like any circle, divisible in degrees. We can start at some point (in degrees) and come back, full *circle*—360 degrees—to the same point.

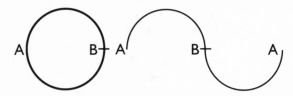

In the diagram, a cycle is represented by a circle transformed in two steps. First, cut the ends of the circle's diameter (points A and B). Then, rotate the bottom half from left to right, using the right cut-point (B) as a hinge. The resulting curve represents a cycle with a peak and a trough, like wakefulness-sleep or body temperature. Notice that the two "A" points on the curve are really the same "A" point of the original circle, meaning that the end of one cycle (rightmost A) is the same level as the beginning of the next (leftmost A). Moreover, like a circle, such a curve can be divided into 360 degrees, that is, 360 units from beginning to end, or from point A through point B back to A. In the diagram, point A is at zero degrees, and point B—halfway through the cycle—is at 180 degrees. The peak is 90 degrees through the cycle, and the trough is 180 degrees from it (270 from the zero point).

The cycles of any two rhythms—sleep-wake and body temperature, for example—are typically non-overlapping, with their peaks (and troughs) out of sync—*out of phase* in the jargon of chronobiology, the study of biological rhythms. An easy way to think of two out-of-phase rhythms is to imagine that you begin breathing in exactly when I begin breathing out, and breathing out when I begin breathing in. As long as the *rate* of our breathing is the same, our breathing rhythms remain out of phase by 180 degrees—as in the two rhythms shown in the next diagram. The light and bold lines are out of phase by 180 degrees, as indicated by the arrow.

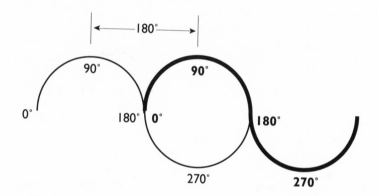

Cycle-somatics

To appreciate the story of rhythm in blues, imagine a trip that requires resetting the internal clock to accommodate a change in time zones, for example, a flight from Texas to Europe that requires a 6-hour change. Many things will happen as a result of such a trip, mostly good no doubt, but one bad thing: disorganization of circadian rhythms, or *circadian dysrhythmia*. The reason is that the body is now 6 hours *out of phase* with the European external clock, that is, one-quarter of the 24-hour distance around the earth (6/24 hours). In other words, your inner clock is 90 *degrees* out of phase, that is, by one-quarter of the 24-

hour distance around the earth (90/360 degrees). Of course, as far as your brain is concerned, you could just as well have stayed home and moved the clock forward six hours. (A more modest version of this is the annual daylight savings bonus imposed on Americans with the one-hour "spring ahead.") Anyway, the time is out of joint and you are out of sorts—with jet lag, that is.

Westerly travel seems to induce less jet lag than does easterly travel. The accommodation of biological rhythms to local conditions after a trip through six time zones takes only about three days if travel is westerly, but nine if easterly. Perhaps the 24.5-hour endogenous rhythm makes it a little easier to extend the day (putting off sleep) than to shorten it (trying to fall asleep earlier than usual). That would explain why "springing ahead" (losing an hour) for daylight savings time is more difficult than "falling back."

Jet lag is less severe for the young, for night people ("owls") compared to morning people ("larks"), and for trips requiring few time-zone crossings. Similarly, clockwise movement from day work (starting 8 A.M.) to the afternoon-evening shift (starting 4 P.M.), or from the afternoon-evening to the night shift (starting midnight), is easier than the reverse. The reason is that, like westerly travel, clockwise changes in shift work accommodate the endogenous tendency to extend the day.

The 24.5-hour endogenous clock can explain Monday morning blues [71]. On weekends we tend to go to sleep and wake up later, as if we were traveling west across time zones. We may advance our sleep-wake cycle an hour or more Friday night, and then again even further Saturday night. By midnight Sunday night, we do the equivalent of returning in an easterly direction across all those time zones, but this time more abruptly. The advisability of getting sleep when the clock indicates midnight clashes with a lack of desire; how can we be sleepy if our biological clock is indicating only 8 or 9 P.M.? Sleep might then be difficult or impossible until much later in the night. Then, we might have only a few hours of sleep before we must awaken to the realities of the first work day of the week. Monday morning blues may thus be a compounding of circadian rhythm disruption and sleep deprivation.

For a better understanding of circadian abnormality, you only have to imagine being an experimental subject paid to live in a room, say for ten days, without clocks, windows, or network TV. Without these familiar zeitgebers, it is completely up to you to decide when to wake up, when to go to sleep, when to have a meal or interact with others. Imagine further that, free from the constraints usually imposed by zeitgebers, your sleep-wake rhythm turns out to be a rather abnormal 30 hours, and your body-temperature rhythm, 25 hours. Having a 30-hour wake-sleep inner day means you get up and go to sleep six hours later relative to each solar day. (Of course, you are unaware of this disparity, but never mind.) After a few of these inner days drift-ing around the clock, you are getting up at night and going to sleep during the solar (external) day. Eventually, you drift back, then away, and so on. You have rhythm, no doubt of that. How-ever, for large chunks of time, you are out of sync with the external world. Furthermore, you—the you that you identify with your wakefulness—would be out of sync with the inner world of body temperature. How would that be?

Well, in the experimental room, your body-temperature rhythm is 25 hours, 5 hours shorter than your 30-hour sleep-wake rhythm. Every 24-hour solar day, your body-temperature rhythm would drift 1 hour relative to the external day-night cycle (25 minus 24), but 5 hours relative to the sleep-wake cycle (30 minus 25). You would be so out of sync that on some inner days the trough of the body-temperature rhythm would occur during wakefulness rather than, as is normal, during sleep. The effect on you would be unpleasant, like feeling chilled and irrita-ble after awaking at 3:00 A.M. Now, at 3:00 A.M, you have a ready explanation for feeling out of sorts, so there's an end to it. But what if you *didn't* have a ready explanation: no weird experiment, no jet lag, no daylight savings? What would you think; how would you *feel?* You might not feel just out of sorts; you might feel depressed.

Though ideal for studying circadian rhythms, zeitgeber-*free* laboratory settings are unnatural. So now imagine a zeitgeber-*shifted* environment, the kind you get with jet travel or with shift work. Ideally, the new zeitgebers would quickly reset the bio-logical clock. Alas, this doesn't happen. Different rhythms shift at different rates, the body-temperature rhythm being one of the slowest. During the period of accommodation, fatigue, insomnia, and dysphoria can persist; these are hallmarks of jet lag. The same thing—a blue-collar jet lag—happens to shift workers who are abruptly shifted from a day to a night job, or *vice versa*. They may be sleepy, out of sorts, and complain of aches, stomach problems, or other bodily discomfort.

Jet lag means a disruption of the normally stable organization of out-of-phase oscillations. Each rhythm takes a different amount of time to accommodate to the different time frame of the new time zone. That is, the phase relations of your rhythms become undone; you may even feel irritable, apprehensive, unhappy—in a word, *dysphoric*. Question: Is the dysphoria you feel anything like that felt by people who are considered depressed? If the answer is yes, then maybe some people feel out of sorts *because* their rhythms are too much out of phase. In other words, the circadian dysrhythmia could be a cause, not just a characteristic, of depression.

Sooner or later

We've been considering dysrhythmia mostly as dissociation of any two rhythms *within a person;* but what about a dissociation between a person and the outside world, that is, between any rhythm and the light-dark rhythm of the external world? One or more rhythms, such as body temperature or hormone activity— even the circadian system as a whole—can be out of phase with the light-dark cycle, peaking either too soon or too late in the 24-hour day. One of the bodily rhythms might be doing "row row row your boat" while the other is already "gently down the stream."

The concept of bodily rhythms out-of-sync with the light-dark rhythm of the external world raises a most intriguing idea that boils down to two testable hypotheses. One is that some depressions are marked by a "too-soon" type of dysrhythmia, with some aspect of bodily rhythms occurring regularly from one to four hours earlier than is normal—that is, showing a one- to four-hour *phase advance*. The other is that some depressions may be marked by a "too-late," or *phase delay* dysrhythmia of perhaps two hours. Consider the "too-late" (phase delay) hypothesis, as suggested by unusual activity of the *pineal gland*, a structure deep within the brain.

With the dimming of natural light toward evening, the pineal gland "awakens" with a burst of activity. The effect of this activity is a dramatic increase in the hormone *melatonin,* sometimes called the "Dracula hormone" because of its nocturnal appearance. Melatonin elevations normally occur around 7:00 P.M., but not until roughly 9:00 P.M. in people suffering from winter SAD, at least according to some preliminary research. What might this apparent two-hour phase delay mean? Phototherapy could provide a clue. Some research finds that, applied *in the morning,* phototherapy has two effects: a rise of melatonin earlier in the evening, closer to the normal time, and a corresponding improvement in mood [271]. These twin effects support the notion of an *abnormally phase-delayed ("too late") clock mechanism that has been normalized by being advanced.*

Other research finds either that the rhythms of winter SAD patients are not necessarily phase delayed, or that phototherapy can be helpful when applied *any time of the day*—even in the evening. Such observations, inconsistent with a phase-delay ("too late") dysrhythmia, suggest the possibility that phototherapy works simply by *energizing* the "slowed" state of mind that characterizes winter SAD [266]. In any case, you have some idea of what investigators are looking for, and the seemingly inconsistent observations that can threaten their favored hypotheses.

Now consider the "too-soon" (phase advance) dysrhythmia hypothesized for those with *typical* (not winter SAD) *depression,* and for those with *premenstrual syndrome (PMS)* whose victims and their relatives have elevated rates of depression. Investigators are finding phase-advance abnormalities in some aspect of one or more rhythms, for example, in the "stop" aspect of the melatonin rhythm that occurs too early in the morning. (The nocturnal "start" and peak output aspects seem to be normal.) In the case of PMS, monthly hormonal changes might drive or aggravate the phase advance that, in turn, makes depression more likely to occur. Rather speculative, no doubt, but this idea could explain an interesting observation. Phototherapy applied in the evening seems to have an antidepressant effect on PMS, as though *an abnormally phase-advanced clock were normalized by being delayed* [244].

A "too-soon" (phase advance) dysrhythmia is also suggested by certain abnormalities of sleep, but this will take a little explaining, starting with this observation. Many people intuitively sense that sleep has something to do with resetting a personal clock. Some years ago, I asked people to imagine that sleep could be eliminated without affecting any other physiological process. They would never be sleepy again, remaining alert 24 hours a day without adverse health consequences. Eliminating sleep would be done by a pill or by an operation that was free of charge and discomfort. While the percentage of people desiring to rid themselves of sleep varied considerably from sample to sample, there was a reliable sex difference. About 20 percent more males than females would take the pill or operation, with more males than females indicating that sleep is a waste of time.

There were many reasons for rejecting the pill or operation. Some had what you might call a neurotic quality—anxiety about being lonely, having nothing to do, or getting into trouble. Others suggested something more hedonistic—the sheer pleasure of drifting off to sleep, or the fun and interest in one's dreams. Another implied that dreaming is an important problem-solving process, a way of getting one's head straight and one's feelings back on an even keel. Finally, there was this important idea, that sleep is a way of starting anew, wiping the slate clean, waking to a new day with new possibilities. The fact that severely depressed people awaken to the worst feelings and thoughts of the day is at least consistent with the idea that something is wrong with their biological clock. This idea takes on further credibility when we consider what is abnormal with the sleep of severely depressed people.

Getting to sleep

Normally, sleep displays a roughly 90-minute rhythm of repeating cycles, about five per night, each one having two parts. One is *REM* (*r*apid *e*ye *m*ovement) sleep, so-called because of the very fast eye movements that give the impression that the sleeping person is scanning a rapidly changing scene. The other part, *NREM* (*n*on-rapid *e*ye *m*ovement) sleep, can be any of four kinds: 1, 2, 3, and 4, with 3 and 4—a distinction we will ignore—called *delta*. Like REM sleep, each of these four

NREM stages comes with its own distinctive brain waves, quality of consciousness, and responsiveness to pain, noises, and the like.

With increasingly deep sleep from Stages 1 to 2 to delta, brain waves become slower, conscious experience more sparse and disjointed, and responsiveness to potentially disturbing noises or other stimuli less reliable or absent. The mind disorganizes and personality dissolves, all most profoundly during the delta sleep which, with its mostly absent consciousness and thinking, can be thought of as an existential vacuum. Each resurrection from delta's depths represents a retracing of steps that can lead to an awakening—to the real world or to a world of dreaming.

With the onset of REM sleep, brain and psyche explode into a unique pattern of activity. The characteristically fast brain waves and rapid eye movements are emblematic of rich mental activity that is easily verified by awakening the person abruptly. Indeed, people thus awakened from REM sleep report vivid, complex, sometimes emotionally charged dream experiences. Not only are these vivid dreams much more common after awakenings from REM than from other kinds of sleep, they have a more *story-like* quality than the typically dreamy and drifting thoughts that characterize NREM sleep. (For more details, see the "Sleep Recording and Dreaming" Appendix note.)

In the figure labeled "Normal Sleep," you can see an example of the nightly rhythm of 90-minute NREM-REM cycles, the first cycle sharply defined in bold lines. The cycle begins with the onset of Stage 2 (ignoring transitional Stage 1) and goes to the onset of the next cycle. The cycle includes a long period of delta sleep and a period of REM sleep that is short by normal nightly standards. Later in the night, the cycles will include less or no delta sleep, and relatively longer periods of REM sleep, which is why you are more likely to recall a dream when you wake up late rather than early in the morning. To appreciate what is often wrong with the sleep of depressed people, consider just the first NREM-REM cycle. Normally, wakefulness (W) plus transitional Stage 1 may last up to 20 minutes. Then true sleep begins with about 90 minutes of NREM sleep filled with Stages 2 and delta, followed by a short REM period with relatively little eye movement.

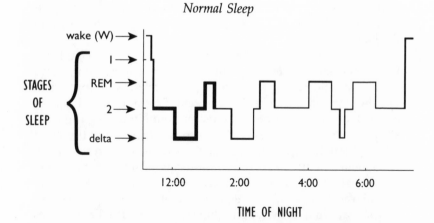

Normal Sleep

Things look different with the sleep of a person suffering from major depression uncomplicated by mania. The figure labeled "Sleep in Depression" shows just one of many possible patterns. This one includes normal sleep onset—the greater the agitation, the longer the sleep onset—plus the characteristic morning insomnia. Moreover, there will be NREM and REM abnormalities, any one of which is found in 90 percent of severely depressed patients. Take, for example, the *abnormally small amount of delta sleep,* especially during the NREM sleep of the first cycle. This anomaly may be a sign of trouble ahead, specifically a tendency toward quicker relapse after recovery from illness.

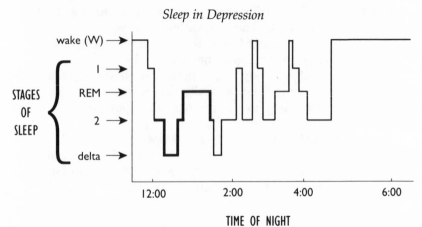

Sleep in Depression

The *initial* REM period of the night typically displays certain abnormal features. For one thing, it lasts too long, as you can see by comparing the two figures. For another, it has an abnormally large amount of eye movement (not shown). Finally, it occurs too quickly relative to the normal 90- to 100-minute standard—30 to 60 minutes after sleep onset, with even earlier onsets (even less than 20 minutes) the older the person or the more delusional the depression. Now, this abnormality, called *short REM-onset latency*, is not specific to depression; for example, it can sometimes occur in schizophrenia. Nevertheless, short REM-onset latency is typical of depression, and, like delta sleep deficiency, it may be a warning sign of poor outcome, including quicker relapses after recovery. More interesting, short REM-onset latency may be a biological marker of *liability* to depression, given that it seems to occur in less marked form in both recovered depressives and in many of their nondepressed first-degree relatives [192].

Do the sleep abnormalities of depression really indicate a "too-early" (phase advance) dysrhythmia capable of overturning psychological well-being? Once again, compare those two figures. What looks like a sleep abnormality *early in the night* would seem less so later in the night. In other words, the first part of depressive sleep looks something like the second part of normal sleep. For example, REM sleep occurring after only 30 to 60 minutes of NREM sleep is abnormal only early in the night. The reason is that the initial NREM period of sleep before the first REM period is, you will recall, roughly 90 minutes long. Look back at that diagram of a whole night's sleep, however, and you will see that NREM periods take up less and less of each subsequent 90-minute NREM-REM cycle. That means less and less NREM before the beginning of each succeeding REM period. Clearly, the first REM period occurring after only 30 to 60 minutes of NREM sleep is quite abnormal.

A "too-soon" dysrhythmia suggests that some aspects of brain function are already in their "sleep mode" hours before bedtime—and therefore that, upon lights out, depressed people are, with respect to those "early-shifted" functions, late for their own sleep. What a peculiar notion. Yet, such a notion could explain one of the oddest observations about depression: Improvement may occur after even one night of sleep deprivation, though without medication the effect is easily lost or even reversed [339]. After a single night of sleep deprivation, a depressed woman became mildly manic with singing and dancing. After napping less than two minutes, she awoke in a severely depressed state that lasted over two hours. Even if temporary, the curious therapeutic effect of sleep deprivation needs explaining.

The effect seems to depend on sleep not occurring during the last four hours of a night. This can be accomplished in either of three ways: (1) allow no sleep, that is, impose total sleep deprivation; (2) allow sleep only during the first four hours of the night by having sleep start at the usual time and imposing early awakening; (3) allow the normal amount of sleep, but have it begin four hours early so it ends before the last four hours of the night. Given all three observations, what does it mean that the effect of sleep deprivation seems to depend more on the timing than amount of lost sleep? A reasonable answer is that the peaks and troughs of some circadian rhythms are occurring too soon relative to the light-dark cycle—a "too-early" (phase advance) dysrhythmia.

Dysrhythmia is speculative, no doubt, yet credible to many investigators [151]. For one thing, it can explain the two-week delay before antidepressant drugs take effect despite their immediate effect on brain chemistry. Perhaps it takes time to normalize the circadian system. Furthermore, a dysrhythmia could explain many of the psychological symptoms of depression, including the physical and psychic pain and the hopelessness that is felt when there is ambiguity about what is wrong and therefore about how to fix it. Circadian dysrhythmia could explain abnormalities connected to a certain time of the day or to events that are known to disrupt circadian rhythms, for example, that deeply depressed people typically feel worst upon awakening, then somewhat better as the day progresses. Finally, the vulnerability to dysrhythmia could explain why depressions can be set off by things that might seem minor or trivial: a change in time zones, routine, seasons.

If inner rhythms make a silent contribution to the texture and organization of experience—if knowledge and sense of self are partly rhythmic—then dysrhythmia might very well disrupt psychological life. The effects might be subtle, for example, sleep problems and poor appetite, or a diminished sense of well-being, and inexplicable dysphoria could prompt continual efforts to feel better through defensive compensation (Chapter 9). A circadian dysrhythmia could have a souring, even unhinging, effect on personal experience. In effect, a person might be sorely pressed to explain seemingly irrational dysphoria and melancholy thoughts. Personality and current events would determine what explanations were given—about life ("Life is meaningless") or self ("I am insufficiently loved or lovable") or fate ("I've run into bad luck"). Usually such thoughts are infrequent, evanescent, easily brushed aside. As a depression deepens into manifest illness, however, such thoughts become persistent, pressing, self-consuming, delusional. With delusional depression, that is, with depression as *psychotic* disorder, we confront the needs, passions, and intelligence of human nature magnified and deformed as if in caricature—in an important sense, *revealed*.

6

TRAGIC PLANE

"My dear fellow," instructs Henry Burlingame, John Barth's wonderful character from *The Sotweed Factor*, "we sit here on a blind rock careening through space; we are all of us rushing headlong into the grave. Think you the worms will care, when anon they make a meal of you, whether you spent your moment sighing wigless in your chamber, or sacked the golden towns of Montezuma? . . . We are dying men, Ebenezer: i'faith, there's time for naught but bold resolves!" Most people can appreciate Burlingame's call for bold resolve, even while rejecting his tragic view of life. After all, being mostly optimistic, they tend to believe in certain basics: that life is meaningful in the sense of there being some sort of unchanging grand plan; that life is knowable through a combination of personal experience and instruction; and finally, that if life isn't always fair, it can be made better through personal efforts to do the right thing.

Reasonably secure in such beliefs, people can go about their business even while suspecting, perhaps if only when alone in the dark, there is some truth to Hamlet's lament that "we are the stuff that dreams are made on, and our little life is rounded with a sleep." Yet, they can hardly be expected to embrace the cynicism of Macbeth about life being a mere "tale told by an idiot, full of sound and fury, signifying nothing"—or worse, the morbid-mindedness of an Ernest Becker. In some of the starkest

imagery to be found on either side of the line separating philosophy from madness, Becker in *The Denial of Death*, speaks of
man's "abject finitude, his physicalness, the likely unreality of
his hopes and dreams . . . man's utter bafflement at the sheer
non-sense of creation. . . . Not only is his body strange, but also
its inner landscape, the memories and dreams. Man's very
insides—his self—are foreign to him. He doesn't know who he
is, why he was born . . . what he is supposed to do, what he
can expect. His own existence is incomprehensible to him . . .
This is the terror: to have emerged from nothing, to have a
name, consciousness of self, deep inner feelings, an excruciating
inner yearning for life and self-expression—and with all this yet
to die. . . . What kind of deity would create such a complex and
fancy worm food?"

Gloomy indeed, these anguished visions of realism, irony,
and negativity—but of what consequence? We may very well
ask, along with American psychologist-philosopher William
James: Are healthy-minded people with no stomach for such
imagery simply too shallow for true philosophical insight, or are
they right to recognize in morbid-mindedness the signs of
unwholesome preoccupation? And how do we distinguish the
insights of gloomy philosophy from the delusions of psychopathology?

Illusory glow

Instinctively optimistic, we overestimate our control over
important events and the likelihood of positive outcomes [316].
Optimistic bias goes with self-reports of being happy, able and
willing to care for others, and capable of working hard and pro-
ductively. Undoubtedly, it facilitates persistence in the face of
failure, persistence sometimes with an inventive twist—as with
the guy who, hung over from scotch and water, bourbon and
water, and rye and water, decided to avoid water. It also facilitates an illusion of invulnerability, an underestimating of unfamiliar hazards such as radiation, and familiar dangers such as
disease [163; 322].

Optimistic bias is expressed in *illusory glow*, the normal tendency to see oneself in an excessively positive light, evidence to
the contrary notwithstanding. Says religious philosopher and

children's book writer C. S. Lewis, "We imply, and often believe, that habitual vices are exceptional single acts, and make the opposite mistake about our virtues—like the bad tennis player who calls his normal form his 'bad days' and mistakes his rare successes for his normal." Thus tending to overrate our performance, competence, and control over current and past events, we take credit for successful outcomes, blame others or external events for failures, and display a self-serving bias in remembering events [142].

Self-enhancing bias is perfectly normal and reinforced in many ways. For example, we select friends with the right amount of smarts, competence, and charm to flatter rather than threaten us by invidious contrast. We incline toward people who are modestly inferior in areas of central importance, thus limiting the competition, and toward people who are superior in other areas, thus flattering ourselves by association. These are just a few of the many protective devices that help us deny negative qualities of our self, or at least their importance, by viewing them as common, inconsequential, or improving. In much of this, we adults are like children: naive and egocentric, with an overblown sense of our ability, goodness, and importance, yet insensitive to our limitations and mortality. With limited capacity for critical self-consciousness, we are poorly equipped to admit error or express remorse, though we can easily find fault in others or in external things. Moreover, like children, we love good stories and prefer self-serving explanations to objective information.

Most of the time, we wear sunglasses—not the blue-gray kind that filter out ultraviolet light, but the rose-colored "blue-blocker" kind that filter out depressing information, turning adult cares into the carelessness of cheerful normalcy. By removing the rose-colored glasses, depression sabotages positive bias and the power of positive thinking, extinguishing defensiveness and with it the illusion of invulnerability. As William James says so eloquently, "a little irritable weakness and the scent of the pain threshold will bring the worm at the core of all our usual springs of delight into full view and turn us into melancholy physicians. The pride of life and glory of the world will shrivel. . . . Let sanguine healthy-mindedness do its best with its strange power of living in the moment and ignoring and forgetting, still the evil background is really there to be thought of, and the skull will grin at the banquet."

Insight out

With deepening depression comes a shifting mixture of certain kinds of abnormal thinking [12]. One, *depressive negativity*, is a Hobbesian vision of the world as alien, hostile, uncontrollable, and of human life as solitary, poor, nasty, brutish, and short. The other, *depressive realism*, can mean just an absence of the usual positive bias. It can also mean an extraordinary ability to see objectively—what Byron called a "fearful gift; what is it but the telescope of truth which strips the distance of its phantasies and brings life near in utter nakedness, making the cold reality too real!"

Thus, it seems that depression might make a philosopher out of an otherwise ordinary person. But does depression really move people beyond illusory glow to true insight into the nature of the world and one's self? Does it make one more aware of one's behavior, for example, aware of the actual degree that one controls events, say, in a game of chance, or how one is perceived by others? Sometimes yes, sometimes no. The answer depends on many things. Our best guess is that depressive realism will be more evident in people who are neither normal nor deeply depressed, but dysphorically in between [4].

The concept of depressive realism suggests two kinds of accurate self-judgment. One, "realistic glow," characterizes supernormal, healthy people who have a thoroughly positive self-concept. The other, a "sadder-but-wiser" kind, characterizes mildly depressed people and nondepressed people with a negative self-concept. Perhaps there are also two forms of *inaccurate* self-judgment. One, "illusory glow," would characterize so-called normal people, as we have said. The other, a delusional form, would characterize mentally ill people whose self-judgment is either delusionally positive (psychopaths, paranoids, manics), delusionally negative (depressives), or just bizarre (schizophrenics).

Imagine those depressed, philosophically gifted people teetering between realism and despair. They apprehend with single-minded intensity things the rest of us usually ignore or deny: the fundamental separateness and isolation of the self, the selfishness and undependability of others, alienation in an indifferent universe, the fundamental incredibility of God. The great Russian novelist Leo Tolstoy describes his morbid transformation from something like a state of grace to a state of damnation—from good mental and physical health, a loving family, admiring friends, wealth, and fame to the ever more frequent and intense sense that none of it meant anything, that his life was and would always be "a foolish and wicked joke." He writes that "it is possible to live only as long as life intoxicates us; as soon as we are sober again we see that it is all a delusion, and a stupid one! In this, indeed, there is nothing either ludicrous or amusing; it is only cruel and absurd." What happens when consciousness is overwhelmed by bizarre ideas and the capacity to deny or philosophize about the tragic aspect of life breaks down?

Deep end

In *The Taming of the Shrew*, Shakespeare called melancholy the "nurse of frenzy." So, too, did Byron (in "The Dream"):

> The lady of his love—oh! she was changed
> As by the sickness of the soul; her mind
> Had wandered from its dwelling, and her eyes
> They had not their own luster, but the look
> Which is not of this earth; she was become
> The queen of the fantastic realm; her thoughts
> Were combinations of disjointed things;
> And forms impalpable and unperceived
> Of other's sight, familiar were to hers.
> And this the world calls frenzy . . .

These days, the operative term is *psychosis,* and in severest melancholia a psychosis is typically hallucinatory or delusional. But note that while all psychotic depressions are severe, not all severe depressions are psychotic; many are without hallucinations or delusions—crazy ideas invented to make sense out of the existential crises and dilemmas imposed by mental illness. In paranoid illness, delusional thinking projects deficiency and malignancy into a "hostile" environment.

In depression, these qualities are accepted as a condition of the self. The mirror reflects someone ugly, repulsive, old, while bodily sensations suggest inner rot. Self-evaluation reveals deficiency, cruelty, stupidity, insensitivity, phoniness. The self is morally reprehensible, guilty of having lied, cheated, swindled, abused—in a word, unlovable. Says Mike Wallace, "you hate yourself so . . . your self-esteem is so damaged . . . you were convinced that everybody thought you were a fraud. . . ." Moreover, themes of personal inadequacy and malignancy may be expressed in dreams. Dream themes include disappointment ("I bought some shoes but they were both for the left foot"), helplessness ("I tried to save my daughter but my feet got stuck in the mud"), criticism ("He called me a crybaby"), failure ("I came in last in the race"), punishment ("I was expelled from school"), and loss ("All my friends have died"). These "loser" qualities appear not just in the dreams of the severely depressed. You can find them in the mildly depressed and even in those with only a vulnerability [32; 41; 150].

In particularly severe depressions, there may be *hypochondriacal* delusions about having a horrible disease. "Below my armpits I'm made of rubber—dead, lifeless rubber. My liver is petrified, my lungs are solid, my bowels have rotted away. Can't you see how my legs have turned crooked? All my blood-vessels have dried up, I'm a shrunken, shrivelled shell." Then there are delusions of *jealousy* involving the unfounded and fantastic belief in the infidelity of a spouse. "She's forever riding the bus . . . one certain bus—and one certain bus driver—I know it is. They even have some sort of signal system—I've heard a queer lot of tootings—three short ones and two long ones—and then I've seen her run to the window. . . . Of course when I accuse her of it she laughs and says I'm crazy. But I know a thing or two . . ." [227].

In most delusional depressions, the delusions fit the mood. A patient complains about being the object of mockery, condemnation, or treachery. The media may be involved, for example, "I know they are writing about me in the papers, but I'm not surprised, I deserve this." In other delusions, culpability is magnified out of all proportion. A patient might say "I am the world's greatest sinner," and believe that public condemnation and punishment are deserved and imminent. In other depressions, delusions seem to involve *mood-incongruent* themes, for example, being illuminated by X-rays, possessing noticeably swollen sex organs, experiencing hands turned into claws, encountering soulless machine-people. Such mood-incongruent delusions have practical significance, indicating over a short term of six months to a year greater symptom persistence, social dysfunction, and occupational impairment than would otherwise be predicted [173].

Perhaps most bizarre are the nihilistic delusions that things are no longer real, relatives and friends have been replaced by doubles, the world has ended and the self is dead. At a meeting of a French psychiatric association held in 1880, Cotard described a delusional syndrome involving denial of the existence of a body part, the entire self, or the external world. One hundred years later, psychiatrists Enoch and Trethowan described the delusions of a severely depressed, agitated, dehydrated woman who apparently believed that she was responsible for the illness of the other patients. Moreover, she had unreal feelings that she was dead and yet that she would live forever. Another patient called herself Madam Zero [99].

This is not just the metaphorical self-expression of philosophic despair. True, severely depressed patients often say something like: "It's like a deep dark bottomless pit—you feel hopeless, like nothing," or "I feel like I were dead." William Styron once described it like this: "I think you're spiritually, morally, and almost physically dead." Nevertheless, severely depressed patients with nihilistic delusions are not saying that it is *like* being dead. Rather, they are saying, "I *am* dead." Yet, like Dracula, Bram Stoker's Transylvanian anti-hero, they also believe, perhaps for just a moment, that they are immortal. In that, curiously, they are like the rest of us. What are we to make of such irrational thinking?

In *The Magic Mountain*, novelist Thomas Mann offers two views on delusion. One is that delusion, as a mixture of actuality and dream, may be a source of insight. Another is that delusions are degenerate thoughts, "luxations of the brain." Somewhere in between is the view that delusions serve to explain ourselves and the world. We all need stories to make sense of existence, to prevent us from being overwhelmed by the absurdity of our lives and the unreality of the world. A psychotic's delusion is a "crazy" version of this principle; it is both philosophy and rationalization, a way of explaining and reconstructing the self [59]. Perhaps all these views are correct, and delusions, like dreams, can be profound, profane, and pragmatic. Yet, the obvious question remains: How can perfectly intelligent people say such crazy things while wide awake?

Willsprings of affect

It's not that mysterious, if we accept the evidence on human nature. History, anthropology, sociology, and psychology teach us about our enduring tendencies toward blind impulse, irrational thinking and destructive sentiment. Says commentator James Burnham, these are all too often "aggressive, disruptive, and injurious to others and to society [and] to the self: seeking pain, suffering, even death . . . are no less integral to the human psyche than those positive impulses pointing toward the liberal ideals" [57]. Likewise, historian Will Durant concludes that humans tend to prefer myth over objective explanation, poetry over logic—that "underneath all civilization, ancient or modern, moved and still moves a sea of magic, superstition, and sorcery. Perhaps they will remain when the works of our reason have passed away" [89]. No wonder, then, that when reason gives way to intense moods, we misinterpret a look or a comment, sometimes in fantastic ways, or we become preoccupied with the meaning of something that is objectively nothing at all. Threatening preoccupations and emotional necessity can have powerful effects on perception, memory, and thinking— from delusional vision that can make something out of nothing, to hysterical blindness that can make nothing out of something.*

The following exotic but instructive example involves an intelligent person with normal vision who nevertheless acts as

*The age-old term *hysteria* applies to three kinds of psychopathology: *histrionic* (personality disorders characterized by dishonesty, egocentricity, theatrics); *dissociative* (including psychogenic amnesia and multiple personality); and *somatoform*—medically inexplicable somatic (bodily) complaints or hypochondriacal preoccupations about pain, discomfort (in breathing, swallowing), or dysfunction (muscle weakness, periodic loss of consciousness), all suggesting inner conflict, role-playing, and illness preoccupation [330].

though blind, and completely without insight. All this was revealed through a diagnostic evaluation done on a chronically dysphoric, sexually conflicted woman. The assessment included the Thematic Apperception Test, or TAT. This projective test uses a set of somewhat ambiguous pictures of people or objects. The task is simple: Tell a story about each card, and be sure to explain what is going on and how things happened. Since there is really no correct answer, the storytelling allows a person to project the contents of mind. From these projections, a clinician tries to fathom the mechanisms of personality. Miss J.'s performance on the TAT is particularly revealing.

Typically, Miss J. would become uncomfortable when shown a card with a sexual implication. Once she sighed, "How can I possibly tell you a story? I can't think of anything that has to do with sex." One TAT card shows a bare-breasted woman lying on a bed with a sheet draped over the lower half of her body. In the foreground is a man covering his face with his arm as though in fatigue or remorse, the picture being purposely ambiguous. Stories given to this card typically describe either an early morning domestic scene or a rape. When Miss J. looked at this card she first burst out into a nervous laugh that suggested disturbance over the sexual implications of the picture. She began to develop a story about the man's drinking behavior. Then she stopped and said, "Oh, I can't think."

Miss J. was giving no indication of having seen what everyone sees: the partially naked woman. Nevertheless, her characteristic emotionality over sexual matters was evident. Apparently, on some level, she had seen the woman. Had she or hadn't she? When asked if she had left anything out, she responded uncertainly, ". . . man, bottle, and some funny looking things that look like a tent." Then she was asked the more specific question: "Is there only one person in the picture?" After looking intently for a few more moments, she then exclaimed, "Oh! There's a female there, with a sheet over her or something. . . . I'm sorry, I didn't see that at all!"

Such a lapse of perception, or negative hallucination, is hard to explain in an intelligent person—that is, without some reference to needs and emotions. Likewise, a delusion is hard to explain in a person who, just a few weeks ago, was known for intelligence and good sense. Granted, there is method in the madness of a depressive's delusion. The *if-then* logic of the delusion can be appreciated despite its overblown first premise, to wit, "I am one of the world's greatest sinners." Even if irrational, if truly believed, it makes sense to say "I deserve to be punished." Then what about that first premise? Can the person really believe it? We believe what we see, but only when we are *dis*passionate, that is, without commitment to see one way or another. Otherwise, we see what we believe, or rather, what our feelings and intuitions make us *willing* to believe. In the end, objective facts don't arouse much feeling or imagination. At best they are dead right, and dead right is cold comfort, certainly not the stuff that dreams are made of.

In all of us, willfulness always finds reasons. Thus, we don't want for having reasons; rather, we have reasons for wanting. We create reasons after the fact to justify and to explain, making much of our philosophizing merely elaborate rationalization. We even will our bodies to comply. A bowler in the grip of intense feeling arches his back and waves his arms as the ball rolls toward the pins. It is as though the ball's trajectory were magically constrained by sheer force of will expressed in intense body language. When confronted, the bowler assuredly knows this body magic is irrational. Nevertheless, in the heat of the moment, it feels right.

Our natural tendency is to respond to what is subjectively real. Even fantastic explanations that are subjectively satisfying may prevail over rational ones that are not. Caring just complicates the process with *need* to see or believe. Heightened motivation validates the slightest fact or thinnest pretext. A depressive may admit that the delusion is impossible. How can she say she is dead and still be talking to you? Yet dead she feels, and that feeling is somehow more compelling than the objective evidence.

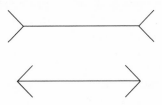

The difference between knowing the facts and feeling otherwise is easily illustrated with a well-known illusion. You are told by an authority that, despite appearances, the shaft of the top "arrow" is actually shorter than that of the bottom one. Nevertheless, you still tend to see the top shaft as longer even after you measure it. And how often, with real-life assumptions, do you get to measure?

Driven by powerful affect, the depressed person *will* have explanations. Sometimes delusional, these explanations may not satisfy an objective observer, but the relevant criterion is the way the person *sees* things, not objective reality. Like illusions and powerful beliefs, delusions remind us that mental life is driven by what we might call the willsprings of affect. The rational element can be brought to bear. Yet, anyone who is hooked on chocolate or tobacco knows how readily we succumb even when we know better and try to resist! Anyone who has been smitten by love also knows how reason can be derailed. Like the song says, "I don't know why I love you like I do; I don't know why, I just do."

Is there a silver lining?

Is there an existential silver lining in the clouds of mental illness? As with any recovery from illness, there is a heightened appreciation of something most people either take for granted or think little about—wellness. But more than that, illnesses such as the manic-depressive, the schizophrenic, and even the epileptic can bring sensuous images, poignant memories, and a sense of *extraordinary* mental wellness. Different voices from diverse fields nevertheless articulate with remarkable consistency the good that can come from illness and from suffering.

Neuropsychiatrist Oliver Sacks describes a patient newly released from Parkinsonian rigidity by the drug L-dopa. "The world becomes wonderfully vivid again. He finds grounds of interest and amazement and amusement all round him—as if he were a child again, or released from jail. He falls in love with reality itself" [273]. In his autobiography, Clifford Beers, describing those aspects of his nervous breakdown that gave him greatest pleasure, writes that "the ecstasy of elation made each conscious hour one of rapturous happiness . . . the floodgates of thought were wide open . . . they seemed to stumble over one another in their mad rush to present themselves to my enthroned ego" [33]. Sacks describes an epileptic patient who, through her dreamy seizure states that she "recaptured a crucial sense of her forgotten, lost childhood. The feeling she had was . . . a trembling, profound and poignant joy. It was, as she said, like the opening of a door—a door which had been stubbornly closed all her life" [275]. Yet, beyond the fascination and pleasure of illusory health—even pockets of real health that may attend an illness—lie two deeper questions about the self.

One question is about the *survival* of the self: Can the core identity of the person survive the severest kinds of mental illness? In most cases the answer is yes, even in cases of schizophrenic or Parkinsonian withdrawal that can last decades before a spontaneous or drug-induced "awakening" that restores the personality. Sacks says it best: "I think the ravages of physical and mental disease are both superficial; that there is something unfathomably deep beyond their reach, that this is the best and strongest and realest thing we have; and that once upon a time this was called the Soul" [273].

The other question is about the *transformation* of the self: Can a nervous breakdown ever lead to a sense of ease and openness with people and with life, a kind of self-renewal? Thoughtful observers from the worlds of literature, religion, and psychology seem to agree that the answer is yes, as exemplified by novelist William Styron's poignant statement that "for those who have dwelled in depression's dark wood . . . whoever has been restored to health has almost always been restored to the capacity for serenity and joy for having endured the despair beyond despair." Likewise religion teaches that wisdom comes from pain and suffering—for example, this hyperbolic pronouncement by journalist Malcolm Muggeridge: "Not success, not happiness, not anything like that. The only thing that really teaches one what life's about—the joy of understanding, the joy of coming in contact with what life really signifies—is suffering, affliction." The value of pain is articulated by religions of the East as well as the West—for example, Zen teacher D. T. Suzuki: "Unless you eat your bread in sorrow, you cannot taste of real life. [Chinese philosopher] Mencius . . . says that when heaven wants to perfect a great man it tries him in every possible way until he comes out triumphantly from all his painful experiences" [302].

Psychology offers the concept of *positive disintegration* by which a new whole arises from old parts of a fragmented personality. The transformation may occur when a person has experienced heightened consciousness, disquieting affect, conflict, and loss of conventional meanings [82]. A psychosis can therefore mean breakthrough as well as breakdown, liberation as well as enslavement. A patient of British psychoanalyst R. D. Laing described it this way: "A new life began for me and from now on I felt different from other people. A self that consisted of conventional lies, shams, self-deceptions, memory images, a self just like that of other people, grew in me again but behind and above it stood a greater and more comprehensive self which impressed me with something of what is eternal, unchanging, immortal and inviolable and which ever since that time has been my protector and refuge" [194].

Can illness really be a portal to an authentic way of being that is superior to, or at least more satisfying than, conventional normalcy? Hans Castorp, hero of Mann's *The Magic Mountain*, has planned a three-week visit to an Alpine sanitarium. There, his sick cousin, Joachim, is being treated for tuberculosis. Increasingly, Castorp is taken by the place, and by the idea of disease. Eventually, he becomes part of what Mann describes as a "charmed circle of isolation and invalidism . . . a sort of substitute existence." Castorp is caught up in a world of disease and with the possibility of death. "In the hermetic, feverish atmosphere of the enchanted mountain, the ordinary stuff of which he is made undergoes a heightening process that makes him capable of adventures in sensual, moral, and intellectual spheres he would never have dreamed of in the 'flatland.' " Castorp has learned a great secret, "one must go through the deep experience of sickness and death to arrive at a higher sanity and health; in just the same way that one must have a knowledge of sin in order to find redemption."

How does one measure heightened experience or personal growth? How does one assess what may turn out to be like a dream written down in a state of ecstatic certitude yet proving inconsequential with further consideration? A few people recovering from deep depression or psychosis may report feeling more secure and at peace. They remember, and they tell their story with touching avidity. But does their new appreciation not become increasingly abstract? Is it not like the insights, resolutions, and relationships that fade after we have awakened from a dream, escaped near-disaster, or returned from exotic lands?

Castorp, lost in a snowstorm, falls into reverie. He dreams about the nature of man. Awakening, he makes a solemn resolution. "I have made a dream poem of humanity. . . . I have taken stock. I will remember. . . . Deep into the snow mountains my search has led me. Now I have it fast. My dream has given it to me, in utter clearness, that I may know it forever." Yet, still in the mountains, Castorp realizes that his dream, seemingly so expansive in space and time, must have taken just a few minutes; this is the illusion of time. Later, in the warmth of the sanitarium after a hearty dinner, both dream and resolutions are barely recalled; this is the illusion of purpose.

For seven years Castorp has been heightened, yet he returns to a flatland convulsing with world war. There, once again, he is an indifferent engineer and now an ordinary foot soldier, doing his best to survive; this is the illusion of growth. What, then, remains when the magic is gone and the memories of pain and suffering are increasingly remote? After the ordeal and postscript philosophizing, is it really back to business as usual, or can the force of habit be broken and enduring freedom be achieved? Can positive self-transformation come from the night journey into the belly of the whale—from the trivial plane of mundane experience to the tragic plane of melancholy insights [185]?

Like Jonah, most depressed people, at least in the short term, can count on some sort of redemption. Even those consumed by the most severe depression may "awaken" from their nightmare of suffering to a relatively more normal life. Nevertheless, most survivors of the belly of the whale will experience no positive change of personality—no spiritual enhancement, no coming to terms with life, no ennobling dream poem of humanity. Without that subtle mix of intellect, humanity, and sensitivity that strengthens more fortunate survivors, psychopathology will promote sentimental inebriation and romantic self-delusion more than good philosophy, self-destructiveness more than genuine growth. Like Jonah, most survivors will seem worse than before—more frustrated, demoralized, and in a few cases, suicidal.

7

FOLIE ADIEU

Mythological hero Sisyphus managed to cheat Death, though only for a little while. Nevertheless, the gods responded by having him for all eternity repeatedly roll a boulder up a hill and then watch it break free just before reaching the top. When is Sisyphus most interesting, asks philosopher Albert Camus in his essay "The Myth of Sisyphus"? Not, says he, while struggling against the boulder. Rather, it is at the moment when, almost to the top, the boulder breaks free, rolling yet again to the bottom. It is his moment of decision to go on rather than quit. Absurd it may be, this endless pushing a boulder up a hill, but it is *his* absurdity to embrace rather than revile. It defines *his* life, gives it meaning, and makes suicide unacceptable.

And what of us? Challenged by illness, loss, or disaster—or by the pressing sense of the absurdity of things—we ordinary mortals nevertheless get rolling again. We manage, no doubt through some instinctive combination of animal spirits, optimism, and a story or two to make sense out of it all. Countless mundane expressions of grace under pressure, for example, in the daily paper, testify to our courage and thus to the heroic quality of human nature. Why, then, does this courageous spirit—or just the animal instinct for survival—sometimes fail in even the most gifted of us? This poignant question is underscored by the haunting image of Castlereagh standing at his window bathed in morning light. He had survived many crises, pushing back from the depths against formidable odds. Why, that fateful Sunday morning, could he not have been, once again, a Sisyphus?

Dirty little secret

Suicide is the eighth leading cause of death in the United States [38]. Internationally, there is much variation in annual rates, expressed as yearly suicides per 100,000 people, from 2 to over 20. The U.S. rate of about 13 per 100,000 people translates into roughly 1 percent of the population committing suicide rather than dying of other causes.

Rates are always questionable, with some suicides detected, but many not. Under-reporting can occur from lack of information, or out of compassion or expediency. "So the sick old man dies at home in his own bed last night," says one compassionate physician. "He was in pain. He was suffering a lot. What good would come from an autopsy that finds some lethal dose? I'm not suspicious of the family. So I sign the death certificate for 'natural causes' " [210]. After agonizing with the family, a doctor agrees to instruct a patient with leukemia in the use of barbiturates to commit suicide. To spare the family, he reports only the leukemia as cause of death. At least 10 percent of doctors know of cases of active euthanasia, some through personal involvement [13]. Only now are physicians beginning to admit helping patients end a life that no longer has quality, and doctoring the evidence to save the family from painful reality.

A major killer, especially of adolescents, is the car accident, yet how many are suicides? Most suspicious are accidents involving a lone driver who supposedly lost control of a vehicle that nevertheless left no skid marks on a route not usually traveled. In one such example [308], a woman had died when her car went over a cliff the day before the deadline for returning embezzled funds. A few years earlier, her husband had found out about her criminal record and had threatened her with divorce if such behavior ever occurred again. Apparently, this "accident" was a way of resolving a seemingly impossible situation.

Even when expected, suicide is personally and socially disorganizing—in an ironic sense, murder on the survivors [10; 61].

Some survivors blame themselves for things they imagine having done or failed to do. Others blame—and feel guilty over blaming—the suicide for being a coward or weakling. In this way, they articulate a view held in many cultures, that suicide is a moral problem and a sign of flawed character. Suicide may create a skeleton in the family closet that can haunt the lives of survivors despite efforts to explain or deny. The effect can last across generations, as we saw with Fitzroy.

For the survivors, then, there is grief, surely, but also guilt and anger and confusion. One of Sigmund Freud's most famous patients, known to the world as the Wolf-Man because of a severe wolf phobia that he developed as a four-year-old, described himself as an innocent third party victimized by his mother's grief over his sister's suicide. "My mother reacted to this tragic event [by arranging] countless masses to be said and [driving] to the cemetery every day to spend many hours at Anna's grave. . . . Her self-torturing thoughts affected her relationship to me, too, and I could not help feeling that after Anna's death her attitude to me became much cooler than it had ever been before and that she was even trying to avoid me."

There is an insidious aspect to the way some people handle suicide, in particular, the attempt to deny that it happened by falsifying the obvious through a process of brainwashing. After witnessing his father's suicide with a shotgun, a boy is urged to imagine that the death was caused by a heart attack. A girl who finds her father's body hanging in a closet is urged to imagine that he died in a car accident. A child persisting with the truth may be discredited, ridiculed, or otherwise intimidated. Being forced to live a lie can be disastrous for personal development [49].

Is it for real?

Most suicides appear to be premeditated rather than impulsive, with between 50 and 80 percent of people who commit suicide having expressed their intent in spoken or written communication or by putting their affairs in order. Yet, most communicators do *not* eventually commit suicide. Put another way, suicide is relatively rare, but often preceded by a communication. In contrast, suicidal communication is relatively more common, but rarely followed by a suicide. Nevertheless, the communication of suicidal intent is a genuine warning signal that should be taken all the more seriously to the extent that certain indicators apply—in particular, a prior suicide attempt, a psychiatric disorder, and a family history of suicide.

The simplified and incomplete family tree in the next figure shows suicide and suicide attempt running together with sometimes virulent, self-destructive forms of alcoholism and drug abuse in the family of playwright Eugene O'Neill who is indicated by the black square. (A horizontal line represents a reproductive link of a man, indicated by a square, and a woman, indicated by a circle.) Eugene was an alcoholic and attempted suicide in 1912. His father and a brother were alcoholics, his mother was a drug abuser (morphine) and had attempted suicide, and his two sons, both drug abusers, committed suicide.

Association between Suicidal and Addictive Behavior in the Eugene O'Neill Family (simplified family tree with Eugene indicated by the black square)

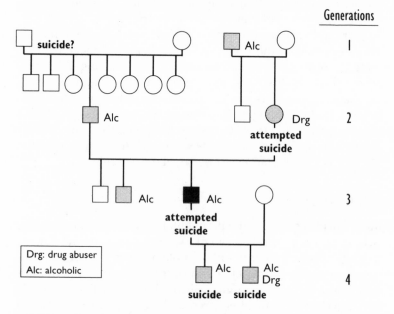

While related, suicide attempt and suicide are not necessarily different versions of the same thing [234]. Compared to the roughly 1 percent lifetime risk for suicide, there is a roughly 2 to 4 percent rate for at least one suicide attempt. Suicide attempt is roughly three times more prevalent in females, but suicide is roughly three times more prevalent in males. In adolescents, the female/male sex ratios are even more discrepant, for suicide attempt (4:1) and for suicide (1:4). The typical suicide completer is an older male. In a state of hopelessness, he uses a firearm in a relatively unambivalent act of self-destruction. By contrast, the typical attempter is a young, depressed, psychologically disturbed female. She uses barbiturates in a suicidal act that reflects desperation and deep ambivalence about dying.

Ten to 20 percent of suicide attempters eventually do kill themselves. Nevertheless, ambivalence about terminating life can often be inferred, for example, in precautions taken to insure discovery by people nearby, or the use of unreliable methods including pills or wrist-slashing. Ambivalence is more obvious in attempts to rectify a reckless act, for example, a woman rushes to the doctor after self-injecting with the AIDS-infected blood of her terminally ill boyfriend [107]. Ambivalence is most dramatically expressed in people who are at war with themselves in being consciously and ostensibly not suicidal, yet having a suicidal alternate personality that sometimes takes over. Suicide attempt is common in multiple personality disorder. According to one study of 236 cases, 72 percent were suicidal and 2.1 percent committed suicide [267]. Many multiples who attempted suicide reported either being amnesic for their suicidal behavior, or having a dissociation, that is, the sense of witnessing their own behavior—actually the behavior of another personality—as if from afar.

The young attempter and her usually sympathetic adolescent peers recognize a cry for help and a way to escape pain. Parents and professionals tend to view the act as hostile, manipulative, and/or coercive. Most observers, regardless of age and sentiment, interpret suicide attempt as a sign of mental illness. The evidence is that attempters usually have three strikes against them. Strike one is a host of psychological problems involving loneliness, isolation, hopelessness. Suicide attempts are nine times more prevalent in people who have ever had a psychiatric disorder than those who have not. Strike two is demoralization by intolerable circumstances such as a failed relationship or personal failure. Suicide attempt is four times more prevalent in separated or divorced people than others, including the widowed. It occurs in about a third of people hospitalized or detained by the criminal justice system, and in as many as 25 percent of people with personality disorder suffering from severe panic disorder as well. Strike three is the inability to see the family as a resource for emotional support; suicide attempters are more likely than others to have experienced parental neglect, abuse, or conflict.

Canary in the mine

Sex differences in suicide rates increase dramatically after middle age, with the relatively higher male rates increasing steadily while female rates level off *or decrease*. Specifically, male rates jump from about 10—remember, these numbers are per 100,000 per year—for young adolescents to about 25 for young adults, remaining at this level during midlife before rising to about 35 for those aged sixty-five to seventy-four, and more steeply to about 60 for the oldest group. In contrast, female rates are a mere 5 per 100,000 during adolescence, peaking in middle age (up to 20), and dropping to less than 10 in the oldest groups.

What psychological reasons explain this age-related sex difference? Given that there is much "conventional wisdom" but no definitive answers, we can only speculate about possible psychological differences. For example, it may be that the menstrual cycle, pregnancy, and breast feeding force women to appreciate their physicality and mortality in a concrete and personal way, not just in theory. Throughout life, they are more accepting of, and better able to "handle" what men are more likely to deny— illness and death. Perhaps when denial no longer works, men are liable to respond with suicide rather than with passive acceptance—doing it before it does them.

Moreover, relative to men, women seem to take greater satisfaction in relationships with children, family, and/or community; identifying with people in an empathetic if not altruistic way translates into a sense of continuity and purpose in life. Men have traditionally been more preoccupied with making things (industry), making people (sex), making it (status), and

making things happen (politics), all of which make their relationships more opportunistic if not exploitive [85; 305]. To that
extent, aging and retirement therefore bring a relatively stronger
preoccupation with lost status and diminished fitness, the effect
being a higher risk of apathy, isolation, or demoralization. Such
a depressed state of mind can be masked, for example, in preoccupations with bodily symptoms, which might explain why,
compared to older females, older males have high rates of suicide yet low rates of diagnosed depression.

Suicide rates have changed dramatically over the last thirty
years. The characteristically high rates of the oldest male groups
have decreased. In contrast, rates for the young have risen
alarmingly, about 300 percent over the last thirty years. By the
1980s, suicide rates for adolescents of the fifteen- to nineteen-
year-old age group had gone from 3.6 per 100,000 (in the early
1960s) to 11.7, while for young men aged twenty to twenty-four,
the rates had increased from roughly 10 to 28. Given that suicide
is the third biggest killer of American adolescents, it is not surprising that a late 1990 Gallup poll found that 15 percent of thir-
teen- to nineteen-year-olds admitted knowing of a teenage
suicide, and 60 percent admitted knowing a teenage suicide
attempter.

An increasing rate of suicide is a sign of troublesome social
and psychological changes. Other signs are increasing rates of
homicide and obesity, diminishing performance on standard-
ized tests like the SAT, and a decreasing sense of security and
opportunity [116]. But whatever its meaning, suicide in the
young is merely the tip of the iceberg. For high schoolers, there
may be as many as 200 to 300 attempts for every completed suicide. Depending on the study, up to 20 percent of college students report having made, or seriously considered making,
some sort of suicide attempt, usually during their high school
years. Some people argue that an increasing rate of suicidal
behavior in young people reflects a declining influence of family
life and a corresponding increase in, even celebration of, egocentric, hedonistic, reckless, self-destructive behavior. Are these
changes like the changing health of that hapless canary, whose
increasingly shaky behavior warns the miners of a quickly deteriorating environment?

Looking for answers

Roughly one hundred years ago, sociologist Emile Durkheim (1858–1917) described two kinds of suicide—*anomic* and *egoistic* [91]. He used the term *anomie* for sudden changes for the better, such as promotion, or for the worse, such as migration, bereavement, financial loss, or medical disaster. These changes increase the risk of suicide by causing dislocating aloneness and normlessness experienced as *acute loss*. On the other hand, *chronic or gradually increasing deficiency* of connection between self and society promotes egoistic suicide, and in two kinds of people. One kind includes rampantly individualistic and destructively self-centered people; these loners or antisocial people have always been self-reliant, indifferent to groups and community, and insufficiently connected to a church or confident in a faith. The other kind includes aging men who are increasingly detached from their social surroundings, cut off from signals that they are supported and that life has meaning. (Another of Durkheim's concepts is noted in the "Altruistic Suicide" Appendix note.)

No doubt suicide rates are affected by what Durkheim called sociological factors—for example, social and personal dislocation caused by economic depression, immigration, or bereavement. This is evident in different suicide rates in different communities, and the *change* of suicide rates across time and circumstances. For example, compared to the host population, immigrants *as a group* have an elevated rate of suicide. In those unable to embrace new alternatives, suicide is a reaction to an unshakable sense of hopelessness about being uprooted from what is familiar and comforting, from what is perceived as minimally acceptable to the spirit. For some, suicide is therefore the final stage of a depressing nostalgia for a lost way of life. Nostalgia can be heightened by special biological liabilities that Durkheim called "neuropathic conditions." Thus some individuals, for genetic reasons prone to anxiety, depression, or alcoholism, are especially vulnerable to anomie. For them especially, says Durkheim, "reality seems valueless by comparison with the dreams of fevered imaginations; reality is therefore abandoned, but so too is possibility when it in turn becomes reality. A thirst arises for novelties, unfamiliar pleasures, nameless sensations, all of which lose their savor once known. Henceforth one has no strength to endure the least reverse. The whole fever subsides and the sterility of all the tumult is apparent, and it is seen that all these new sensations in their infinite quantity cannot form a solid foundation of happiness to support one during days of trial."

The question, then, is not whether, but *how much* weight we should assign to sociological and psychological factors, and that depends on perspective. Surely sociological factors are paramount for explaining *changes* in suicide rates, but less certain for explaining group or individual differences. What accounts for individual differences in responsiveness to environmental factors? Searching for clues to unexpected suicides in young people will often yield evidence of what makes people especially vulnerable—being perfectionistic, for example, or having been a "difficult" or isolated child. Young suicides had more than their fair share of problem traits; they usually had at least one diagnosable psychiatric disorder, the most typical being a depressive and/or personality disorder. Depressive, antisocial, addictive, unstable, self-destructive qualities all contribute to anger, resentment, and isolation. A suicidal adolescent may be so friendless, isolated, *invisible*, that the death is not discovered for days. Further complicating the problem are broken relationships, humiliating experiences, social disruption and/or physical impairment. Up to 30 percent of teen suicides are homosexual—mostly male, often effeminate, and often abusive of alcohol or other drugs [209].

Stress and psychopathology combine to increase the liability to suicide in vulnerable adolescents or young adults. The interaction may be triggered by the suicide of a close friend or media personality. During the ten-day period after such an event, suicide rates increase significantly. The increase occurs as a cluster in some locale such as a school, or in an area served by the media publicizing the event. However, mere exposure will not trigger suicide without a vulnerability to which the vast majority is mostly immune [84; 138].

The vulnerability may involve a personality disorder or perhaps the comforting sense that suicide is something rational, romantic, even noble. Thus, like the Cynics and Stoics of ancient Rome, some people rationalize suicide as a logical, even dignified way to end a life that has lost continuity and meaning. Others imagine it as a sign of mental superiority, even genius, and as a creative way to thumb one's nose at a stupid, insensitive world. Others view suicide as a portal to the mystery of life. Playing with death, they gamble for knowledge of the ultimate secret, but often end up with a sense of nothingness and of having been swindled [14]. In this, they are like the melancholy knight in filmmaker Ingmar Bergman's *The Seventh Seal* who discovers through playing (chess) with Death the horror that there is no revelation at the end; not even Death has privileged knowledge.

A swimming lesson

Durkheim's analysis helps us appreciate two different but intimately related aspects of the suicide question: rate and liability. The question of *rate* is about why a small percentage of people commit suicide, and why that number changes from year to year. The question of *liability* is about why, whatever the rate, some people are at relatively greater risk. This distinction between liability and rate, a key concept explored in Part 1, can be appreciated all the more when it is applied to the problem of suicide. To that end, imagine the social environment to be a great swimming pool with swimmers who spend their time swimming or resting (at the shallow end).

Obviously, long-term survival depends on many factors: pool factors such as depth and lighting; social factors such as crowding and competition for desirable locations; and person factors such as ability to swim and height (for standing at greater depths). Although there are many other factors—for example, inventiveness with a flotation device and shrewdness about securing aid from others—most of the individual differences in liability can be explained by just a few major factors. Assume, then, that everyone is a good swimmer and socially astute, so that the really big difference between survival boils down to differences in just two big factors: depth of the pool and height of the swimmers.

The average depth of our pool varies from five to seven feet. People less than five feet tall obviously have the highest risk; for all others, risk varies, with the tallest swimmers having the least or no risk. Note that height and risk of going under are related, whatever the overall rate. That is, *even if no one drowns* during a given time period, there will still be *individual differences in risk.* Moreover, these differences can be explained. Since individual differences in height are mostly genetic, liability to going under in our metaphorical pool is perforce highly heritable.

But the heritability of liability is only one answer to one question about the "problem of survival" in our pool; environmental factors are also important. To appreciate what this really means, consider *average risk,* that is, ignore individual differences. Average risk reflects the average height of the swimmers (big genetic factor) and the average depth of the pool (big environmental factor). However, any *change* in risk will depend on a change in average height and depth, *and this must be environmental* because detectable genetic change cannot occur so fast. For example, average risk can be decreased by boosting the height of all swimmers with a height-enhancing pill or reducing the depth of the pool by removing some water. (Remember, it's our metaphor so we can do what we like.)

You can think of liability as a line-up, with those at highest risk at the head of the line. Clearly, a change in pool or person characteristics can change average risk. But, while it may increase or decrease everyone's risk, it has greatest practical implication for those at the head of the line. But whatever we do environmentally to change the people or the pool, *the highly heritable individual differences in height will remain* because, even in our imaginary pool, there is no pill to make everyone the same height; as long as there is variation, some will always be at higher risk than others.

It is clear why the "genes or environment" question is naive: a radically different mix of causes underlies a *rate,* or average, and the *individual differences,* or variation around that average. In our pool, the *average* risk at any point in time is completely genetic *and* environmental—genes and environment are *both* essential. However, a *change* in the average risk is *entirely* environmental, while *liability* is mostly genetic. You see, asking about the relative importance of genetic or environmental causes makes sense only when a particular aspect of the problem is specified.

Our pool metaphor makes it easy to understand the two questions about suicide—rates versus liability—that we posed at the outset of this section. Accordingly, we let the pool represent the social environment, and variation in its depth represent variation in the stressfulness of social life. Thus, a *difference* between any two locations represents a difference in the stressfulness of living conditions, while a *change* to a new location represents a change in the stressfulness of living conditions. Moreover, we let height represent *suicidality*, a psychological trait that disposes people to commit suicide. Like other graded traits such as extraversion, suicidality runs from none/mild (normalcy) to moderate/severe (abnormality). In our scenario, extreme shortness represents *extreme suicidality*, a potentially lethal kind of abnormality that can be brought out or suppressed by environmental conditions.

Our pool metaphor thus addresses *two* distinct but related questions. First question: Why is the *average risk* of a population (for the pool) high or low compared to other populations or this population at an earlier time? The answer, not surprisingly, is largely environmental. Second question: Why are some individuals within a population (shorts versus talls) at *more or less risk?* The answer, perhaps surprisingly, is largely genetic, but to appreciate in what way, first consider the familial link between suicide and depression.

Unlocking the liability

Investigations of suicide frequently uncover depression—at least behavior such as excessive drinking that suggests depression, or living conditions such as isolation and infirmity that are good reasons to be depressed. But what is the causal connection between depression and suicide? To get answers, researchers can start with diagnosed depression, following up patients to see what happens. For example, studies of the depressed suggest that their lifetime rate of suicide is 15 to 20 percent, a staggering fifteen to twenty times the corresponding population rate

[134; 152]. Most investigations, however, start with the suicidal act and try to reconstruct its antecedents. Evidently, over 90 percent of adults who commit suicide were diagnosable with some mental illness, with depression as the primary or secondary problem. Most suffered from depressive disorder or depression associated with alcohol abuse, as the O'Neill family tree clearly illustrates. Organic, schizophrenic, and other disorders are also represented, and these too are frequently associated with depression. More than 70 percent of people who commit suicide were in psychiatric treatment, with as many as 20 percent being inpatients [260].

Risk of suicide increases the more that certain factors apply: being male, forty-five years old or older, unemployed or retired, separated, divorced, or widowed, living alone, being in poor physical health, and having recently been treated for a medical or psychiatric condition. More obvious factors include having expressed ideas about committing suicide or having made an attempt, and having a family history of suicide. Risk increases during the descent into a depression, but falls during the depths of a depressive episode, probably because of low energy and passivity. Risk rises six to nine months after discharge from the hospital, though not as dramatically as initially during descent into illness. What explains the elevated risk of suicide during what otherwise appears to be a period of recovery? One hypothesis assumes a conscious effort to deceive by orchestrating the appearance of getting better despite having made the decision to end it all. Another hypothesis notes the hopelessness and despair caused by an actual or imagined return of symptoms. A third recognizes the intolerable idea of having to return to some demoralizing situation at home or at work [183].

Like depression, suicide is *familial*, with relatives of suicides having a roughly ten times higher risk of suicide than that of the population. Moreover, up to 50 percent of adolescent suicidals—10 percent of nonsuicidals—have at least one suicidal first-degree relative (parent, child, or sibling). For a concrete illustration of the familiality of suicide, take a look at the family tree showing suicide (S) and suicidal tendencies (s) running through three generations, from top to bottom in the figure. At the top, you can see how one man (square) who eventually committed suicide is linked to two women (circles). The children of the first link (to the left) include a son who committed suicide. The children of the subsequent link include one son with suicidal tendencies whose daughter is suicidal.

Familial Association of Suicide (S) and Suicidal Tendencies (s)

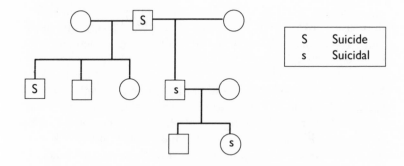

S	Suicide
s	Suicidal

More definitive are two observations suggesting that the familial suicidal disposition is heritable. First, it is the *biological*, not adoptive, relatives of depressed and/or suicidal people who have the elevated rates of suicide [285; 327]. For example, suicide is roughly ten times more prevalent in the biological than the adoptive relatives of adoptees who are ill with depressive disorder. Second, identical twins are roughly 15 percent concordant for suicide—about 15 percent of the co-twins of identical-twin suicides also commit suicide. That seemingly low rate is quite large when compared to the near-zero percent for fraternal twins [168; 269].

Let's return for a moment to suicide and depression because the connection raises an intriguing question about *exactly* why familial suicide is heritable. That suicide and depression tend to run together in families is especially evident in the Old Order Amish community. There, 73 percent of the suicides came from just four pedigrees (connected families) and, over four or five generations, twenty-four out of twenty-six of the suicides were clearly associated with affective disorder [94]. The next figure illustrates the familial connection between depression and suicide across five generations of one of those pedigrees (again, with squares representing males, circles females).

Suicide and Affective Disorder in an
Old-Order Amish Family (five generations)

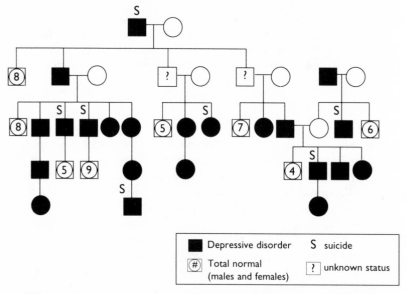

Depressive disorder   S suicide

(#) Total normal
(males and females)

? unknown status

The connection between suicide and depression is probably exaggerated in this special, close-knit, drug-free community where suicide is explained by few if any reasons (personality disorder, alcoholism, or social isolation) other than depressive disease. Nevertheless, the connection between depression and suicide may be less straightforward than it appears. Conventional wisdom says that depression explains why people commit suicide, but which people? Relatively few even severely depressed psychiatric patients commit suicide—maybe only 20 percent. What, then, is the missing ingredient that takes a person beyond depression to self-annihilation?

Put the question this way: Is there an *independent* liability to suicide, and is depression, though not necessary, nevertheless uniquely suited to unlock that suicidal liability? An affirmative answer would surely explain why, given suicide, you often discover depression, but given depression you often *don't* get suicide. So, too, would it explain why the relatives of a suicide have higher rates of suicide than do members of other, psychiatrically comparable, families. No wonder, then, that elevated rates of suicide characterize the *biological* (not adoptive) relatives of depressed adoptees, *but only if the adoptees have committed suicide* [284]. This observation is at least consistent with the albeit speculative idea of a distinct and heritable liability to suicide that can be unlocked preferentially by a depressive state of mind. (The physiological basis of suicide is unknown. One possibility is briefly described in the "Serotonin and Suicide" Appendix note.)

Jumping ship

We need to examine the psyche of the suicidal person to appreciate how the will to live can be overthrown. Suicidologist Edwin Shneidman suggests four suicidal qualities that have been illuminated by research [31; 288]. The first, *perturbation*, usually starts with a personally undermining setback. This fall from prosperity can mean loss of employment, relationship, status, freedom, health. Sometimes it is an intimation of another episode of depression, an experience the person feels might become a permanent state. Liability is elevated in the bereaved and recently divorced, and in people rejected by a close friend or spurned by a loved one. It is elevated in immigrants with their loss of friends and familiar environment, and in those with acute disability or sudden awareness of fatal disease. For young people, the typical stress is a broken relationship that precipitates intolerable feelings of abandonment. Says Shneidman, "The victim's best eggs are in the other person's flawed basket. He (and his figurative eggs) are crushed" [289].

Inimicality, the second suicidal quality, involves an intensely painful kind of self-consciousness, the kind that comes with exposure, or the threat of exposure, of one's inferiority, impotence, or culpability; it is the threat that makes an enemy of the self and of life. This explains why even a promotion can trigger suicidal behavior, that is, unlocking anxiety about being unmasked as inadequate or unworthy with no way to master the situation or escape embarrassment. Says an anonymous, unhappy soul: "We are indeed flattering ourselves if we have the illusion that we can jump out of ourselves like a genie whenever we please and start anew. No, it's a whole rotten package. My solution is to wrap it up and burn it all. A little stench, a few ashes, but nothing more." Such inimical thinking can take on delusional and hallucinatory aspects, whipping up intolerably morbid conceits of decay, death, and the absurdity of life. In such a state of mind, there are overwhelming impulses to annihilate the self.

Constricted thinking, the third suicidal quality, strips away curiosity and conviction, an appreciation of different perspectives, and capacity for caring. In the constricted state, thinking becomes overly focused on hopelessness and compelling images of suicide: tree limbs, guns, closed garages, all of them. There may even be a little comfort in knowing that with knife or pills at the ready, one can always escape. Nevertheless, constricted thinking produces mostly a grinding sense of endless here and now, stereotyped thoughts about the deck of life being stacked, and a desire for comforting routine.

Yet, with thinking constricted, behavior becomes aimless, reactive, or impulsive. A riot of pain-induced self-aggression and uninhibited pleasure seeking can become self-consuming. For example, an alcoholic binge or reckless driving can take over before the final denouement. Sometimes self-destructiveness is more subtle, idiosyncratic, inventive. One person would heedlessly and in ritualistic fashion walk head down back and forth across a busy highway. It was as if he were engaged in a kind of Russian roulette, as if he had thereby reduced to crap-game status Hamlet's question, to be or not to be [80]. Two opposing forces seem to be operating simultaneously. One is an embracing of death, sampling it bit by bit, acknowledging its inevitability and maybe its desirability through a kind of invocation of providence. The other is a denial of death, a playing with fate, a thumbing of one's nose at the gods.

The idea of *cessation*, the fourth suicidal quality, is tied up with a desire for relief from pain and crushing emptiness, but also with the fantasy of continuation. Cessation means self-annihilation—"a sweet thought," says one person, "the only thought that puts me to sleep at night"—but also something else—a kind of magical transcendence involving fantastic notions of rebirth, reunion, revenge, and control over others, all of which deny cessation. For example, some potential suicides may have fantasies of continuing beyond death, floating above the scene to assess the situation, perhaps enjoying the unhappiness caused by the act. People will finally pay attention! The distinction between escape from pain and reunion with someone is illustrated by the suicides in Shakespeare's plays [100]. For Romeo and Juliet, suicide is a means to escape the pain of irreparable loss. For Antony and Cleopatra, it means avoiding humiliation and more, the restoration of honor and reunion after death.

An irresistible sense of power and magic can explain how suicide may be employed as either a personal or political statement, supporting what William James said—that suicide can make a true heroic figure out of an ordinary little "genius." For is that person not our superior who can fling away that to which we cling? What an odd condition that combines potency and heroism with weakness and defeat. These observations may also explain why, in some cases, an essential part of the act is the method—contrived, elaborate, operatic.

The trigger for the definitive suicidal act may be a rather trivial event—a last straw that sets in motion a landslide of suppressed pain. Yet it may be a real setback normally brushed off or managed with aplomb. Goethe describes a young girl who grows up in hopelessly dreary conditions of spiritless drudgery. Eventually, her hopes and passions coalesce around a young man who promises deliverance from her stale existence. "With her consciousness dulled, she wavers in the anticipation of happiness and reaches the highest possible degree of tension. At last she stretches out her arms to grasp all she desires—and her lover leaves her. Petrified, out of her mind, she stands in front of the abyss. All is darkness around her, she has no comfort, nothing to hope for, because he, in whom she had her being, has left her. She doesn't see the world in front of her nor the many people who might make up for what she has lost. She feels alone, abandoned; and blindly, cornered by the horrible need in her heart, she jumps and drowns her torment in the embrace of death." Utter hopelessness can undo even great minds and noble souls. Thus it was with Castlereagh, and countless others.

Checking out

Suicidal impulses are surely born in the *passion* of suffering—in the grief, embarrassment, rage, or physical pain that is unendurable because it is hopeless. Here, suicide means jumping ship to escape personal loss or defeat—Jonah crying out in angry humiliation over the apparent failure of his prophecy: "It is better for me to die than to live."

Suicidal impulses are also born in other kinds of suffering, the suffering of being an outsider, of being alone even in company, sometimes because of tragic circumstances. Theodore Dreiser describes a vision of a city with a wall about it. "Men were posted at the gates. You could not get in. Those inside did not care to come out to see who you were. They were so merry inside there that all those outside were forgotten, and he was on the outside." Another kind of "outsider" suffering—what is sometimes called existential—is consciousness of self as empty and existence as meaningless.

With the outsider kinds of suffering, suicide means checking out, recognizing being defeated or being on empty with no filling station in sight. For older people, the problem is a falling out, a loss of purpose and vitality. One who must remain anonymous says, "Now tell me honestly, a man who has nothing whatsoever to look forward to, who is gradually losing the capability to love and what is worse, is even incapable of receiving love, who has no clear-cut set of ideals or moral values of life, who has no interest in anything in life be it big or small, who is too weak to struggle yet too proud to admit defeat—what should he do?" An even more inimical condition is Jonah's at the end of his story—really, at the end of his rope. Having moved from protest to despair, he sits demoralized and alone outside of Nineveh, without insight into God's mind and wishing for death.

Strangely ironic are the suicides of people who look so calm, so normal, with seemingly everything to live for, like poet E. A. Robinson's tragic hero Richard Cory:

> And he was rich—yes, richer than a king—
> And admirably schooled in every grace:
> In fine, we thought that he was everything
> To make us wish that we were in his place.

Despite all, Richard Cory "one calm summer night, went home and put a bullet through his head." We might say, with Viktor

Frankl, that the Richard Corys of the world "have enough to live by but nothing to live for; they have the means but no meaning" [113]. The subjective sense of meaninglessness, the feeling that life is simply not worth the trouble, can defy rational assessment. It is as if the person lacked some psychological enzyme to digest objective evidence to the contrary. About to become a grandmother for the first time, a woman calmly swallows over one hundred pills but is discovered before succumbing. Four months later she shows no remorse for the act nor gratitude for being alive. There is no abatement of her suicidal thoughts despite joy when holding her grandson and despite genuine interest in his future [196].

The more passionate and the more existential suffering are different kinds of depression. The one can turn into the other with the cumulative losses of status, connections, and purpose that demoralize the elderly. When combined in a sensitive temperament, they can turn hopelessness into lethal impulse. In 1941, at the age of fifty-nine, Virginia Woolf finally succumbed to manic-depressive disease. Wearing an overcoat weighed down with a stone, she drowned herself in a river near her Sussex home. A letter to her husband explained that the depression and voices of her madness were once again becoming overwhelming. "I don't think two people could have been happier till this terrible disease came. I can't fight any longer. I know that I am spoiling your life. . . ." With no hope of recovery, only suicide made any sense.

It really does seem that the key is hopelessness, a quality of mind we can distinguish from pain or indifference [2]. As with depression, with suicide we can ask, "How about your prospects for the future?" as well as, "How depressed do you feel?" In severe depressions, painful feelings and hopelessness occur together, but not in equal measure in different people. Nevertheless, their distinct effects can be separately measured with a statistical trick. In effect, we remove variation in either the dysphoric feeling or the hopelessness to see if the remaining variation in the other still correlates with suicide risk. What we find is interesting though not all that surprising.

Suicidal risk is strongly correlated with hopelessness even when variation in depression is removed statistically. It seems we can tolerate all sorts of pain and suffering if we can remain even vaguely optimistic that things will get better, or that there is meaning to life. In contrast, suicide risk is poorly correlated with depressed feelings when variation in hopelessness is removed. Thus, a key factor in suicide is less the urgent feeling of sadness than the utter sense of hopelessness. The suicide-hopelessness connection explains why the elderly male population has a high rate of suicide despite a low rate of the kind of manifest depression seen more clearly in younger groups. It also suggests that, in younger people, the much more evident suicide-depression connection with its strong alloy of manifest anger and frustration, is forged by a deeper sense of hopelessness [69].

It seems strange that suicide happens in only a few severely depressed people—stranger still that it happens in people who appear not at all depressed. That it can happen to the best and brightest, to the Castlereaghs and Corys, is also difficult to fathom. Perhaps some people, for genetic reasons and regardless of age, are doomed to a continual consciousness of emptiness and meaninglessness. If so, many of them will feel hopeless and some will commit suicide, sometimes seemingly out of the blue. Moreover, this will happen despite freedom from adversity and dysphoria, or even great triumphs in realms of love and work. And it will happen despite what we know and what we try to do.

8

POLAR EXPLORATION

"Everything seems out of nature in this strange chaos of levity and ferocity. . . . In viewing this monstrous tragicomic scene, the most opposite passions necessarily succeed, and sometimes mix with each other in the mind; alternate contempt and indignation; alternate laughter and tears; alternate scorn and horror." Thus did political philosopher Edmund Burke describe the French Revolution. He might have been describing a form of mental illness that has preoccupied physicians ever since Hippocrates. Seemingly worlds apart, mania and depression prove to be two poles of one world.

The manic pole

Not unlike a cocaine high, a manic episode involves an abnormally elevated, expansive, *or irritable* mood plus at least three additional criteria—four if the mood is mainly irritable (just to be sure it's mania and not something else):

- inflated self-esteem,
- decreased need for sleep,
- extreme talkativeness,
- flight of ideas or subjective sense of thoughts racing,

- distractibility,
- overblown needs or grandiose plans,
- reckless self-indulgence.

These symptoms can impair ability to work or function interpersonally, all of which may require hospitalization to prevent harm to the self or to others.

First occurring during the second decade of life in up to a third of the cases, manic episodes can be precipitated by just about anything, even acute loss where grief would be expected. It could be social stress that triggers anxiety about admission to a college, dating situations, or some occupational crisis, such as conflict with the boss. It might be a circadian dysrhythmia set off during adjustment to a new time zone. Finally, even alcohol intoxication or antidepressant medication might bring out a manic potential. The severest episodes tend to be the shortest, perhaps only two weeks; moderately severe episodes can last six months; mild ones as much as a year or more. Generally, a manic illness tends to be chronic or recurrent, even when treated with lithium carbonate ("lithium"). Nevertheless, social or occupational adjustment may be reasonably favorable in the short term, say during eighteen months after discharge from the hospital.

Euphoric or irritable, the manic is energetic, extravagant, and intoxicated on overblown egoism. All the world's a stage, and the manic is the central player. Whereas the depressive is impotent, the manic is all-powerful, revved up, engorged with readiness. Said one patient, "I can't sit; I need to stand, to walk, to move around, you know, like I have this energy, this feeling that keeps me going. I'm a dancer, you know; I'm into movement, moving like I think I could go on forever" [295]. The rest of us lack the energy, but also the wit, courage, imagination, artistry of the manic.

Manics are loquacious, their speech loud, rapid-fire, even clever. A manic English woman realizes she is speaking to someone with a newly conferred title. She comments: "Well Sir Alexander, since I had the pleasure of seeing you last, I have been benighted and you have been knighted" [291]. The manic quality of mind spills into behavior. Fantastic plans are made and airplane trips are taken all over the country as the manic literally takes flight. Waiters are overtipped. Outrageously expensive gifts are bought for business contacts. Checks for thousands, even millions, are written to pay for fabulous projects and deals. Letters, sometimes with elaborate drawings or graphic designs, are written to the famous and powerful. Scientists are informed of a secret formula, corporate presidents of a brilliant invention, senators of imagined intrusions by the CIA. Sexual impulses are more intense, and indiscretions are not uncommon. Gambling to excess, like alcoholic binging, can be as much a joy to the manic as it is a nightmare for the family [103].

When euphoric, manics are jolly, amiable, facetious, playful, and flirtatious, sometimes to the point of indecency. When irritable, they are impatient, sarcastic, fractious, abrasive. If frustrated, they can be paranoid, even physically abusive. "Why, I can and will lick anyone who gets in my way!" may not be an idle threat, as abused spouses can testify. The potentially dangerous mixture of euphoric and irritable mood was described by Jelliffe, an astute psychiatrist of three generations ago. "[J]ust as the person who while slightly intoxicated is good-natured, generous, careless, mischievous, and perhaps lewd, when more deeply intoxicated becomes irritable, combative, and incoherent; so the manic as his condition deepens exhibits a tendency to angry rather than pleasurable excitement."

States of malignant well-being, euphoria, omnipotence, or exaltation can occur in addiction, epilepsy, and schizophrenia; mania is no exception. In *A Mind That Found Itself*, Clifford Beers noted, of his ecstatic and rapturous experience in a manic state, that "a man abnormally elated may be swayed irresistibly by his best instincts, and that while under the spell of an exaltation, idealistic in degree, he may not only be willing, but eager to assume risks and endure hardships which under normal conditions he would assume reluctantly, if at all." Of course, the well-being of manic disorder is mostly illusory and misleading, in that it is often mixed with dysphoric feelings, it is fundamentally selfish, egocentric and destructive, and it is a signal of a liability to depression and suicide.

Manic delusions tend to be grandiose and sometimes paranoid, with sexual, political, or religious themes involving spouses, colleagues, government, or providence. The mixture of ambition and suspicion is illustrated by the high school physical education teacher who becomes increasingly disheveled, agitated, and disruptive, insisting that he has been named head coach of the Olympic track team. He makes calls all over the country to recruit assistant coaches, and he interprets any interference as a sign of communist conspiracy [240]. The sense of having special powers of invention or vital secrets that will change the world is illustrated by a manic patient who explains how "I had expected to leave Chicago this morning had you folks not detained me. I expect to meet some fellows there who will put this thing across. They are big men, with big brains and big money, and when I explain this they will jump clear over their chairs to get first whack at it. They'll probably form a corporation, make me chairman of the board, and we'll have to organize a foreign sales department at once, because this is a world beater. You think I'm crazy, but just remember—that's what they said about Fulton and Isaac Watt and all the rest of us!"

Manics, especially males, tend to abuse alcohol and other drugs. The reasons are diverse but seem to boil down to poor judgment. An altered sense of well-being drives manics to more frequent, intense social interactions—for example, in after-hour bars—in order to share ideas that might develop into exciting prospects for action. During a manic episode, stimulants like cocaine may be used to enhance euphoric and sexual feelings. Because of their depressant effect on brain activity, alcohol or heroin may also be used, even to the point of abuse, in an effort to self-medicate manic states that are dysphoric because of anxiety, despair, irritability, and delusional notions involving sin or persecution.

There may also be a sort of silver lining, however, to relatively mild mania, the kind that seems as much a trait of personality as a symptom of disease. After all, by boosting energy, ambitiousness, courage, or just chutzpah, manic temperament can contribute in no small measure to the makings of productive and magnetic personalities—a Martin Luther or a Van Gogh, for example—without whom societies would be diminished if not impoverished.

The two poles of mood

Mania is of interest in its own right, but also in its link to depression. First, *within an episode*, pathological mania may alternate, or even co-occur with, depression; one can be anxious, irritable, and unhappy as one hurtles forward in manic thought and action. Second, *across episodes*, mania can become less euphoric, more irritable, and more painful—more "depressive." Moreover, manic episodes are increasingly likely to be followed by periods of emptiness or melancholy, even episodes of full-blown depression, as described over 300 years ago by Spanish dramatist and poet Calderon de la Barca who characterized the condition as a dream in which, "drunk with excess of majesty and pride, methought I towered so high and swelled so wide that of myself I burst the glittering bubble that my ambition had about me blown, and all again was darkness." Third, the *familial connection* between mania and depression means that depressive illness is typically found, not only in people who suffer from manic illness, but in their relatives. These three observations support the ancient notion that mania is but one pole of *bipolar* illness.

With most bipolar illness, the bipolar switch in and out of a manic or depressive episode can take months, even years. Discrete episodes can alternate with long periods of *relative* normalcy—relative because mood and personality disturbances can often be found. Between-episode disturbances may be compounded by an apprehensive preoccupation with the recurrence of illness, justifiable given that aging often means more frequent and severe episodes. A worsening course of the disorder can even cause demoralization and a heightened risk of suicide, as evident in the story of Robert Fitzroy.

Up to 15 percent of bipolar patients experience *rapid cycling*, meaning at least four, but typically more than twenty, discrete episodes of mania or depression per year [29; 337]. In some cases, the bipolar mood shifts are too precipitous and frequent to be considered episodes in the usual sense. A bipolar patient may go to bed depressed and wake up manic, or shift between moods on an hourly basis. A shift may occur virtually in minutes. In one case, a male clinician attending to a depressed female patient was momentarily distracted. While his back was turned, he felt his behind being pinched by none other than his patient, who had suddenly been galvanized by mania into impish action. Because it is an extreme and terrible bipolar condition that responds poorly to lithium treatment, rapid cycling bipolar disorder carries a relatively high risk for suicide.

Bipolar depression is just one of many similar-looking illnesses, and trying to understand them is like trying to assemble a jigsaw puzzle. As in a puzzle, you begin by searching for edge pieces that define boundaries and other pieces of similar pattern and color that represent prominent features. During the last hundred years, researchers have located the equivalent of many edge pieces that, pieced together, reveal quite a bit of the boundary between depression and related disorders. Moreover, interior pieces have been connected to form islands of recognizable form. One island—the affective-disorder part of the puzzle—appears to be composed of manic-depressive and "pure" depressive pieces; other islands suggest different disorders. There still are a few gaps, but we now have a reasonable idea how the puzzle will turn out.

Moody clues: Culprit 1

The most obvious place to find key pieces of the puzzle is in the differences between depressive illness associated with mania—that is, bipolar depression—and *depression-only* illnesses—that is *unipolar depression*. Comparisons between bipolar illness and unipolar illness yield differences, even when only the depressions of bipolar illness are compared to unipolar depressions. Taken together, the distinctions listed in the table below—we need not dwell on them all—suggest that bipolar and unipolar depressive illnesses are qualitatively different. Finding out in what sense this is true and what it all means turns out to be quite a challenge. We proceed, keeping in mind that, depending on context, the term *disorder*—as in "bipolar disorder"—can mean an observable illness (syndrome) but also an inferable pathology (disease) that explains illness.

CHARACTERISTICS OF BIPOLAR AND UNIPOLAR ILLNESS

Characteristics	Bipolar Illness	Unipolar Illness
Lifetime risk of an illness indicating the respective disorder	1%	4%
Age at first episode	20s	30s and older
Heritability of implied liability	high	modest
Characteristic symptom pattern	retarded depression	agitated depression
Male:female risk (M:F ratio)	same (1:1)	different (1:3)
Socioeconomic groups disproportionately affected	highest	none
Illnesses to which biological relatives are at greatest risk	bipolar, unipolar	unipolar

Consider the question of heritability. Almost all investigators agree that the liability to bipolar illness is highly heritable, given that bipolar concordance is *five times* greater for identical twins than for fraternal twins. Compare that to unipolar concordance, which is "only" three times greater for identicals than for fraternals. In effect, an estimated heritability of about 0.7 puts liability to bipolar illness in the genetic big leagues along with the liability to schizophrenic illness, while an estimated heritability of at most 0.4 to 0.5 puts liability to unipolar illness in a somewhat less exalted league along with liability to some anxiety disorders [175]. What can we make of this and other bipolar/unipolar differences?

Recall that modern efforts to explain depressive illness originate with Emil Kraepelin. If depression with mania and straight depression were homicide cases, detective Kraepelin might suspect one culprit, *manic-depressive disease*, with two ways of killing (bipolar and unipolar illnesses). This *one-culprit solution*, diagrammed in the figure below, raises a most interesting question: How can depression-only (unipolar) illness come from manic-depressive disease? Manicless manic-depressive illness sounds like more cheeseless cheeseburger, but Kraepelin would say, *only if you stick with surface appearances without digging to get at the underlying disease.* Let's take a closer look.

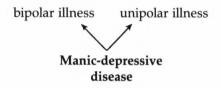

bipolar illness   unipolar illness

**Manic-depressive
disease**

Our inquiry begins with a simple observation: The manic aspect of a bipolar depressive disorder can vary in severity. If the mania is severe, researchers call the bipolar disorder *bipolar I*; if it is moderate, they call it *bipolar II.* We will mostly ignore the bipolar I/II distinction, calling both kinds bipolar on the assumption that each is a variant of the same manic-depressive disease. Fine, but what about depressive illnesses associated with little or no mania? Do we automatically dismiss the possibility that there is anything more to the depressive illness than the straight (unipolar) depression that we see? No, because hidden bipolarity may, in some cases, be revealed by getting past the mask of unipolar illness.

First, we may simply wait to see what happens because up to 20 percent of unipolars will eventually display manic symptoms that warrant a bipolar diagnosis; call these people "bipolar late." (It may take antidepressant medication to bring out the hidden bipolarity in what is sometimes called "manic overshoot.") Since people who suffer from bipolar disorder are at some risk for hypertension and even diabetes, and tend to be heavy around the middle, a girthy unipolar patient with these other characteristics would at least be a "bipolar suspect."

Second, we may extend our search beyond the affected person because some of the bipolar-late depressives plus additional "unipolars" will give *indirect* evidence of bipolarity. Think of a young woman's parents who have just been informed about a serious new boyfriend. Surely they will want to do more than study his appearance and behavior; they will want to inquire about his family to get an even better sense of his potential and prospects. Likewise, a depressed person's diagnostician may inquire about close relatives to get a better idea of potential (liability) and prospects (prognosis) than can be had merely from direct observation.

Finding outright manic behavior in depressed people's close relatives will suggest that the depressive-only (unipolar) illness is "crypto-bipolar," that is, manic-depressive deep down; recall suicidally depressed Castlereagh whose connection to the manifestly manic (as well as depressive) FitzRoy permitted the speculation about hidden manic-depressive disease. So, just as labels *bipolar I* and *bipolar II* indicate depressive illness associated with manifest mania *in the afflicted person*, the label *bipolar III* indicates depressive illness associated with manifest mania only *in a first-degree relative*.

The story of bipolar III is particularly important. Considering the behavior of relatives—in effect, asking about what is running in the family—makes the bipolar III diagnosis a *hypothesis* about causality rather than a mere descriptive summary of behavior. Thus, we understand things, not just by appearances (manifest illness), but by what those appearances really mean (disease, or liability). A bat may look like a bird, but no bat ever laid an egg—or claim to a robin's ancestors.

The plot thickens: Enter culprit 2

Well, a one-culprit solution won't do, and for a couple of good reasons. First, compared to bipolar illness, unipolar illness seems heterogeneous—too many patterns to be explained by just one disease. We suspect that a depression-only illness is like a fever that can indicate anything from flu to TB, or like a headache that can indicate anything from tension to tumor. In short, the seeming heterogeneity of unipolar illness suggests that a one-culprit solution, though mercifully simple, is simplistic.

Second, some unipolar illnesses, however severe they may be, nevertheless give *no evidence of any manic element*, either in the affected person or in the relatives. Suspect mania all you like, you can't find it. For example, *brief recurrent depression* shows the full range of sometimes incapacitating depressive symptoms with a relatively high risk of suicide. Episodes can erupt in a matter of hours, last from two to five days, and recur twenty times a year. Victims are apprehensive, if not demoralized, because they cannot predict the onset or severity of an episode. Remarkably stable over the years, the illness nevertheless shows no tendency toward manic development [232].

It is always possible that, with more sensitive diagnostic devices, a manic element will be found in seemingly pure-depressive disease, in which case, diagnosis becomes simpler. Until then, the heterogeneous, frequently manicless qualities of unipolar illness suggests a *two-culprit solution*. Such a solution would, of course, include Kraepelin's "two-way" culprit (manic-depressive disease), but also a "one-way" culprit (pure-depressive disease). The two-culprit solution is represented in the new figure by an additional component (in boldface on the right side of the diagram).

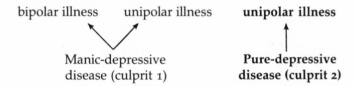

A good detective worries about having missed that all-important clue that might overturn even a seemingly ironclad solution. What, then, about the not-so-ironclad two-culprit solution? Might it yet be overturned, or at least seriously threatened, by something we have overlooked? In fact, the earlier discussion of the relative heritability and heterogeneity of unipolar illness provides two such clues, but these two must be considered together as a key that unlocks a better solution than the one we have. So, we consider this question: Why is unipolar illness *apparently* less heritable than bipolar illness? Consider three possibilities.

The simplest is that, whatever their origins, unipolar illnesses are just what they seem: less heritable. Moreover, as the earlier table indicated, the relatives of bipolar patients have markedly elevated rates of bipolar *and unipolar* illness; in contrast, the relatives of unipolar patients have markedly elevated rates of unipolar illness only. Indeed, a bipolar depression does apparently indicate a stronger liability, and in the light of the genetic evidence, a bigger dose of "bad genes."

A second possibility is that the lower heritability could, *to some extent,* be an artifact of mixing depressive "apples" and "oranges"—say, the highly heritable "unipolar" apples of manic-depressive disease (culprit 1), and the less heritable unipolar oranges of pure-depressive disease (culprit 2). But consider a third possibility, one that turns out to be the key we are seeking: Both the apple and orange kinds of depressive illness are, in fact, more heritable than they seem—maybe even as heritable as bipolar depression. They only *seem* less heritable because mixed in with *them* is other, less heritable "fruit," in other words, genetically less determined depression from an entirely different source—a *third culprit.*

A three-culprit solution

The possibility of a third culprit raises the critical question of *motive.* To appreciate what this means, think of depression as murder by either of two killers, each with a distinctive style. One is the "manic-depressive," or *two-way,* style of culprit 1 (manic-depressive disease). The other is the "pure-depressive," or *one-way,* style of culprit 2 (pure-depressive disease). Psychiatrists call both of these culprits *primary depression.* But there is a third possible culprit. This culprit 3 would be analogous to a person who kills unwittingly, that is, who commits manslaughter without intent or relish. The depression caused by culprit 3 is associated with psychological and medical disorders other than affective disorder, which is why psychiatrists speak of *secondary depression.*

We now have a *three-culprit solution* that distinguishes the primary depressions of affective disorder (culprits 1 and 2) from the secondary depressions of all other disorders (collectively represented as culprit 3). Our three-culprit solution calls for a simple addition to our earlier diagram (in boldface on the right of the new figure).

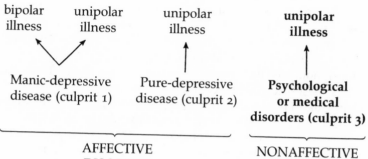

The obvious practical question is: How can we ever know what a seriously depressed person is *really* suffering from? Does the depression represent affective disorder (culprits 1 or 2) or something else, and if something else (culprit 3), is it psychological or medical? For example, how do we distinguish between the depression of affective disorder and the depression of personality disorder? We suspect that the underlying problem is affective disorder when there is evidence of insomnia and short REM latency, an *agitated* pattern of vegetative symptoms (for example, insomnia and loss of appetite), a positive response to certain antidepressant drugs, and, of course, mania in self or relatives.

On the other hand, we suspect nonaffective depressive disorder when there is a different pattern of symptoms, for example, mood fluctuations that are highly reactive to situations, a *retarded* (slowed) pattern of vegetative symptoms (for example, excessive sleeping and eating), and a positive responsive to different kinds of antidepressants. It stands to reason that where there are problems with being responsible or handling frustration, trouble with caring for others, and difficulties with feeling alive and real, there is a dramatically increased risk for depressive illness, in part because of the depressing conditions inevitably created by such traits. Therefore, we suspect that the underlying problem is personality disorder when there are lifelong patterns of immaturity, dependency, egocentricity, irrational thinking, emotional volatility, impulsivity, and low self-esteem, with a family history of alcoholism or antisocial behavior.

A depressive illness can reflect a disorder of personality and a disorder of affect, each aggravating the other to create a "crazy" pattern of behavior. A striking example seems to have been Freud's case of the Wolf-Man (born Sergei Pankejeff) [56]. Throughout his life right up into his eighties, he suffered episodes of severe depression that would end abruptly with his feeling like a new man. The first episode occurred after his sister died; he was just nineteen. "After the death of Anna," he writes, "I fell into a state of deepest depression. The mental agony I now suffered would often increase to the intensity of physical pain. In this condition I could not interest myself in anything. Everything repelled me and thoughts of suicide went around in my mind the whole time without, however, my having the courage to carry them out." Another probable episode occurred when his wife committed suicide; he was thirty-eight. There would be many more episodes, not always connected to adverse events. Moreover, he would have to deal with demoralizing suicidal impulses.

His relatives, especially on his father's side, were manic, depressive, and suicidal. His paternal grandmother suffered depression and committed suicide after one of her daughters died. His father, who probably committed suicide after many hospitalizations for depression, had been diagnosed by Kraepelin as manic-depressive, and Freud had concurred. His sister, believing herself to be ugly and unworthy, committed suicide by poison. Given his and his relatives' behavior, Wolf-Man's depressive illness may have been a severe bipolar III condition. But, whatever the affective disorder, personality and other non-affective disorders seem also to have been part of the picture, again as suggested by his and his relatives' behavior. He had multiple problems, many of them first appearing in childhood. These included phobias, obsessionality, cruelty to animals, hypochondria, recurrent constipation, conflict over homosexual inclinations, and an irritable, sometimes violent temper. At one point, Wolf-Man developed the delusion about a large hole in his nose. He was also consumed by delusional hostility toward his doctors whom he threatened to kill. His behavior made him seem like one of his paternal uncles who, besides being an eccentric, was hospitalized as a paranoid recluse.

"Weak sisters" may be "tough mothers"

Until now, our focus has been on severe depressions of the bipolar and unipolar kinds. But what about those more common, less severe kinds that we can more readily identify with—mixtures of pleasureless disinterest, irritable despondency, and just plain misery that are closer to home? Of course, those depressions can always be explained by invoking the usual suspects: an unsatisfying job, financial disappointments, a stressful marriage, and the like—but wait. Many people with such problems, or worse, are *not* depressed, while others who seem to have it all are nevertheless depressed. Are we not dealing with something more than merely matters of circumstance? If so, what is that "something?"

Moderately severe mood disorders are sometimes called *sub*-syndromes, but don't be fooled by that little prefix. Subsyndromes are "sub" only in failing to meet all the criteria for severe, full-syndrome depression. Despite their "weak-sister" appearance, subsyndromes are real syndromes representing a middle ground between severe mood disorder that is clearly pathological and mild moodiness that is clearly normal. Though less spectacular than their full-syndrome counterparts, subsyndromes are nevertheless easier to identify with. That is why understanding them brings the problem of depression closer to home.

If the causes of full-syndrome illness are like culprits who commit homicide, then the causes of subsyndromes are like culprits who commit *near-homicide,* that is, bodily harm *almost* to the point of death. Some subsyndromes are caused by affective disorder (culprits 1 or 2); others are caused by something *other than* affective disorder (culprit 3). But how do we decide if a subsyndromal depression represents affective disorder (culprits 1 and 2) or nonaffective disorder (culprit 3)? Clearing up the ambiguity is no easy matter.

Briefly, we suspect affective disorder when the subsyndrome seems to arise spontaneously, when it is relatively unresponsive to positive events, or when it is connected to clear-cut affective disorder. An obvious example is residual demoralization after "recovery" from an episode of bipolar illness, manic or depressive [6;9]. Another example is a between-episode depressiveness with which some sufferers come to identify in a personal way. The more or less chronic mood is experienced as familiar, even comforting, but more, as an essential part of self-definition. Periods of normalcy or even mania may be enjoyed, but only as excursions from the "home" condition. As one former patient explained: "I would never want to let go entirely of my depression because it's the only thing that's been stable throughout my whole life. I can always count on it to be there; no one person or thing has been so responsible."

We suspect personality disorder—a *nonaffective* pathology—in emptiness and boredom, and in deficiencies of character or antisocial behavior involving traits such as impulsivity, emotional instability and promiscuity, hostile and self-destructive tendencies, or a histrionic and paranoid outlook. Another clue is the eruption of a depression triggered by childhood memories of an incestuous relationship that made the person a wife to her father and mother to her siblings [122]. Depressions of abused, especially sexually abused, women involve unshakable dispiritedness, low self-esteem, powerlessness, desire to get away—even self-destructive, if not suicidal, tendencies.

Consider, now, only the *affective* subsyndromes. These are

- *hypomania* (subsyndromal mania), recognizable in boundless energy, impulsivity, abrasiveness, optimism, ambition, confidence, and can-do expansiveness coupled with hail-fellow-well-met sociability;
- *dysthymia* (subsyndromal depression), recognizable in gloomy apprehensiveness, moody sensitivity, obsessive self-consciousness, and brooding intellectuality; and
- *cyclothymia* (subsyndromal mania and depression), involving cyclic shifts between dysthymic and hypomanic mood from barely noticed to dramatically evident.

Depressive illness can be better understood by examining the connections between affective subsyndromes and their full-syndrome counterparts, for example, the *developmental* connection. Even seemingly ordinary moodiness can, sometimes for "no good reason," ripen into a severe, life-threatening, illness. Genetic influence as it changes over the course of a lifetime can alter brain activity and therefore personality and behavior. Personal decisions, social interactions, drug-taking, even luck have cumulative effects on self and circumstances. Over time, a darkening of temperament and/or accumulation of adversity can make troubled people even more so—more intolerant, suspicious, supercilious; more penurious, prudish, self-deprecatory; more volatile, theatrical, self-destructive. What begins with the blues or mere indifference may end with melancholia or even suicide. A case in point is F. Scott Fitzgerald's "crackup" that began with a gradually deepening depressed state of mind. He says that "for two years my life had been drawing on resources that I did not possess, that I had been mortgaging myself physically and spiritually up to the hilt. [Moreover] I saw that for a long time I had not liked people and things, but only followed the rickety old pretense of liking. I saw that even my love for those closest to me was become only an attempt to love. . . ."

A mild depression can be as innocuous as it seems; it can also be something more serious, even insidious. Consider one study in which one hundred so-called "neurotic" depressives were selected on the basis of having mild-to-moderate (subsyndromal) depression with anxiousness, immaturity, and/or excessive reactivity to stress, but no delusions [7]. After three to four years, 40 percent could be rediagnosed as full-syndrome unipolar (22 percent) and bipolar (18 percent)—culprits 1 and 2. Other subjects in the study were clearly diagnosable with personality disorder and other psychological problems—culprit 3. All of which again makes the obvious point that a mild depression, in one sense, may be a symptom of disease, and in another sense, it may be a quality of personality. That is, it can be something you have, like diabetes, and it can be something you are, something that defines your self.

One last observation leads us to perhaps the most intriguing implication of subsyndromes: The relatives of subsyndromals have elevated rates not only of subsyndromes, but of *full* syndromes too. There is really nothing surprising about mood problems running in families. What *is* surprising, however, is this: The *same* elevated rates of depression and suicide that are found in the relatives of people with full-syndrome (bipolar) illness can be found in the relatives of people with subsyndrome (cyclothymic) illness [8]. Apparently, people with subsyndromes—at least those with a manic element—may carry the *same* genetic liability that full-syndrome people carry. This means that a subsyndrome need not be the complete expression of a weak genetic liability; it may be the *partial expression of a strong genetic liability*. Given the evidence of high heritability for the affective disorders, we could say that what looks like a behavioral "weak sister" may be a genetic "tough mother."

Elevated liability can be carried and transmitted not just by subsyndromals, but *even by people who look normal*—people who might be called "nonsyndromals." Recall again from Chapter 2 the study of identical twins discordant for bipolar disorder. The offspring of the manifestly bipolar twins had an elevated rate of bipolar illness—roughly 10 percent—*but so did the offspring of the not-ill co-twins*. Equal rates of illness despite major differences in environment suggest equally strong genetic components of liability.

A liability need not show up, however, not even in a relatively mild subsyndrome. We don't yet know why, but the lesson is clear: Understanding mental illness means going beyond behaviors that, like bat and bird, may look similar but reflect different causes. Also, it means discovering disorder (liability) even where there may be no disorder (illness). Finally, it means recognizing that mental illnesses may not be what they seem— or that they may be what they seem not to be.

PART THREE
THE CLAY *IS* THE POTTER

For in the Market-place, one Dusk of Day,
I watch'd the Potter thumping his wet Clay:
And with its all obliterated Tongue
It murmur'd—"Gently, Brother, gently, pray!"

—OMAR KHAYYAM–EDWARD FITZGERALD
Rubáiyát of Omar Khayyám

9

MASKED BAWL

Whatever their cause, depressive subsyndromes represent personality struggling with threats to its integrity. The result is often a quiet desperation at the core of the soul. If even our best and brightest secretly despair—if an optimist and literary giant like Goethe finally admits that underneath it all, life is mostly pain and burden—how must it be with the rest of us? The answer, says William James, is that self- and world-weariness lie just below the surface of bubble enthusiasms. "Make the human being's sensitivities a little greater, carry him a little farther over the misery-threshold, and the good quality of the successful moments themselves when they occur is spoiled and vitiated. All natural goods perish. Riches take wings; fame is a breath; love is a cheat; youth and health and pleasure vanish."

Such thoughts can become really depressing unless banished from consciousness, if not from the psyche. One way to achieve this denial is with "happy" activity whose true nature is revealed by compulsive, hostile, or otherwise unhappy qualities that color or break through the facade—a "fake smile" or untoward outburst of meanness, for example. Another way is with unhappy activity whose self-effacing quality can sometimes put off a more deeply dysphoric condition. Through almost any activity involving denial, self-deception, and social role-playing, one's true state of mind as well as one's deepest vulnerabilities can be masked from others and from oneself.

Confronting the depression behind the mask can occur dramatically in nervous breakdowns. More often, it occurs subtly, as illustrated by the two seemingly innocent drawings shown here. Complying with a request to draw a person, a college woman draws the happy-faced, childlike cartoonish figure shown on the left. That this drawing represents an incomplete self-expression is suggested by what happens next. First, she cancels the drawing, but with a light wavy line suggesting some ambivalence. Then, on the other side of the page, she makes a second drawing whose facial expression, background shading, and floating quality suggest a distinctly somber mood. Here, on the back side of the page, is the dark side of personality, the dysphoric state of mind behind the mask. The second drawing is not more valid, only more courageous. It begins to remove the mask.

Comic mask

It is said that the saddest among us are those who wear the jester's motley garb. A classic version of this notion is told by nineteenth-century criminologist Cesare Lombroso. A depressed man is advised by his physician to take advantage of the circus being in town, and to be sure to see that greatest of harlequins, Joseph Grimaldi. "You need amusement; go and hear Grimaldi; he will make you laugh, and that will be better for you than any drugs." "My God," the man replies, "but I *am* Grimaldi." This little story symbolizes a long-held view that suffering lies just below the surface of histrionic enthusiasms. "It is good to laugh," says Herman Melville in *Mardi*, "though the laugh be hollow. Women sob and are rid of their grief; men laugh and retain it. Ha! ha! how demoniacs shout; how all skeletons grin; we all die with a rattle."

Never mind, say the experts, an active life is the best therapy. Have goals and keep active to create those felicitous thoughts and comforting feelings. What better antidepressive than always having something to do—better yet, something meaningful that gives purpose to life. Forceful activity, even when contrived, can defend against melancholy, for a while at least. "Everyone was crying," exclaims the movie character Zorba the Greek. "Me, I got up and danced. They said Zorba is mad. But it was the dancing—only the dancing—that stopped the pain." Lurking behind the cacophony of such urgent comedy is the possibility of succumbing to sadness.

The harlequin happy-face may work for a while. In time, however, the effects wear thin. People become increasingly put out by the put-ons, and the old tricks cease to work their magic. Nagging doubts arise and dysphoria percolates, as in neurotics whose coping with depression is especially desperate, transparent, and pathetic. Sometimes they seem to be on empty: bored, goalless, indifferent. Other times they seem to be filled to overflowing, as if on an emotional roller coaster that shuttles them between the heights of manic-like grandiosity, rapturous infatuations, and idealization of a loved one, and the depths of depressive self-devaluation, hostile disillusionment, and cynical world view. Empty or full, they struggle with a poor sense of self and/or weak and shifting values.

Such problems with identity can also mean impulsive recklessness in just about any aspect of living: money (foolish investing), sex (promiscuity), drugs (alcohol abuse), food (binge eating), traveling (reckless driving), shopping (shoplifting), or even personal commitments (impulsive marriage). Hypersensitive to perceived rejection or abandonment, neurotics may even resort to self-mutilation or suicidal gestures. Behind what one expert calls pseudovitality lies the potential for depression, "a deep sense of uncared-for worthlessness and rejection, an incessant hunger for response, a yearning for reassurance" [186].

Consider a twenty-year-old college student, Brian, who seeks a diagnostic examination as the first step to getting help for a growing sense of emptiness and a loss of motivation. Brian is hurting, yet in the diagnostic testing situation, he mobilizes denial and other defenses against the twin threats of exposure and change. Face to face with the examiner and the attendant dangers of intimacy, the problem and the solution are no longer abstract. Instinct kicks in to derail reason, the effect of which is procrastination, defensiveness, and back-sliding. Clever banter, suggestive comments, facetiousness: all these Brian uses in a battle of wits whose unconscious goal, to diminish the impact of the interview, requires making light of procedures and disarming the examiner.

Despite the posturing and clowning, Brian's insecurity and self-contempt show through, as confirmed by his sometimes touching comments written later in the comparative safety of his apartment. The signs of chronic dispiritedness and demoralization are evident in his self-description as "bland and undirected, with definite ideas but no ambition or concentration even on subjects and projects which interest me . . . conservative and easily discouraged." Rather than succumbing, denial again comes into play. Yet it lacks the anxiety-driven brashness, gusto, and conviction displayed during the interview. "Since coming to college, I've abandoned high goals and purposes. My ideal would be to make myself a Phi Beta Kappa Rhodes scholar holding down a very lucrative legal practice in civil law. I see myself fighting my great heart out in the courtroom, and on the campaign trail for the American way—whatever that is. But that's the rainbow that you never quite can reach. Now about all I want is a job, a wife, kids, a home, a car, a fire on cold nights and a big easy chair. And these will be hard enough to come by. . . ."

Antisocial mask

Dysphoric states can be masked by devotion to sensory and symbolic adventures that can make a mechanical life seem more meaningful, an empty self seem real. Such devotion may not suffice to hide the lack of feeling, the inner emptiness, the zero state that lies at the core of the self [341]. In that case, more manifestly antisocial defenses may come into play. Risky, rebellious, aggressive, and addictive behavior: all these can serve as antidepressants. Later, we'll look at the more aggressive pattern. Here, consider two examples of antisocial defense—first, a brief one involving kleptomania, then a longer one involving drug abuse.

An otherwise law-abiding person suffering unbearable psychological tension finds relief in compulsive shoplifting. Despite appearances, the kleptomania is a matter of irresistible impulse more than calculating premeditation, emptiness more than opportunism. The suspicion that the psychopathology is depressive more than psychopathic is supported by two additional observations: that thefts are followed by genuine remorse, even acts of restitution, and that compulsive shoplifters and their relatives have strikingly elevated rates of depressive, not antisocial, disorders [221].

Observers have noted ominous psychological trends in our increasingly fast-paced, materialistic, and impersonal modern Western culture. They see fewer inner-directed, work-oriented, self-reliant, personally responsible selves, but more outer-directed, socially skillful yet fragile, spiritually empty selves [81]. Empty selves are bereft of inner meaning and identity. With their ambiguous and shifting values, they are ever ready to act upon expedient and self-indulgent impulses. Salient signs of empty-self psychology are legion. They include consumerism, political fanaticism, and zealous devotion to fads, cults, self-help seminars, and spiritual training. They also include eating disorders and drug abuse.

The antidepressant effect of drugs comes from their ability to bring self-centered pleasure and reassuring diversions. Psychoactive drugs like LSD and cocaine create an inner world of vivid imagery, intense feeling, heightened meaning, transcendent purpose, and a renewed sense of self. In short, they bring an awakening out of sterile experience, a heightened sense of the "utterly utter," as William James called it. Alcohol, he says, liberates the spirit so often crushed by the cold facts of life. "Sobriety diminishes, discriminates, and says no; drunkenness expands, unites, and says yes. It is in fact the great exciter of the *Yes* function in man [making] him for the moment one with truth. Not through mere perversity do men run after it."

As a neural depressant, alcohol works by weakening the conscience while focusing attention on impulses or feelings of the moment. The result is a greater willingness to take risks, for example, in relationships, with gambling, and in self-disclosure. Alcohol thus makes the adult more childlike, which means more egocentric, volatile, irrational, antisocial. To be effective, however, the psychological myopia produced by alcohol must be filled with antidepressive experience, for example, doing fun things with fun people. Otherwise, intoxication will just intensify the dysphoria or emptiness that initially motivated the drinking, kindling deeper depressions than might have been [297].

Somatic mask

A depressed state can be denied in still other ways, also egocentric but less obviously so. Consider a form of denial that is played out in somatic complaints and help-seeking behavior. Your body hurts, you feel weak, you've lost your appetite and you are not sleeping well. It might be situational stress or even the flu, but it might also be something more personal, something hidden that, if conscious, might stir unpleasant feelings. Nevertheless, you don't feel anxious or sad. What could be wrong? The following remarkable study illustrates how somatic complaints can signal a hidden state of mind, in this example, a repressed conflict [294].

Hypnotized male subjects were instructed to imagine having a sexually provocative encounter with a seductive older woman. However—here's where the conflict comes in—they were told that they would experience increasing anxiety and conflict culminating in the urge to flee her apartment and repress the whole affair. In other words, the subjects were given an *Oedipal* experience, one supposedly connected unconsciously to a boy's doomed proprietary infatuation with his mother. In the posthypnotic state, special stimuli (spoken numbers) connected to the hypnotically induced fantasy were used to elicit increasing desire and provoke clearer memory, in effect, to increase conflict between desire and need to repress. In response to a probe stimulus, one subject gave the following report. "I'm starting to feel nervous again; kind of the same feeling I have after a date. [Another probe stimulus] I notice cold again; I feel my leg shaking. . . . [another probe] I noticed my jaw is tense again and in the area of my temples; I think it is either warmer or colder in the area of my genitals. . . ." Subjects reported heart pounding, coldness in extremities, shortness of breath, shakiness, bladder sensations, or other somatic symptoms, but they could not say why they were experiencing these things.

Such research on inner conflict suggests how dysphoric states of mind can remain hidden, unrecognized by oneself or others, masked by somatic complaints, for example, about insomnia, loss of appetite, or fatigue. Feeling achy or tired might be just what it seems, or it might be a symptom of that sadless depression that poet Samuel Taylor Coleridge (in "Dejection: An Ode") described as:

> A grief without a pang, void, dark, and drear,
>   A stifled, drowsy, unimpassioned grief,
>   Which finds no natural outlet, no relief,
>   In word, or sigh, or tear—

Some investigators consider sadless depression to be a core condition—a somatic common denominator recognizable throughout the world. Superimposed on that common denominator are depressions whose distinctive expression in what a person feels and what other people see depends on personality and culture. In Western cultures, the mostly hidden core state is usually expressed in anxious, guilt-ridden, angry, and melancholic ways [16; 151]. What if these symptoms are absent in a person who displays only the somatic symptoms? Is the reasonable implication sadness *defended against*, and therefore the proper diagnosis *masked depression* [198]? Maybe, but diagnosing someone as having a masked depression is rather controversial, if only because somatic symptoms are inherently ambiguous; they might have other explanations. They need not be matters of repression but an inability to "read" any feeling, unpleasant or pleasant. This inability to read—a sort of dyslexia of feeling— is sometimes called *alexithymia*, meaning without *(a)* words *(lexi)* for mood *(thymia)* [290; 310]. Alexithymics are literal-minded, detail-driven, and externally oriented. Their inner life is devoid of metaphor and imagery. They have trouble distinguishing feelings from bodily states and translating feelings into words, all of which makes them deficient in self-understanding and empathy.

It's not that depressed alexithymics can't recognize a loss of appetite or even nervousness and dysphoria; they may even know in some abstract sense that their problem is depression. It's that they don't *feel* depressed. It is as if in one sense they are depressed yet in another they are not. They are worried, but they aren't quite sure what is wrong. "I guess I'm depressed. [What do you mean?] Well, it's always on my mind. [What is?] I'd like to feel all right . . . I used to feel all right. [And how do you feel now?] Well, I'm worried about how I feel" [128]. Even after responding favorably to antidepressant medication, they may not fully appreciate that they have recovered from depression.

How can the nature of somatic complaints be understood? True, somatic complaints are common in people with major depression, and depression is common in people with somatic complaints. Nevertheless, the statistical connection doesn't mean that complaints, say, of pain or sleeplessness indicate depression in either the masked or alexithymic sense. To make the inference stick, you need additional evidence, for example, of a depressing environment at home or on the job, responsiveness to antidepressants or a felicitous change of circumstances, and an elevated rate of depression in first-degree relatives.

In some cases, somatic symptoms prevent the feeling of depression by distracting attention from depressing thoughts. Better to worry about the body than the soul. As a victim of "medical" problems, the hypochondriac need not face head-on the distressing personal realities of loneliness or failure. Inadvertently, the physician may play into this game of hide and seek by providing the more comforting physical explanation: "Don't worry, you're a little run down; get more sleep and maybe change your diet."

The somatic mask of depression has a more bizarre aspect. Occasionally, a person complains of lost eyesight, a paralyzed limb, difficulty swallowing, or blackouts—even seizures. Typically, these symptoms are elicited by life crises such as impending separation from a spouse or therapist. Often, with a change in circumstances, they disappear as suddenly as they began. At first they look medical, then psychological in the sense of being highly motivated and self-serving, motivated, that is, by frustrated needs and inner conflict, and self-serving in the manipulation of others to get attention, escape dangers, or avoid responsibility. It is as if anger, sadness, or helplessness were converted into a language of bodily dysfunction—hence the term, *conversion* symptoms.

People with conversion symptoms initially display a peculiar indifference to their dysfunctions. A closer look often reveals dysphoria and hopelessness, sometimes outright depression. Moreover, that conversion symptoms may be a sign of hidden liability to depression is suggested by the fact that the relatives of a person with conversion symptoms have elevated rates of depressive disorder, possibly comparable to the elevated rates observed for relatives of depressed patients [74; 268].

Tragic mask

Masks come in many guises, not just a happy face with its accompanying expansive, aggressive, or theatric behavior. One can put on an *un*happy face, for example, cultivate spiteful self-pity while railing indignantly against the mindless and the mediocre. One can embrace a tragic philosophy that recognizes the absurdity of existence, like Shakespeare's melancholy Jacques indulging in sweet sorrow that denies a deeper, less felicitous sadness. Finally, one can cultivate a guilty attitude and a self-punitive interpersonal style. In these and other "tragic" ways, a greater unhappiness can thus be avoided, at least momentarily, either by decreasing painful self-consciousness or by increasing the sense—perhaps only the illusion—of the self as potent, sensitive, and good.

Consider an experimental study in which subjects periodically received, sometimes, positive feedback (green light) but sometimes negative feedback (electric shock), both supposedly from someone situated out of view. (In truth, no one was there, as the feedback was systematically controlled by the experimenter.) After each green light or shock, the subject had to choose from among three possible responses, and all had to be used by the end of the study. That is, he could give the other person a green light or a shock, or he could deliver a shock to himself. Acceptance of painful negative feedback was measured by the number of shocks a subject administered to himself versus to the other person. Against this measure, depressed people were relatively more "masochistic." Moreover, a blood pressure index of distress and relaxation suggested that they were more comfortable shocking themselves, in contrast to nondepressed subjects who preferred delivering shock to someone else [108].

Such laboratory behavior supports an idea about self-denial, self-recrimination, even masochistic behavior: Self-directed put-downs, especially when they prevent loss of support or affection, are more tolerable when preemptively metered by oneself than when acutely administered by someone else. Moreover, they carry a hidden advantage, namely the comforting sense of doing the right thing and being good. In his novel *The American*, Henry James described it in a character who, he said, was "a saint, and persecution is all that she needs to bring out her saintliness and make her perfect." Perfect, and powerful too, for there is power—perhaps from an illusion of superiority—in being so good. At bottom, then, the false humility of practiced self-diminution is, as psychoanalyst Roy Schafer once called it, an age-old trick of turning necessity into virtue. It is one of many largely unconscious ploys that put neurotics out of touch, not only with those about whom they pretend to care, but also with themselves about whom they pretend to know.

When 2 + 2 = 5

In normal people coping with personal flaws, short-term problems, and occasional tragedy, defensiveness is understandable. In neurotic and antisocial people coping with crippling vulnerabilities and irrational fears, defensiveness is baffling and off-putting—in a word, pathological. No wonder, for many troubled people, the greatest dangers seem to lie not so much in conflicts between the environment and the person, but within the personality—in destructive impulses, dependency needs, existential angst, mental instability, loneliness, or memories of child abuse. (For a more formal presentation of defensiveness, see the "Ego Problems" Appendix note.)

Defensiveness in otherwise well-adjusted people is intensified in situations that range from the emotionally challenging to the personally threatening. In maladjusted people, however, defensiveness is a kind of change-resistant *character armor* [258]. Like the metallic kind, it may even look good while it works, at least for a time, protecting against vulnerability. However, it is weighty, inflexible, and carried at great cost, imprisoning and exhausting the wearer. Historian Arnold Toynbee has made this very point on a much broader scale [317]. He describes *arrested civilizations* that face otherwise impossible circumstances yet manage to survive through audacious but inflexible and all-consuming feats of strength, skill, or ingenuity. Classic examples of such *tours de force* are ocean sailing by the Polynesians, Arctic seal hunting by the Eskimos, and stockbreeding by Asian steppe Nomads. *Tour-de-force* accomplishments teeter between further development and total defeat. What Toynbee calls perilous immobility at high tension is reminiscent of psychoanalytic descriptions of the neurotic fixations and repetition compulsions of arrested personalities defended by character armor.

Pathological defensiveness takes its personal toll in persistent low-grade unhappiness, debilitating self-consciousness, feelings of emptiness, and even a sense of the general absurdity of things. There is an interpersonal toll in relationships strained or broken by constant demands, accusations, and deception. Dependency increases while suspicion is cast on any efforts to comfort. It is an approach-avoidance game guaranteed to alienate others and aggravate the problem. The need for reassurance becomes increasingly desperate while the effort to accommodate to social demands becomes increasingly artificial and obligatory [76]. There may also be a physiological toll. The greater the stress, the greater the incidence of illness and disease, including cardiovascular disease, tuberculosis, skin disorders, pregnancy complications, even accidents [26].

But there is something deeper behind the masks of neurotic and psychopathic posturing. That "something deeper" may, from casual evaluations of conventional behavior, seem self-diminishing and, in the long run, self-destructive; yet it is self-serving, an instinctive survival mechanism as automatic if not imperious as any devoted to preserving the physical self. In *Notes from Underground*, Dostoevsky warns against taking the "whole register of human advantages from the averages of statistical figures. . . ." Why? Because, he says, theories about what motivates behavior on average leave out the possibility— no, the *likelihood*—that individual behavior will contradict social and psychological generalizations when there is a deeper advantage. And that advantage lies in self-survival, what Dostoevsky describes as "most precious and most important—that is, our personality, our individuality." To ensure self-survival, says the novelist, a person may find it necessary to resist lining up with others like so many piano keys played by events according to conventional rules. To ensure self-survival, a person will contemplate with satisfaction that two plus two might equal five.

Make no mistake, there is method in this "madness," though it may be lost in statistical principles such as the general responsiveness of behavior to reinforcement. Yes, behavior is encouraged by rewards and discouraged by punishment, *other things being equal*. But other things often are *not* equal, in particular the unique needs, responsiveness, and capacities of individuals seeking their perceived advantage while challenged by ego-threats from within as well as from external circumstances.

10

SOUL SURVIVAL

Psychological defensiveness, whether normal or abnormal, represents adaptability in the face of life's challenges and its threats to the ego. Understanding this aspect of our psychology means knowing not just how depressive illness is brought on by adversity, but why it *doesn't* occur in such circumstances, that is, when common sense and our theories say it should occur. Answers to such vexing questions do more than reveal the unpredictability of behavior and the tragic aspect of the human condition. Ultimately, they illuminate the resilient and heroic qualities of human nature.

The brain behind the defense

While inner threats to ego survival are usually matters of the self—of dysfunctional temperament or malignant ways of thinking that make up one's personality—they can be matters of a traumatized brain whose damage threatens the integrity and security of the self. We can learn a lot about the nature of defensiveness even when, as the following example shows, it involves bizarre changes in behavior. Brain damage can produce marked changes in intelligence, but also in personality and emotion. While left-hemisphere damage causes anxious, angry, depressed feelings, right-hemisphere damage may cause facetiousness, silliness, or extraordinary indifference. Patients with damage to the right hemisphere may even deny they have a problem in the face of severe dysfunction. In some cases, the denial is nothing short of spectacular. A person blinded by damage in the visual area of the brain may complain about poor lighting when asked questions about objects in the room—an article of clothing, for example, or a newspaper. The patient tries to fill in the blanks, sometimes by inventing a story. A red comb is held up in full view. "Now look hard at it. Can you see it now?" asks the neurologist. "Yes." "Really and truly?" "Of course." "What color is it?" "Brown and white." Two thousand years ago, the Roman philosopher-statesman and orator Seneca wrote to a friend about a "silly woman" who would not admit to being blind. "She keeps asking the housekeeper to change her living-quarters; she says her apartments are too dark" [78].

These admittedly extreme examples make clear how a defensive solution can become a problem, yet one that may be of little consequence to suffering people. Like imperious children clamoring to satisfy immediate needs, they struggle against immediate threats while ignoring the big picture. They may claim that they want to change when really all they want is to feel better. This makes many a psychotherapy less an honest effort to change than a struggle to justify the self against hostile intrusion from the agent of change. Every psychoanalyst understands that defensive self-organization means resistance to change. That is why all psychoanalytic treatment proceeds by analyzing the so-called resistances. In fact, the first stage of treatment deals with the resistance to the treatment itself.

To a question about what it would take to change, a depressed patient replied that it would mean becoming someone else [208]. Perhaps this is how it must be, with even a positive transformation sensed as a kind of death; no wonder we resist. Some people do seem willing to change; dependent, timid people may wish to become more independent, assertive—to be masters rather than victims. Nevertheless, the motive for change often turns out to be less than genuine, and the change less than real. All too often it is a matter of the same self-serving mechanism in a new guise, the same personality sporting the new vocabulary of yet another self-delusion. There is an ironic message in all these examples, namely that the resistance of an abnormal personality to change toward health, and the resistance of a *normal* personality to change toward illness, seem to be two sides of the same "coin," or basic rule. The rule is that *all* living things are devoted to defending or restoring their security, their ways of being.

As a living system, personality is no different in this regard. When challenged by threats, whether internal (a neurotic trait, a damaged brain) or external (an abusive environment), it will mobilize its self-organizing forces to defend, or to effect a return to, its habitual, largely instinctive ways of being. Like personality, the brain compensates after damage by tumor, stroke, or trauma. Defensive compensation can occur when undamaged neurons become increasingly sensitive to chemical messengers, perhaps by sprouting new branches to make up for lost connections. Compensation can also occur when other, undamaged parts of the brain take over. For example, after damage to a language center of the left hemisphere, a normally subsidiary area of the right hemisphere becomes more active. Such compensations can explain the near-miraculous recovery of language and other functions that seemed forever lost.

An undamaged brain can compensate by radically changing its organization in response to altered sensory input from a part of the body, for example, after a finger is surgically removed [110]. Every part of the body is represented in maplike fashion in the cerebral cortex. This mapping enables an organism to *make sense* out of sensory information coming from any part of the body's interior and surface. After surgery, the usual signals from the now-removed finger no longer stream to the finger section of the cortical "map." Without the usual input, that part of the map no longer makes sense. Being senseless, it is no longer useful; no longer useful, it gradually disappears. This happens when the input-deprived neurons that used to map the now-missing finger shift allegiance to sensory input from a remaining adjacent finger. In effect, they become part of a new *four-finger* map that allows the organism to remain as handy as possible with one less finger. You could say that, by changing the way it makes sense of important information, the cortex is putting its best foot—or rather its best four fingers—forward. Isn't this, in a sense, what a personality does when it compensates for some personal weakness by modifying the way it perceives and thinks?

Exotic examples of brain compensation include special cases of congenital hydrocephaly—what used to be called water on the brain. In people with this condition, much of the developing brain is destroyed by internal pressure that builds from cerebrospinal fluid that cannot properly drain. Brain scans give the impression that from 50 to 90 percent of the tissue making up the cerebral mass is missing. An abnormally thin layer of highly active neural tissue surrounds a hollow, fluid-filled cavity. The organization of brain structure and activity is clearly aberrant. Whether neurons and connections are reduced or highly compressed is yet uncertain, though some reduction is likely.

Profound retardation is the typical effect, yet in the occasional person, something remarkable happens—little or no evident psychological devastation [200]. After inspecting the brain scans, what neurologist would predict that *any* hydrocephalic child would grow up to have a seemingly normal personality and even the abilities necessary to excel at college? Such observations certainly defy conventional wisdom regarding not so much what is typical, but what is necessary. What marvelous machinery, the human brain, that it could *ever* manage such heroics against such odds—no wonder, then, the resiliency of personality.

The gods must be crazy

Defensiveness is aligned against depressing facts of internal and external life. Sometimes, as we have just seen, it must be arrayed against a rare kind of inner enemy imposed willy-nilly from the outside: the threat to self that comes with unpredictable acute brain damage. More often, the inner enemy is intrinsic to the self, an unshakable tendency to be self-critical, self-conscious, or just plain unhappy. The tendency to be morbid-minded or self-destructive is aggravated by an intellect that recognizes tragedy rather than irony or comedy in the depressing facts of life—for example, the intellect of a Melville who, historian V. L. Parrington describes as, "forever comparing a wife in her morning kimono with the Helen of his dreams," or the intellect of a Camus, who describes himself as seeing something inhuman in men who seem to "secrete the inhuman. At certain moments of lucidity, the mechanical aspect of their gestures, their meaningless pantomime makes silly everything that surrounds them. . . . Likewise the stranger who . . . comes to meet us in a mirror. . . ."

Still other depressing facts of life come from external sources, some created by one's own behavior, but some—loss, deprivation, or trauma—for which one is largely or entirely not responsible. Irremediable erosion of fortune, family, and fellowship may not come from anything specific or localizable; it may be chalked up to bad luck. It is only when adversity comes to *seem* purposeful that it may produce increasing alienation, fatalism, demoralization. But most people have a reservoir of optimism, confidence, and an extraordinary resiliency that will get them through crisis, for example, enabling them to cope with cancer [64; 311; 312].

Mothers of dying leukemic children often adopt strategies that appear nothing short of neurotic. One mother might have a cold, aggressively intellectual attitude toward her child's disease and therapy. Another might use denial, in an effort to convince herself that, despite objective evidence, things are not so bad and may be getting better. A third adopts a hostile, questioning, accusatory attitude toward the sick child's doctors. Such strategies help a mother comprehend her child's disease and continue to function in the world. Eventually, inordinate defensiveness gives way to acceptance, often before the child succumbs. The healing process involves habituation, but also a search for meaning. What, we wonder, is the nature of the recovery, how real the apparent wellness? That is, we want to understand why people get sick and how they get well, but also how well they really get.

Depressing circumstances may be traumatic or may be just an accumulation of reminders that people are stinkers and life is unfair. Such events may cause grief without demoralization, challenging a person to display a resiliency and fortitude that others recognize as competence, courage, and character—in a word, virtue. In his novel *Far from the Madding Crowd*, Thomas Hardy describes the effect of a disastrous investment on his main character, Gabriel Oak. "He had passed through an ordeal of wretchedness which had given him more than it had taken away. He had sunk from his modest elevation as pastoral king into the very slime-pits of Siddim; but there was left to him a dignified calm he had never before known, and that indifference to fate which, though it often makes a villain of a man, is the basis of his sublimity when it does not. And thus the abasement had been exaltation, and the loss gain." It is more than just resilient temperament, but the mundane facts of life, of love and work, that divert most people. To the extent that these areas of life are secure, at least hopeful, there is little room for gloomy thoughts.

Usually, it takes something external to threaten happiness and bring on depression, though it need not be traumatic or catastrophic. Little things will do. Everyday life is full of mostly minor, isolated hassles and stresses, and the occasional seemingly impossible condition. Some problems are mundane, though wearing—a loveless or conflict-ridden marriage or a recurrently stressful work situation, where even the little things grind a person down. Other problems are traumatic, such as divorce, being fired, or physical and/or sexual abuse. What happens when organisms confront conditions that frustrate their deepest needs? Answers, or at least clues, to deep questions about real-world behavior can sometimes be found in the laboratory.

Rats can be shocked for pressing a bar, which they have previously learned will get them food when hungry. Act and get shocked; don't act and stay hungry. In such life-threatening situations, rats display the intensely agitated behavior emblematic of frustration. First, they will try to escape. But with no way out, many will develop so-called *experimental neuroses*. These are frantic and chaotic behaviors (anxiety), stereotyped and repetitive behaviors (compulsivity), or complete inactivity (demoralization) in many ways reminiscent of neurotic patterns of behavior in humans. And like the human kind, these neurotic reactions can be self-defeating; they don't solve the problem and they persist even when the situation changes and a solution (escape) becomes possible.

In his classic analysis of communist society, *The Captive Mind*, social philosopher Czeslaw Milosz describes two psychological

(with their genetic overlap of 50 percent), resemblance on IQ tests is usually between .30 and .40, and it remains in that range throughout childhood and young adulthood. For *genetically unrelated* adult siblings—adoptees and their adoptive siblings—resemblance of about 0.15 during childhood drops to .00 by adulthood. To date, published correlations—two negative (−.03, −.09), and two positive (.02, and .05)—add up to *virtually no correlation* [43].

Despite their common rearing and shared experiences, genetically unrelated adult siblings are apparently no more similar to each other than to people picked at random from the population. Yet, they *do* show a modest resemblance to their biological siblings whom they've never met [203]. In sum, like the genetic traits of a species, the heritable traits of the individual—those variations on species themes—tend to unfold according to inner lines of force. They have a life of their own, displaying a natural conservatism in their resistance to change and in their reversion to type.

Perhaps you can teach introverts to party or melancholics to look for the silver lining or to act more assertively, even aggressively—but how convincingly, for how long, and with what emotional effect? We may howl like wolves despite being sheep in wolf's clothing. Or, we may baa like sheep despite being wolves in sheep's clothing. You might help a psychopath do a good deed, make amends, strive for redemption—even experience rebirth. Perhaps you can teach self-centered, materialistic college students to be generous and socially conscious—but, again, how convincingly, for how long, and with what emotional effect? Undergraduates, says political scientist Fred Baumann, are encouraged by campus life and course curricula to deny their true nature through the celebration of other, especially noncapitalist, cultures. Yet most of them turn out to be irredeemably bourgeois, students who "pretend to be [cultural] relativists but who are really believers in rights and individual responsibility. Underneath the high-toned moralism, they are lovers of wealth and comfort. Furthermore, the lives they lead when they graduate will overwhelmingly be bourgeois lives, composed of the usual professional and commercial careers, condominiums, divorces, therapies, and retirements" [30].

The call of the wild is more than animals reverting both to

their species-typical and individually unique, *heritable* ways. Like pigs and other living things, we are what we are—uniquely and in common with other members of our species—despite what we, too, are forced to do. Because we are biased to learn, remember, do, and enjoy certain things, no wonder that, like porcine "bankers," we revert from imposed toward preferred ways of being. We can bank on it.

Moving targets

Heritable traits, those inner central tendencies of personality, have a life of their own. Unfolding from within, they follow mostly normal but sometimes pathological developmental pathways laid down by brain maturation and experience. This unfolding—sometimes smooth, sometimes zig-zaggy, sometimes regressive—will be imperfectly reflected in behavioral changes generally toward greater maturity, but sometimes toward abnormality. Traits are therefore, in a sense, like moving targets that "attract" behavior. These inner dispositions tend to make behavior trait-consistent, while promoting reversion in externally imposed behaviors that are trait-inconsistent—including setbacks caused by trauma and improvements caused by educational / therapeutic intervention. Moreover, reversion will tend to occur despite the illusion of fundamental and enduring change that comes from observing situational reactions and learned accommodations.

Messy kids will respond to threats or promises by putting away their toys or picking up their clothes, but they are likely to be messy tomorrow or next week, that is, when the promises or threats are forgotten. Enforced neatness is the social responsibility of parents who should act as though their efforts will make a difference, as surely will be true, to some extent. However, enforced neatness is not change in the deepest sense if, *in their hearts,* the children remain indifferent to messiness, and if they revert to messiness in time. What, then, is the psychological effect of rewards or punishments, the modeling of behavior and the training to standards, whether it be children exposed to educational programs or children exposed to rearing conditions?

Apparent change may thus be enduring, like deep currents that move by unseen forces; momentary, like surface water blown about by the wind; or something in between, a habit whose persistence depends on circumstances. *Sometimes, it is none of these.* Consider a statistical fact of life that has a surprising explanation. After being punished for behaving extraordinarily badly or poorly, children usually behave better the next time. If you think you know why, then explain this: After being praised for doing extraordinarily well, children usually do *worse.* Here's a conundrum, an apparent asymmetry: Punishment generally seems to have desirable effects, and reward has undesirable effects. What's going on? Could it be that, to some extent, the apparent effects of our rewards and punishments are illusory?

To shed light on the question, imagine those same children playing a dice game in which throwing a "12" is considered extraordinarily good performance, a "2" extraordinarily poor performance. Now we make the same observation as before (though here it will seem odd), to wit: After being punished for doing extraordinarily poorly (rolling a "2"), children usually do better the next time. On the other hand, after being praised for doing extraordinarily well (rolling a "12"), children usually do worse. Can there be any surprise, given that rewards and punishments after a dice roll have no effect on the outcome of the next roll? The point is that extraordinary events based solely on chance are, by definition, unreliable. So, regardless of what we have just seen, whether "12," "2," or any other number, our best bet is the expected, or *ordinary,* value—that value with the greatest prior probability—which in the case of dice is "7." Moreover, we should expect the ordinary value *regardless of praise or punishment.*

But, you argue, surely that dice game is inappropriate for modeling children's behavior. Surely there is something systematic about the changes in their behavior, especially after the application of rewards or punishments. Alas, it ain't necessarily so, at least, not entirely, and here's why. Any extraordinary behavior—scoring high on an IQ test, for example—is the result of two things. One, called "true" or "real," is systematic—in our example, true intelligence, that quality of the nervous system that is reliable, meaning that you can count on it next time. The other, called "false" or "erroneous," is a matter of chance—good fortune, "lucking out," rolling a "12." Next time, of course, a

"2" might just as likely come up, making the test score—reflecting true intelligence plus luck—that much lower.

For any unusual behavior, the question must be: *To what extent* is it systematic (predictable) and to what extent unsystematic (chance)? Regardless of appearances, to the extent that chance is operative, a second observation or measurement, say a week from now, will reveal behavior that is less extreme, more ordinary. Moreover, this will be true *regardless of any attempts to reinforce or discourage the behavior with rewards or punishments.* But we are easily fooled because rewards and punishments do have immediate, often striking, effects on behavior. It's just that we can't tell if those immediate reactions are relevant to the *long-term* learning of traits that we want to reinforce or discourage. Question: Is the child who displays extraordinary behavior *really* different now, and after being rewarded or punished, any different than would have been the case *had the parents done nothing?*

In sum, extraordinary behavior may reflect something systematic—talent, character, liability, learning—*but also something random.* If the systematic element is operative; we can count on it the next time; if not, we can't. So, ABC: always bet on chance. Or at least keep in mind that random factor which, along with heritability, you are often apt to underestimate. (For more on this and related questions, see the Appendix note "Capitalizing on Chance.")

Paint your wagon

As a species, we are naturally sociable, curious, and adventurous—also somewhat anxious and irritable. These and other genetically determined qualities make us liable to depression in the face of loss. To some extent—heritability estimates tell us the extent—some of us have more (or fewer) of these human qualities; some of us are relatively more (or less) sociable, dependent, irritable, moody, and liable to depression. The heritability of depression, like the heritability of any trait, suggests that individual differences reflect genetic variation on our species' themes.

The genetic blueprint of an individual lacks continuity in that only a *random half* of its genetic elements gets passed on to each offspring. Clearly, then, there can be immortality, but only for individual genes, not your unique genetic blueprint. For a generation or two, elements of your heritable self survive in close relatives—as with the manic-depressive elements of Castlereagh and Fitzroy. But the continuities weaken with increasing genetic distance within and across generations. There's some of you in your siblings but less in your cousins, some in your parents or kids but less in your grandparents or grandchildren. Across four to five links, just about all similarity in personality disappears. A person no more resembles a fifth-generation (or any fifth-degree) relative than someone of the same sex and ethnic group chosen at random. A melancholy fact, perhaps, yet what better argument for the specialness of the individual than this: that, at the deepest level of our being lies a blueprint which, subject to unique circumstances including a random roll of genetic dice, inspires development of a person about whom it can be said, there never has been nor ever will be another.

Specialness, yes, but what of freedom in the face of the genetic roll of the dice and other biological facts of life? On the one hand, biological determination has always been suggested by the "id" aspects of our nature, including the imperious quality of survival needs, and the pressing quality of our distinctive dispositions that serve those needs. But freedom is suggested by those "higher" yet no less biologically determined creative and humane qualities of ego, imagination, and intellect that free us—at least seem to free us—from the demands of both id and conventional reality.

There is impulse, but also inhibition. There are physical limitations, yes, but we can exercise reluctant muscles and improve our appearance. There are intellectual limitations, but we can study hard and project a smarter image. A person may know evil, but not succumb; stumble, but not collapse. There are moral and spiritual limitations, but even when threatened, we may give over to heroism rather than give in to fear. As Albert Camus said, "freedom is nothing else but a chance to be better." Yes, and sometimes *surprisingly* better. Viktor Frankl tells of seemingly ordinary people who, despite the horrors of the concentration camp, showed their courage, compassion, and generosity in offers of comfort or even a last crust of bread. "They may have been few in number, but they offer sufficient proof that everything can be taken from a man but one thing: the last of the human freedoms—to choose one's attitude . . . to choose one's own way." Yet, what does choosing one's own way really mean?

Think about the question this way: Exposed to similar challenges in other concentration camps, the *identical twins* of such courageous people might likewise behave courageously, perhaps to the last detail, environment permitting. If so, would we want to say that the heroes of Frankl's story were really free to choose? For all we know, unexpected behavior—even behavior so different from prior behavior that it seems to come from nowhere—may be just as determined as predictable behavior. Granted, the determinism may be a looser, more ambiguous kind arising from complex human potentials interacting sometimes competitively with each other and with unpredictable events.

If ego and intellect are as biologically determined as id, then it seems safe to say that, in the personal as well as biological sense, we are determined to be ourselves, *however unpredictable the behavioral details, and whatever inferences about free will we derive from making choices.* Yes, we can paint our wagons, but we are probably stuck with them. Yet, our choice of colors and mode of application are more than mere matters of chance or free will. Surely they, too, arise from sources outside our personal volition: dispositions that push us inexorably from within, and influences that coerce and seduce from without. Dispositions remain, while external pressures and their manifest effects change or dissolve. In time, fashionable paint jobs wear thin, crack, and flake off, revealing inner grain. Thus does the telling comment, I open my mouth and out comes the voice of my father/mother, strike middle-aged people with a mixture of surprise and rueful amusement.

Genetic determination is no mere philosophical notion, but rather, an empirical generalization. Correlational evidence of striking psychological resemblance between identical twins reared apart is convincing enough. Perhaps more compelling are the remarkable, sometimes mind-boggling coincidences that such reared-apart identical twins display even for unusual or idiosyncratic behaviors. As described by University of Minnesota investigators, one pair had both been using Vademecum toothpaste, Canoe shaving lotion, Vitalis hair tonic, and Lucky Strike cigarettes. In another of many such unlikely coincidences, the investigators made this observation: "Only two of the more than 200 individual twins reared apart were afraid to enter the acoustically shielded chamber used in our [research], but both separately agreed to continue if the door was wired open—they were a pair of [identical twins reared apart]. When at the beach, both women had always insisted on entering the water backwards and then only up to their knees." Such coincidences have rarely if ever been observed for fraternal twins reared apart *or together* [207].

Identical twins reared apart are remarkably similar even in characteristics thought to be shaped mainly by common experience, for example, conservative attitudes. Their surprisingly high heritability prompted psychologist David Lykken to raise an intriguing rhetorical question: Could William F. Buckley—like any other conservative, or liberal for that matter—have resisted developing his particular views on politics, religion, capital punishment, abortion, and the rest [206]? The question is rhetorical, but the implication (like the evidence) is becoming increasingly clear. Each of us will come to resemble others with similar blueprints. Find someone with your exact genetic blueprint, and discover much of yourself.

Wild goose story

Human behavior can be flexible, inventive, reflective, but also rigid, mechanical, impulsive, and defensive—sometimes so much so it has the appearance of a fixed action reminiscent of a lower animal. To illustrate, consider two stories, the first one told by ethologist Konrad Lorenz. The story, not the goose, is wild [204].

Martina was a greylag goose raised from birth and nightly housed in Lorenz' second-floor bedroom. Greylag geese don't like to be touched. So, rather than be carried, Martina was allowed to walk up the stairs. Greylags move toward light when in a state of uncertainty. Upon entering the house, Martina would walk to a hall window before turning back to the stairs. Then she would continue, climbing each step along its left, or window, side. In time, her detour became less pronounced, persisting as a subtle, ritual-like *fixed habit*. But, the subtlety of habits can belie their psychological importance. One day, Martina was let in long after the customary time. Apparently in a state of agitation, she rushed directly up the stairs along their right side, the shortest distance from the front door to the second floor. *Upon reaching the fifth stair she showed signs of anxiety, crying out and extending her neck as if to take off. Immediately, she retraced her steps, "and set forth resolutely, like someone on a very important mission, on her original path to the window and back. This time, she mounted the steps according to her former custom from the left side. On the fifth step she stopped again, looked around, shook herself and greeted, behavior mechanisms regularly seen in greylags when anxious tension has given place to relief."*

Martina's story takes on a special poignancy when related to the behavior of Samuel Johnson (1709–1784), one of England's great literary figures. Poet, essayist, lexicographer, journalist, and conversationalist, Johnson was more than a bit peculiar in appearance and behavior. In a classic biography, John Boswell describes some real eccentricities. One was Johnson's superstitious habit of anxiously taking "care to go out or in at a door or passage, by a certain number of steps from a certain point, or at least so as that either his right or his left foot . . . should constantly make the first actual movement when he came close to the door passage. Thus I conjecture: for I have, upon innumerable occasions, observed him *suddenly stop, and then seem to count his steps with a deep earnestness; and when he had neglected or gone wrong in this sort of magical movement, I have seen him go back again, put himself in a proper posture to begin the ceremony, and, having gone through it, break from his abstraction, walk briskly on, and join his companion."* (Italics are added to facilitate comparison.)

What a daffy image: Samuel Johnson, supersimian literatus, stuck in greylagian ritual. Yet how singularly apt to express two key points. First, human nature, in its universal themes and unique variations, is part of something larger and older, something unconsciously organized and resistant to change. Second, our freedom as well as determination are matters of our biological heritage. Our instincts, the fixed and the flexible, make us the creative geniuses of all species, and through genetic variation, some of us the creative geniuses of our species. Instinct can explain our tendencies to be superstitious and inclined to ritual. It can also explain why we are liable to depression, but also why we are able to resist the liability.

We humans are smart mammals, but with a primitive core, the legacy of a more distant evolutionary time. Our distinctive ways of being come from what psychologist Thomas Bouchard calls the prehistoric tune sung by the genes [44]. For a brief moment in time, our song is heard, with all its comic, heroic, and tragic overtones, as we participate in a great play of potentialities—a process that yields across the generations imperfect, sometimes abnormal, re-creations of ancient patterns of temperament, talent, and character. For a brief moment, we represent history, past and future—that infinitely creative process by which old truths are rediscovered and little chips become familiar old blocks.

12

INSIDE STORY

We appreciate the simple truth that organisms are in the business of being what they are supposed to be. But what about us as self-conscious individuals: how do we know what *we* are supposed to be—how do we recognize what C. S. Lewis calls the secret signature of our self—and how confident can we be in the knowledge? Self-knowledge can be accurate, but not when misleading distractions, fanciful images, or self-serving notions bias thinking—delusional thinking, as we have seen, but even conventional thinking, which is notoriously subjective if not irrational.

Accurate or not, our explanations can nevertheless reveal important, often hidden aspects of our psychology. We therefore take a closer look at the nature of explanation directed both toward our selves and toward the outside world. That means exploring, first, the question of self-concepts and their possible effect on liability to depression (this chapter), and second, how we theorize either about *individual acts,* such as suicide (Chapter 13), or about *individual differences* in intelligence and personality (Chapter 14). Later chapters extend our exploration into the political area where ideological explanations about individual differences—mainly about why some people are labeled mentally ill—clash with more scientific explanations. In all of this, we deepen our understanding of both the nature of abnormal behavior and the nature of human nature.

Script behind the play

We appreciate people and things through the stories we create in our dreams, fantasies, recollections, and explanations. But deeper understanding means getting at the narrative behind experience. To understand a troubled person we ask not only what's the matter but also what's the story. Digging deeper, we try to get the story *behind* the story, the experience behind the words, the social and biological substance behind the symbolism. Psychotherapy is surely an elaborate extension of this basic principle of digging below the surface to illuminate the story [49].

Problems with pathological self-doubt, inhibition, and low self-esteem may reflect too much story—vivid experiences and memories saturated with self-demeaning themes of incompetence or unworthiness. On the other hand, crippling feelings of emptiness and a lack of personal identity may reflect too little story—amorphous or isolated experiences and memories lacking a consistent theme. Finally, chronic dissatisfaction and bodily symptoms may reflect traumatically painful experiences that are inaccessible until walls of repression are breached in stormy episodes of vivid recollection. It may be incestuous, physical, or more subtle abuse involving threat, ridicule, and neglect, even when the victim is another person. An extreme example is illustrated by the case of a woman who, through psychotherapy, recalled an incident that appeared to have been repressed for twenty years. She had witnessed her father sexually assault and bludgeon to death her eight-year-old girlfriend. A court, mindful of the possibility of false recall, supported her story and found the father guilty of murder [213].

The human psyche may be haunted by all kinds of soul-sabotaging, depressing narratives—demeaning, deficient, demoralizing at the time they are experienced and laid down in memory. But are they the elements of psychogenesis rooted in early trauma and in failures of the rearing process, that is, an exogenous liability at the core of the self? The question is raised by those who understand the inventive powers of the mind, the instinct for a good story whose script may be matters of imagination more than objective fact. Some of those sudden recollections of child abuse turn out to be suspect if not false, though how often and for what purpose continues to be debated [146].

Mental causality is complicated by the fact that thinking is mostly intuitive and unreflective. We infer intuitive thinking from a baby's surprised look and searching behavior after seeing a ball roll into one end of a cylinder but not out the other. Intuitive thinking is an inarticulate attraction to a person or a tip-of-the-tongue knowing or a *déjà-vu* feeling. It is the irrational sense of danger felt by a phobic for the same elevator she willingly lets her beloved child ride. Intuitive thinking is outwardly directed toward the world of people and events, but it is also egocentric. That is, much of what we know apparently involves memories colored by personal experience, and this self-centered knowledge biases our thinking, from what we perceive and learn to what we remember. You can think of it as the scripts for the play of personal experience—scripts that help determine whether we feel worthy or unworthy, optimistic or hopeless. Negative scripts can explain why, even in the face of success, some people are predictably burdened by self-doubt, guilt, or self-loathing.

During early childhood, experience is highly egocentric, fantastic, subjective, and scattershot. "I can pedal my feet . . . only boys have penises, not girls," trumpets a two-year-old boy exalting in his newly achieved mastery of the three-wheeler. Not very grown-up, this curious exaltation, and the reason is simple. Growing up means an increasing ability to think logically and to develop more realistic self-concepts through self-monitoring. The increasingly competent actor develops the skills of a director who uses personal evaluation and propaganda to promote the play.

Self-development, though highly heritable, depends on external conditions that contribute to *particular* experiences. In other words, the director has *some* freedom to interpret, even go beyond, the script, depending on how well the play seems to be unfolding. Perhaps dreaming contributes to self-development by consolidating recent learning, strengthening personality defenses, and creating self-serving solutions to emotionally significant problems. The self-expressive process of dreaming may thus be an egocentric REMembering of things past that shapes our future, making a healthy person healthier, a neurotic more neurotic.

The survival of a coherent self is threatened when self-scripts are inherently inadequate or when they are ruined by revision and vandalism imposed from outside. A self can be fragile, amorphous, fragmented, conflict-ridden. Relevant clues about the self can be found in what people say, feel, and do. Some people have difficulty feeling sufficiently beautiful, competent, and lovable; therefore they are unable to feel confident and worthy. One melancholic referred to life as a bowl of pits and to himself as the wooden spoon. Others feel insubstantial, unreal, disembodied, rootless. One patient describes his false (public) self observed by a detached, disembodied (private) self [193]. Another, in a Freudian slip, describes his "fetal—I mean feeble attempt at individuality." Still other people seem to be two or more persons—mutually incompatible or conflict-ridden personalities isolated by amnesia. In most cases of inconsistent behavior, the dissociation is less exotic. Perhaps there are just two personalities—one for daytime, one for night—or merely amnesia for large chunks of personal history.

A dysfunctional self has many guises, some in the form of negative self-concepts consciously experienced and willingly admitted. Others are in the form of unconsciously expressed neurotic traits that may be transparent even to the casual observer or misleading even to intimates. For, as psychotherapist Andras Angyal noted, a neurotic may "cover his assumed worthlessness with practiced pretenses. . . . If one cannot be loved, at least one can have fame, prestige, a reputation, titles, and other external trappings; the person himself becomes an appendage of his badges. In other cases, genuine wishes or wants are replaced by obligations, and life becomes a set of hated demands one halfheartedly tries to fulfill. There are many ways of selling out, of exchanging being for appearing; [there is that] wish to get *at least* something. . . ." [17]. Thus personality disorder creates depressing circumstances that involve the alienation of others and the self, and thereby aggravates any latent affective disorder, for example, a manic-depressive disease.

Know thyself?

Being yourself is one thing, knowing yourself is quite another. We may not know ourselves as well as we think we do, for lack of courage or other reasons. Like the blind person who complains about poor illumination, we may not know that we don't know. Some unusual examples will illustrate why the injunction, "Know thyself," is easier said than done.

Patients with damage deep in their temporal lobes can learn a task without knowing that they are learning. One task might involve tracing geometric shapes seen in a mirror—that is, front-to-back mirror-reversed. Another involves reading text printed backwards and / or upside down. (Try it.)

People find this task rather difficult at first, but less so after they have worked at it for some time.

Despite increased skillfulness from day to day, at the start of each new practice session the patient with temporal lobe damage always experiences the task as novel and expresses surprise at doing so well. At the start of each visit, he reacts to his doctor or the researcher without recognition. The same joke repeatedly told elicits the same hearty response, as long as the patient is briefly distracted between each telling. New people, places, newspaper stories: nothing seems to stick. He is like the rest of us after looking up an unfamiliar telephone number—a little distraction and the memory is gone. "Right now," he says most poignantly, "I'm wondering, have I done or said anything amiss? You see, at this moment everything looks clear to me, but what happened just before? That's what worries me. It's like waking from a dream. I just don't remember" [229].

Here is a person who does things that moments later he cannot declare having done. In other words, he displays *procedural* knowledge without *declarative* knowledge—know-how without know-that. He is like that epileptic physician who once examined a patient, arriving at a valid diagnosis all the while being in an epileptic absence—a nonconvulsive seizure with momentary lapse of personal consciousness and no memory after recovery [39].

Consider another example of the dissociation of procedural and declarative knowing [155]. A man, brought up since early childhood in an English-speaking Japanese-American family, says he is no longer able to speak or understand Japanese. During hypnotic regression to age three, he begins speaking Japanese. Progressed to age seven, he reverts to English. During another session, he continues to speak English even when regressed to age three—until the experimenter says Hi! Responding as if it were the Japanese word for yes *(hai)*, he lapses into Japanese. Hearing the tape recording in the posthypnotic state, he is unable to understand any of it. Moreover, he reports having had a dissociated sense of himself mouthing sounds he could not be sure made any sense. Apparently, the "hi" sound was the key that unlocked long-forgotten procedural knowledge.

As epileptics or sleepwalkers, or even just as motorists engaged in conversation with no thought to the passing scene or the action at the wheel, how often do we pass through life—mechanically more than apperceptively—as in a sort of dream? And how often, without giving it any thought, do we awaken to a higher consciousness of self and surroundings, yet without recall for the prior experience or with the illusion of having been awake and in full control?

We need not rely on extreme examples of procedural knowing dissociated from declarative knowing. Everyday experience instructs. Imagine a ball attached to a string. Holding the end of the string, make the ball fly in a circular path around your head, then release the string. Disregarding the effects of gravity, the ball flies away *in a straight line.* Nevertheless, many adults say that the ball would follow a curved trajectory [219]. All chimneys stand vertical, that is, perpendicular to the horizon, yet children draw them sticking out at an angle, perpendicular to the angled line of the roof. Many adults, even some college students, seem unable to draw on natural principles that come from vast personal experience with the physical world. Given a drawing of a water-filled glass *(A)* and asked to show how water would look if the glass were tilted, some draw a line parallel, not to the inferred horizon, but to the bottom of the glass *(B).* It is as if they cannot declare, in the act of drawing, this basic principle: Water *always* remains level regardless of how much a container is tilted. Nevertheless, many still don't get it even after practicing with an apparatus that focuses attention on how water behaves in tilted glasses [314].

A　　　　　　　**B**

It does seem strange that we may not learn what is plain as the nose on our face—or the face of a telephone. How many people can draw accurately from memory the arrangement of the buttons? (Try it.) How many draw ABC on the button marked "1"? How many of us can precisely describe the appearance of something we handle every day, such as a penny (which way does Lincoln face)? Clearly, we use the telephone and the penny without necessarily understanding—without *needing* to understand—how it is laid out or how it works. In other words, most of us most of the time seem to get by rather well procedurally, even though we may be deficient in declarative knowledge—in accurate understanding of things and ourselves.

We err in presuming to understand all the iceberg when we have flawed knowledge of only the tip. We are mostly unconscious of external stimuli, habits of thought, and personal biases—never mind the subterranean stuff of Freudian fancy. If asked, we can report what we like to do—play the piano, work on computers, keep house—yet with little insight into deepest reasons. To appreciate our sociability, for example, is not to understand its origin. Sociability might come from good fortune, good looks, or felicitous living conditions. Its deeper sources could be genuine extraversion and good will, or inferiority feelings and dependency needs. It might be manic-depressive spiritedness or psychopathic charm. We may also be happily unaware just how much fabricating is involved in our after-the-fact explanations. It would seem that we sometimes really don't know what we are up to or what we are talking about.

Here are some striking examples in evidence [239]. In one

study, subjects are either handed, or allowed to select, a 50¢ lottery ticket. Later, they are asked what they'd take for their ticket. Those who had selected their ticket act as if it carried a higher probability of winning. They indicate a willingness to sell the ticket for about $9. The others want about $2 [197]. In another study, all subjects get a placebo, usually an inert or sugar pill with no inherent psychological effect. Compared to those who think it is a "relaxing pill," subjects who think it is an "anxiety" pill accept higher levels of shock. Explanation: Aversive experience is tolerated more easily when one has a credible explanation. Thus, more shock is tolerated by subjects who can attribute some of the shock-induced distress to an "anxiety pill." Sounds reasonable—people tend to accept adversity when they believe there is a good reason for it—but here's the odd thing. Subjects often deny that the pill has—even could have—anything to do with their willingness to accept more shock.

Ask people how good they are at detecting a lie; ask them what kinds of clues they would consider important, for example, evasiveness, a phony smile, poor eye contact. Then, test them against videotapes of other people lying or telling the truth. It turns out that observers are easily fooled. Generally, they achieve about 60 percent accuracy relative to 50 percent chance. Moreover, there is no relation between accuracy and either confidence in lie-detecting ability or reports about what clues they would use [95]. However, this observation goes beyond mere lie detection. One fellow insists incorrectly but confidently that tomatoes are vegetables. His more timid companion, while sensing that a tomato is more like a plum than a string bean, nevertheless yields to the more authoritative colleague. A little thing, and yet we wonder. How often do both confidence and lack of confidence prove unjustified?

Under some conditions, lack of personal insight can be striking. Subjects are asked to articulate a view that contradicts one previously noted on a self-report questionnaire—to make a pro-busing speech if they are anti-busing, or an anti-busing speech if they are pro-busing. No rewards or threats are used to induce compliance with the request, so there is no obvious external reason for compliance that occurs. Subjects therefore seem to believe that their compliance stems from a personally held attitude. What else could explain why, later on, their viewpoint shifts toward their speech and away from their original rating. Incredibly, some subjects are completely unaware of the change, even though it may involve a shift from pro to anti or *vice versa*. Such a self-serving explanation for behavior, lacking both accuracy and insight, often arises because of needs or biases that are largely unconscious.

People often display a lack of awareness that their reluctance or willingness to help someone in distress may be determined simply by the presence or absence of others—that the larger the group, the less apt they are to help. Moreover, they are equally unaware of a position bias regarding the brand that they are likely to choose while shopping—a tendency to pick the brand (of nylon stockings, for example) displayed rightmost on the store's shelf. Ask people why they didn't help or why they didn't choose the leftmost item and you will discover that they make up stories, often convincing, even inventive, stories, that may have nothing to do with the actual causes of the behavior. We might very well wonder how often this is true of stories that professionals make up—theories that may sound good while proving inadequate for explaining the actual causes of behavior.

The heart has its reasons

What we are can be masked by what we think we are. All it takes is a little denial or repression, a storyteller's instinct for explanations, and something else: a self-concept, usually with positive spin. Accuracy often takes a back seat to the more compelling affective criterion of good feelings if not just less distress. Let's take a look from an unusual angle.

Life-threatening epileptic seizures can be remediated by a "split-brain" procedure that severs the neural bridge, or *corpus callosum*, connecting the left and right hemispheres. In effect, the verbally inarticulate right hemisphere can no longer communicate directly with the speaking, self-conscious left hemisphere. Nevertheless, the right hemisphere can express what it knows through emotion or by pointing to relevant things with the *left* hand that it controls. Remember, each hemisphere receives information from the opposite half of the body and external world, and each controls the opposite half of the body.

In most situations, the split-brain person's behavior seems

quite normal. However, under special laboratory conditions, intriguing things can happen [121]. Consider a male subject sitting in front of a screen, staring at a focal point at its center. A sexually arousing stimulus—for example, the word "kiss" or a Playmate centerfold—is flashed for a split second to the left half of the screen. In this way, it is locked in the right hemisphere. Remember, it must be flashed for only a moment—just long enough to get the half-screen information into one hemisphere, but short enough so that subsequent eye movements will not bring the information to both hemispheres.

The stimulus is flashed, and the subject is aroused. An unconscious part of him—the right hemisphere—recognizes the stimulus. Nevertheless, he—the he of subjective consciousness constructed by the left hemisphere—has no idea what the stimulus might have been. Here's a rather peculiar situation—being emotionally aroused with no idea why. Having no idea is like being without a story, and this can be most disconcerting. Stories, the objective and the fanciful, are designed to fill in the blanks and enhance the self. Filling in the blanks—especially *our* blanks—is a matter of achieving a coherent story from partial information.

Imagine again the split-brain patient staring at the center of a blank screen. For a moment, two pictures are flashed to either side of the fixation point: a chicken claw to the right, a snow scene to the left. The patient—actually, his verbally proficient left hemisphere—reports seeing a chicken claw in the right visual field, but nothing in the left. At the same time, his right hemisphere, incapable of speech, mutely perceives a snow scene in the left visual field, but nothing in the right. Immediately after the screen goes blank, the perceived pictures are memories locked in each hemisphere. Now the subject must look at a set of pictures, say eight pictures lined up in a row on the table, and point to *one* that relates best to what had just been seen. Can you predict what happens?

The right hand—servant of a left hemisphere that remembers the chicken claw—points to a chicken head. This is a good conceptual match, but wait. At the same time, the left hand—servant of a right hemisphere that remembers the snow scene—points to a shovel. This, too, is a good match and evidence that the right hemisphere, though dumb, is no dummy. Now what?

The personally conscious subject—actually, his left hemi-sphere—has only one thing in mind, namely left-hemisphere stuff (chicken claw). Yet, he perceives himself acting as if having *two* things in mind. Since no one likes to get caught in a bizarre inconsistency, and since neither denial nor blame will work, only one solution seems evident. Make up a good story to neu-tralize the inconsistency: "I saw a claw and I picked the chicken, *and you have to clean out the chicken shed with a shovel.*" Bingo!

Here is necessity as mother of invention revealing the story-teller instinct and raising a question about the personal stories codified in self-concepts. Can we trust them? How do we distin-guish the reasonably accurate from the distorted and contrived? How do we know what's missing from conscious awareness? Without answers, how confident can we be in our knowledge about ourselves or, for that matter, in our relationships to other selves? Moreover, what does all this tell us about the role that self-concepts play in liability to depression or other kinds of dis-order?

Many factors outside personal consciousness determine mood and thinking. Subjects in one study have no appreciation that their preference for certain meaningless tones or geometric shapes depends on familiarity—simply on the number of pre-sentations [191; 342]. Subjects in another study react emotion-ally to information they cannot recognize. In one task, a stream of words heard through the right earphone must be reported out loud, continuously and without error. This task requires much attention. Therefore, anything presented softly in the left channel will be ignored. Even threatening words like disease or tragedy will not be consciously recognized or recalled later. Nevertheless, they will disrupt the performance of anxious peo-ple even more than other people [218].

Clinical work provides striking examples of abnormal behav-ior whose meaning lies buried in unconscious realms. Consider just two examples. A sexually abused five-year-old describes "funny feelings" in her tummy whenever a finger is pointed at her. The meaning of these feelings is unclear until confiscated pornographic photos reveal an erect penis touching the same area on the girl when she was 15 to 18 months old. Of these experiences, she has no conscious memory [313]. A psychotic man claims to feel head pressure caused by miracles of God.

This delusional hallucination turns out to be a bizarre reminiscence. His father was a pedagogue whose peculiar if not sadistic views on child rearing and discipline were published in a how-to book complete with pictures. Techniques included various apparatuses designed to force rigid compliance in conduct and posture. One was headgear that could be strapped tightly to restrain jaw movement and to put pressure around the head [282].

Research and clinical observation thus confirm Pascal's aphorism that the heart has its reasons, which reason (intellect) does not know. Much of what we are about, much of what moves us, is locked up in unconscious realms of mindless impulse, intuitive disposition, prelogical memory, nonverbal thought. It is what psychologist Henry Murray called that whispering gallery where "voices echo past events, currents of contending complexes, plots and counterplots, hopeful intimations and ideals . . . a full Congress of orators and pressure groups, of children, demagogues, communists, isolationists, war-mongers, mugwumps, grafters, log-rollers, lobbyists, Caesars and Christs, Machiavellis and Judases, Tories and Promethean revolutionists" [235]. Some of these elements of self may be kept unconscious through repression, but many are simply incompatible with the verbal-logic keys of an adult's conscious thought processes. That is why trying to apprehend our self is like trying to remember dreams or childhood experiences—and why we sometimes make things up when we can't make them out.

But the problem of insight is more than an inability to recognize the diverse signatures of our self in the "whispering gallery" of mental life. It is an inability to integrate the *behavioral* evidence—evidence from our own everyday experience to anomalies such as multiple personality. That we are many things is an old notion. Roughly 400 years ago the great French essayist Montaigne argued that each part of our nature "plays, every moment, its own game, and there is as much difference betwixt us and ourselves as between us and others." More contemporary essayist and novelist E. M. Forster, observes that: "For the purpose of living one has to assume that the personality is solid, and the 'self' is an entity, and to ignore all contrary evidence." If knowing oneself means knowing its many components, and if our knowledge of those components is unclear, then how accurate can any unifying generalization about our self ever be?

If it ain't broke . . .

Compounding the problem of self-knowledge is the tendency not to keep tabs on the self. Now, most of the time, self-monitoring is not necessary; it can even reduce the efficiency of well-learned skills like playing the piano or riding a bike. Like all reflective thinking, self-monitoring works best in novel or problematic situations. The operative rule is: If it ain't (obviously) broke, don't fix it. Since selves normally ain't broke, they tend not to be looked at with a mind to fixin'. Reflective self-monitoring therefore tends to be reactive more than habitual, something provoked by external stresses or dysphoric feelings that heighten self-consciousness and put a negative spin on experience. Evidently, some of what we think about ourselves—why we did or didn't do such and such—is reconstructed after the fact in a state of perturbation where distortions and misinterpretations can occur.

The tendency not to reflect is a matter of efficiency but also of motivation. Self-directed attention is avoided insofar as it is difficult and aversive. It is difficult because the object of self-directed attention is abstract or ambiguous. Self-data are hard to identify and interpret. We have little difficulty invoking competence, disposition, or other traits to explain *other* people's behavior. For our own behavior, however, we invoke situational factors, especially when our behavior represents some kind of failure. Perhaps this readiness to explain ourselves by tangible external factors is a legacy of childhood ways of thinking—"It wasn't my fault, it was Billy's!"

Self-directed attention is also avoided because it promotes infelicitous comparison with others and with standards of excellence. So, we may succumb to what Samuel Johnson called the arrogance of pretending that our faults escape notice. Self-directed attention may also promote what William James called an irremediable sense of precariousness. Even the well-endowed, well-adjusted person enjoying good fortune may rightly wonder that his fate might be otherwise.

Psychological changes that occur along with self-directed

attention are reminiscent of a mildly depressed state with negative mood, lowered self-confidence, and an increased sense of personal responsibility. These changes may occur even when people are not conscious that the situation has directed attention to the self. Example: A tape of one's own voice, even when unrecognized, produces an elevated skin-conductance reaction like that measured by lie-detector tests [272]. Most people will try to avoid situations that unrelievedly focus attention on the self; others seem addicted to self-scrutiny.

In normal people who are on the self-conscious side, self-scrutiny may bring accurate knowledge with relatively little emotional cost. Their ratings of their own extrovertedness, aggressiveness, or sociability tend to predict how they actually behave at a later time [283]. In neurotics and others given to self-critical rumination, however, self-scrutiny can be a burden. For the romantic soul, it manifests in a sense of the futility of things. "My summer was a complete failure," confides one. "I did not even finish the job which I assigned to myself. Here, neither time nor place matters, it is the basic lazy little me within myself which is the source of all evils. My life seems to be a series of little escapes—escapes from nowhere to nowhere. Quite sad, isn't it?"

Love and understanding

How important are negative self-concepts in causing seemingly normal people to become mentally ill? As features of personality disorder, negative self-concepts are obviously associated with elevated liability to depression. Yet, negative self-concepts, even when enlivened by reflective thinking, need not indicate personality disorder. Moreover, they need not promote depression, as suggested by studies of nondepressed people. Subjects with either positive or negative self-concepts receive written first impressions from hidden observers. In fact, there are no observers, and the bogus positive or negative impressions are randomly assigned. Nevertheless, compared to others, negative self-view subjects tend to rate a negative impression of themselves as accurate. It's not that they like getting such feedback; it's just that they consider it acceptable.

Negative self-verification need not merely be accepted when

it occurs; it may be actively sought out and actively cultivated [304]. People with negative self-concepts tend to focus on negative self-relevant information. They tend to behave in ways that give clues about their negative self-concepts. For example, they display excessive deference and self-denigration with friends and spouses who can provide the requisite self-verification along with needed affection. True, unflattering behavior in the service of negative self-concepts tends to diminish personal appeal and therefore threatens that affection. Nevertheless, behavior consistent with a negative self-concept does increase the likelihood of being understood, and this, no less than affection, serves the need for self-preservation. Dostoevsky says "man may consciously, purposely, desire what is injurious to himself, what is stupid, very stupid [if] it preserves for us what is most precious and most important—that is, our personality, our individuality." Negative self-verification creates an existential dilemma to the extent that the pain of unworthiness dilutes the pleasure of praise [303]. Thus is the need to be loved sometimes confounded by the need to be understood, a dilemma exaggerated in neurotic personalities where conflicts are intense. Endlessly seeking and cultivating feedback to verify and enhance the self can create inconsistencies and apparent flip-flopping that can confuse and alienate others.

Initially, people can give the impression of having either a positive or a negative self-concept. Nevertheless, appearances can be deceiving and the facts surprising. First, consider people who initially appear to have a positive self-concept. Of course, many are what they seem to be—true positives who are competent and happy people with every good reason to be pleased with themselves. However, others prove to be *false positives*. Like sheep in wolves' clothing, their inner sense of being inadequate, unattractive, and unworthy is masked by grandiosity and self-promotion, yet their urgent, abrasive, and self-defeating qualities suggest an antidepressant function. Thus can false-positive behavior and manifest depression be merely different faces of the same coin. That is, false positives are indeed depressive, either below the surface (state of mind) or down the line (liability).

Now consider people who appear to have a negative self-concept. Some prove to be *false negatives*. Like wolves in sheep's clothing, these are people whose disarming embrace of criticism may mask overblown narcissism and a sense of moral superiority. But we are tempted to reiterate what former Israeli Prime Minister Golda Meir supposedly once quipped, "Don't be so humble, you're not that great." Of course, other negative self-concept people do prove to be what they seem—*true negatives.* Their charming though disingenuous self-diminution constitutes a relatively unthreatening means of expressing a sense of inadequacy.

But what of true negatives who really do lack skill, beauty, talent, confidence or charm, yet willingly tell it like it is; what keeps so many of them from getting depressed? One possible answer is *defect*—an inability to recognize inner states of mind, as with the alexithymics mentioned in Chapter 9. Another is *defensiveness*—turning poorly controlled dysphoric feelings into better-controlled ideas, for example, admitting personal inadequacies before others discover them. A third possibility is *compensation*—supportive, hopeful, or redeeming behavior that corrects an imbalance. Compensation can come from almost anything: a talent, a tolerant friend, service to the community—even mundane little pleasures afforded by books, TV programs, or Walter Mitty fantasies. The point is really quite simple. Even great misfortunes may be tolerated reasonably well as long as life has hope and meaning. Without these, even small misfortunes can lead to overwhelming sadness and despair.

Melancholy self

We have looked at the negative self-concept of people who, superficially at least, are not manifestly depressed when we suspect they ought to be. What about the negative self-concept of the manifestly depressed person? May it not be *false* negative, the temporary product of an illness? Healthy people with the flu can become miserable and socially maladroit. Likewise, competent people with high self-esteem can develop a depression that sabotages their sense of well-being, their ability to think objectively, and their capacity to act in a socially desirable manner. For such otherwise true positives, mental illness exaggerates the experience of not being oneself—it creates a false-negative self—

while remission of symptoms means recovery of the true-positive self.

On the other hand, the depressed person's negative self-concept may be roughly *accurate* (true negative). First, it may reflect real change. Unshakable depression can, finally, and in some cases irreparably, undermine the self, turning it into something meaner and less competent than before. This transformation can occur in older people who have long suffered with depressive disorder, but also in younger people who have long suffered a sense of meaninglessness and ennui. Second, in the light of depressive realism, the self-concept may reveal a fact of personal history, confirming what the true-negative person always knew while revealing what the false-positive person has been hiding. That is bad news indeed for the false positives, for they will surely have a hard time returning to pretense and posturing once their depression lifts.

Mental illness can put even more than the usual self-serving spin on self-concepts, making them inaccurate, sometimes even delusionally so. The spin may be positive though transparently false, such as in weak, indifferent people who view themselves as unusually competent and caring. The spin may also be negative. Normally competent and caring people debilitated by depression view themselves as weak and indifferent to others. Depressed people show better recall for negative words they rated as characteristic of themselves than for positive words they rated as uncharacteristic—just the opposite of normal people [88]. Depressed people blame themselves for even minor events that really can't be helped—a soiled shirt, a clumsy child, a flat tire, an unsuccessful party.

Depressives can be their own greatest critics. However painful or self-destructive, their self-critical ways of thinking are readily used and stubbornly defended. Depressed people pay particular attention to whatever seems to confirm their negative self-concepts. It's not that they dislike hearing nice things about themselves; in fact, some of their behaviors—the comic, the tragic, the clever, even the outrageous—are designed to get positive reactions. It's just that the impulse to go for something positive is blunted or derailed by a chronic or depression-induced negative self-concept. Having a negative self-concept is like having a digestive system that lacks a critical enzyme. Because it can't assimilate and grow with positive information, the good stuff just doesn't sink in.

People with such a negative self-concept want to be loved, but they can't become more lovable. If they are to be loved, it must be for who they are. Yet, if they are not lovable, being loved is always suspect, never secure. More than others, depressed and neurotic people are caught in an existential dilemma—what hope of being loved with understanding, yet what use being loved through misunderstanding? There are two solutions to this dilemma, openness or distance. Choosing openness means forging ahead in being oneself, risking love while cultivating self-verification. Choosing distance means avoiding contact, or maintaining a psychological distance with masking behaviors that limit being both loved and understood.

It stands to reason that how one thinks of oneself should determine the choice, should determine whether depressing events will be magnified or buffered. Holding to impossible standards, making unrealistic assumptions, and having irrational expectations all dispose a person to view the self as inadequate, incompetent, unworthy, and all these should increase the risk of depression. Yet finding credible evidence for assumptions about just how and how much the self-concept figures in depression turns out to be more daunting than at first it seems. Suppose you find *nondepressed* people whose positive or negative self-concept predicts whether they will suffer a depressive illness within five years. That would make the self-concept seem important to liability. But what if a negative self-concept were merely an early expression of a temperamental disposition that can unfold regardless of what one thinks about oneself. In that case, a negative self-concept would seem unimportant to liability. So, until researchers measure the power of negative self-concept relative to other factors, the idea that it is a powerful *independent* aspect of liability to depressive illness must remain a credible but unproved assumption.

It's not just this but all kinds of assumptions about human behavior that we must question. Assumptions that appeal to intuition and common sense may yet be false; if true, they may have limited application. Like a mine field at night, they should be scrutinized, especially the mysterious and enigmatic kind that involve causes hidden in subterranean realms of unconscious mind and in symbolic language of dreams and behaviors. Repressed memories, unconscious conflicts, and dream meanings: These make for good stories, but they are supported by anecdote or personal testimony more often than by scientific test. Yet the call for scrutiny also holds for assumptions based on scientific research. Take those reasonable facsimiles of neurotic disorder created in laboratory animals, experimental neuroses involving anxiety, compulsivity, and depressed behavior. These occur when, driven by starvation, shock, or confinement, an animal's ability to cope is frustrated by conflicting signals of shock versus food or safety. Experimental neuroses may be adequate explanations, but only if they accurately model real disorders, *and* if the experimental conditions represent real-world conditions. Otherwise, they are the moral equivalent of parlor tricks, diversions that teach us less about what happens than about what can be made to happen.

The call for scrutiny recognizes that the fabric of thought often seems to have more subjective warp than critical woof. We easily recognize malignant forms of subjectivity in the obsessive apprehensions, compensatory rationalizations, egotistical denials, bizarre delusions, and the fanatic ideologies of extraordinary people. It is the common but more pervasive forms of subjectivity that we so readily overlook—even our most reasonable explanations tend to be self-serving more than truth-serving, and not just in the passionate heat of the moment. How much easier than critical thought come self-enhancing memories, heartfelt beliefs, and self-deceiving fantasies. If our explanations rest on reasons of the heart as much as, perhaps more than, matters of fact, then virtually anything can be justified no matter how cruel or stupid, denied no matter how evident, and believed no matter how improbable or fantastical. If we can be as irrational as objective, then however rational our behavior may seem to be, how do we know when our explanations *aren't* self-serving more than truth-serving, or when conventional reasons are off base, while delusional reasons are closer to the target?

13

BACK-ASKED QUESTIONS

Figuring out where mental illness comes from means finding its connections to other factors. These factors could be personality traits, the effects of drug abuse, qualities of the environment, or the behavior of close relatives. Some depressions seem caused by negative events triggering negative habits of thinking learned in the school of hard knocks. But are most depressions thus explained? What about the really serious cases that require hospitalization? Perhaps you know someone whose hospitalization was triggered by hopeless conflicts at home or by stress-related physical illness. Why, then, are some people relatively immune to those depressing conditions of hostility, indifference, or failure that seem to explain depression in others? Why are some people subject to depression despite positive conditions of love, support, or personal achievement—even having a baby—that seem to explain the *absence* of depression in others [77]?

Missing the mark

The broader question goes beyond depression or even mental illness to individual differences in talent, temperament, and intelligence. It is about why people turn out differently from what we would have confidently predicted. Such impertinent questions challenge not only our own notions, but also conventional wisdom. Answering such questions is more than a bit daunting, and not just because of the complexity of the problem. Another reason, our tendency toward subjective thinking—part intuition, part sentiment, all self-serving—was neatly described four hundred years ago by philosopher-statesman Francis Bacon: "For what a man had rather were true he more readily believes. Therefore he rejects difficult things from impatience of research; sober things, because they narrow hope; the deeper things of nature, from superstition; the light of experience, from arrogance and pride, lest his mind should seem to be preoccupied with things mean and transitory; things not commonly believed, out of deference to opinion of the vulgar. Numberless in short are the ways, and sometimes imperceptible, in which the affections color and infect the understanding."

Subjective thinking can make us clever, cunning, and resourceful, but also prejudiced, gullible, unprincipled. In a pinch, subjectivity may work better than rational thinking or even common sense—in "psyching out" another person, for example, or in leading to more immediate and effective action that might be derailed by being objective. Our subjectivity can, however, sometimes get us into trouble with problems—the problems of depression and mental illness—that are best approached by a rational consideration of the facts placed in their proper statistical context.

Something that seems too good to be true probably is—or so we say, but do we act on such understanding? Sometimes not, and with potentially disastrous consequences. Mathematician John Paulos describes a compelling con game by a stock-market adviser in which people pay for what seems to be a sure thing—it is a sure thing, but not what they think [246]. Once a week during a six-week period, they receive a letter correctly predicting the direction of the stock market during the following week. In the last letter, they are asked to pay $500 for the next week's prediction. Sounds reasonable, except for one thing: The claim that the accuracy of the predictions is due to special skills, computer programs, and inside information *that can be counted on each time* is false. Paulos tells why.

The adviser begins by sending out 32,000 letters, half predicting the market will be higher, half predicting it will be lower, during the following week. Half of these predictions will be true, and to the people who received the correct prediction, another letter is sent. Half of these 16,000 letters have a correct prediction, and to the 8,000 people getting the correct prediction, a third letter is sent. Again, half of these will get a correct prediction and these are sent a fourth letter, and so on, until a fraction of the original have received six letters, each with a correct prediction *based solely on chance.* Therefore, betting that $500 is, literally, capitalizing on chance. Even without the adviser's "explanation" of his powers of prediction, investors would likely dream up an explanation involving special skills or deliberate actions. In the face of randomness we must fill in the blanks, reconstruct what must have happened, explain that which cries out for explanation; our storyteller's instinct is devoted to extracting order out of chaos—to survival.

Yes, we are sometimes distracted or misled, but not always for emotional reasons. Sometimes it's just that relevant information can't be brought to mind. To illustrate, consider the following example. Six-year-olds are asked to imagine how they might retrieve a bead floating in a little water inside a stationary test tube. Some of the children achieve a float-up solution: Pour more water in to make the bead float to the top. Nevertheless, half of these successful little problem solvers can't solve the same problem later when shown a real bead floating in a real test tube affixed to a table. Distracted by various bottles, tweezers, and other irrelevant things, they can't mobilize their pertinent knowledge: the memory of their float-up solution [42].

Adults, too, can get distracted and have trouble mobilizing pertinent knowledge, especially about relevant statistical facts of life. Consider the question of airline safety [296]. We understand that a commercial airliner is highly unlikely to crash. Such statistical facts are called *prior probabilities—priors*, for short— because they exist prior to any pertinent information that might suggest a different probability. For example, given the priors, we assume a very low probability that our airliner will crash. However, learning something pertinent—for example, that *our* airplane is past its prime or that it has been badly serviced— should make us raise the probability quite a few notches.

Now, what if we learn something that seems pertinent but isn't? For example, reading in the papers about a plane crash shouldn't affect our estimate. Crashes do occasionally happen;

that's why the priors aren't zero. Nevertheless, the story of a plane crash makes us *feel* that our risk is higher than we would have thought. That's just human nature—identifying with people in scary situations and following our feelings and imagery when reason and computers tell us something else. Like the children with the float-up problem, we succumb to provocative but irrelevant, therefore distracting information. We will sometimes miss the mark when it comes to explaining socially or personally important events, behaviors, and experiences—even when, in the abstract, we know better.

Chasing tails

Knowing better is no help when our intelligence is derailed by needs and fantasies. People send in that sweepstakes envelope or buy that lottery ticket. Yet their chance of winning big (virtually zero) is about the same if they resist the temptation (zero). Their enthusiasm stirred by advertisements for *near-zero*-probability positive events, such as winning a state lottery jackpot (1 out of 55 million in one recent case) is matched by their distress caused by reports of near-zero-probability negative events, such as dying in a plane crash (1 out of 200 million departures). Yet many of these people seem indifferent to *much more likely* events, like getting killed while riding on a bike (1/75,000 killed per year) or in a car (1/5,300 per year). How many unbelted children die in car crashes while sitting on the lap of a parent who was more impressed by the message of Ed McMahon than of prior probabilities?

Miss Euphoria Grand has just won her state lottery. The chance she will win again within the year is almost nil. Nevertheless, somewhere, *someone* will win twice; a double win has a better than even chance of occurring during any ten-year period. There is nothing spectacular about this if one realizes how many lotteries and participants there are. In short, the probability of recurrence is different for an event (a double winner somewhere) and a *specific instance* of an event (Miss Grand winning twice). The former has a good chance, the latter, virtually none at all—even less than the virtually zero chance that *you* will win.

And never mind your premonitions, portentous dreams, and uncanny feelings about your lottery ticket numbers. Someone wins the lottery after dreaming of winning—compelling, except for one thing. Given the millions of nightly dreams and millions of annual lottery tickets, there *must* be coincidences between premonitions and winnings. Nothing magical or metaphysical need be invoked, no need for notions like precognition. So too with misfortune. A woman *feels that* her miscarriage is some kind of punishment for transgressions even though she *knows about* prior probability and the many rational explanations. She is simply overcome by magical thinking, like the hand-washing compulsive who knows her idea of being contaminated is nutty [158].

The combination of intuition, hedonism, and sheer willfulness is irresistible. It can make even normal people do things that, in more dispassionate moments, they know to be hopeless, irrational, even harmful. What is the effect of learning that 500 to 1,000 Americans die *each day* from the effects of smoking—in two months, at least as many as died in the Vietnam War? How many smokers, learning this, would stop smoking—and remain nonsmokers? And being educated provides no sure defense. College students know that averages are more reliable than individual events. They know, for example, that auto statistics or college course surveys are more reliable than personal testimony. In practice, however, even a single comment about an experience with a car or course can divert our attention from pertinent knowledge and unduly influence decision-making. The inability to apply formal knowledge can happen even when the comment is known to be atypical and thus unreliable *and* misleading.

We prefer particulars, anecdotes, and personal experience. We are swayed by explanations that can be brought to life in imagination and feeling. Remote concepts, though fully understood, don't move us; they aren't readily embraced, recalled, or put to use. To illustrate, we can use an example based on the work of psychologists Amos Tversky and Daniel Kahneman [319]. Imagine that you are in a Las Vegas casino. You watch a man drift away after working a slot machine about 20 or 30 times with no payoff. What now? You could play his machine on the assumption that it's due, but there are two other choices. Assume that each pull is an *independent* event unaffected by prior pulls; each has the same payoff likelihood, say 90 cents on the dollar (the legal minimum can be as low as 83). It's all a matter of mechanics, not motivation; there is no "dueness." So, being rational, we might do either of two things. One of these— choose at random—assumes that all the machines have approximately the same bias. The other—play a different machine— assumes that occasionally a stingy machine is defective.

Students understand all this in the abstract, like the kids given the float-up problem that they solved in principle but failed in practice. One student had earlier explained that each toss of a coin is an independent event, such that heads or tails is just as likely after flipping a head or a tail. Yet, caught up in the imagery of the casino, she failed to apply that knowledge. Expressing a preference for the first (it's due) option, she seemed to imply two impossible characteristics of such machines: a memory for the prior 20 or 30 pulls and a sense of fair play to decide someone is due! Of course she didn't really mean either of these. Clearly she understood that, with coins and one-armed bandits, each event is independent of any other, such that you are just as likely to lose (or win) after a loss as after a win. Well, knowing is one thing, acting on that knowledge is quite another. Sometimes, statistical knowledge simply cannot compete with intuition. We go with what feels right, even when it derails the engine of logic and the capacity to appreciate the statistical facts of life.

Make no mistake about it: Not even the smartest people are immune from being distracted by irrelevant information, especially when there is a personal stake in seeing things a certain way. For example, consider the sex difference in performance on the SAT test of math ability. Observed for over thirty years, that difference—appearing in the figure as incompletely overlapping test-score distributions—begins at puberty and favors males. The math SAT scores in this illustration come from a study of seventh, eighth, and ninth graders who, passing preliminary tests of mathematical talent, were given the opportunity to take the SAT test that is normally taken by high school seniors.

Sex Differences on the Math SAT

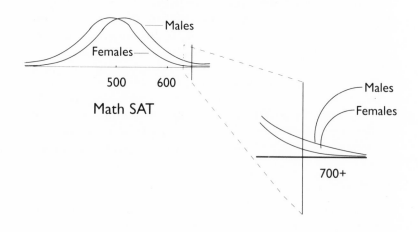

A researcher, apparently offended by the sexist implication of the observations, points out, quite correctly, that there is much overlap in the male and female distributions of ability. You can see this in the figure showing the bell-shaped curves. These indicate the percentage of people scoring at each point on an ability dimension. The male average is just a wee bit higher. So of what practical relevance can such a difference be? Picking boy-girl pairs at random and predicting that the boy is better at math will be correct only about 65 percent of the time—not so great when chance (assuming no real differences) is 50 percent. Then, what's the problem? The problem is that, despite a seemingly small *mean* difference, a surprisingly large difference favoring males exists *at the rightmost tail end of the distribution*— see the magnified area in the figure. That is the region where, by convention, the highest-scoring kids are located (with lowest scorers placed to the far left). Moreover, the higher the standard of excellence—the higher the cutoff point beyond which you consider someone highly able—the bigger the sex difference. In one study, a modest cutoff point (around SAT = 600) yielded a 4 to 1 male-to-female ratio [34; 35]. For higher cutoff points (above 700), the ratio was 13 to 1.

Our investigator has missed the point. A big sex difference

exists, but one ought to look not so much in the obvious place around the center of the curves but in the less obvious, "off center" location, exactly where the sex difference is most embarrassing—in the area of extraordinary math ability, an intellectual resource that is invaluable to a vibrant, competitive, technological society. (The psychological reasons for this difference are entirely different and surely arguable matters—that is, unless you deny the test's established validity, which, given the evidence, would be like blaming the messenger who brings the bad news [329].) Here, then, is a clear example of how subjective and ideological biases can distract attention from the simplest facts.

Butter and eggs

We may get derailed when overlooking little things that make all the difference or when paying too much attention to personal experience or anecdote. Nevertheless, with the proper caution, we can make use of personal experience and anecdote to illustrate concepts and suggest alternative ideas that can advance our understanding. In that spirit, consider the following story that illustrates how adversity affects different personalities as heat softens the butter while it hardens the egg.

Baseball legend Jackie Robinson was graced with extraordinary athleticism and courage. Incredibly, in the late 40s, he defied segregationist convention that viewed him simply as a bad egg, breaking the color barrier at the Brooklyn Dodgers' Ebbets Field to help turn "dem bums" into the immortal Jackie Robinson Brooklyn Dodgers. Roger Kahn lovingly describes how an indefatigable Robinson, beyond his glory days, "had suffered a biblical curse; his first-born was struck dead. His entire circulatory system was breaking down. Not only blindness but possible leg amputations lurked in his future. And yet there was no sorrow to the man, and despair was alien in the kingdom where he lived" [170]. In contrast, Jackie Robinson, Jr., seemed unable to cope in the face of adversity. He lacked his father's inner strength—a spiritual quality, Red Barber called it. For the son, economic and social advantages could not compensate for racism, invidious comparisons, and a host of other factors that combined with self-pity, drug-abuse, and deceitful character to sabotage a life.

The difference between this father and son symbolize the difference between vulnerability and resiliency in the face of stress. "The soil is everything," declared microbe hunter Louis Pasteur, meaning that the susceptibility of the host (individual liability) determines the power of the microbe (stress). What, then, is the nature of liability (soil)? How much is genetic and how much social—or, in an old-fashioned way of speaking, is the liability mostly God-given (soul) or man-made? Answers will of course depend on the specific illness. Liability to manic-depression, for example, looks more heritable than does liability to other depression, but we still need to know about environmental factors that can boost that liability.

Consider the idea that parental loss during childhood increases the liability to suicidal depression. That was one of the possibilities we raised at the end of the Castlereagh story. Trouble is, the statistical connection between loss and suicide is rather weak. Early parental loss is therefore neither necessary nor sufficient to create the liability. It isn't necessary, since most suicidally depressed people never experienced early mother loss; and it isn't sufficient, since most people who did experience such loss do not develop suicidal depression. At most, the connection may mean that early loss *contributes* to liability in those who are most vulnerable.

Even such pallid causality may be illusory, as the following observations suggest [174]. The loss-depression connection holds for separation from father as well as from mother, which raises questions about a special maternal element in liability. And this connection holds only for separation by divorce, not by death, which raises questions about what separation really means. Does it signal a familial instability that in parents manifests itself as divorce and maybe depression, and in offspring as depression and maybe divorce? Another possibility, explored in the next chapter, is that we are measuring, not manifest causes and effects, but different aspects of a common but hidden cause.

Risk for depression is elevated in people on whom many unreasonable demands are being made without emotional support—people exploited, isolated, neglected or otherwise abused, and unable to share their problems. Nevertheless, there is some question about why most people seem comparatively immune, at least to depressive illness if not to depressive symptoms.

Stressed people may be irritable and otherwise dysphoric, they may yell at their spouse or kids, but they usually don't require hospitalization. Repeatedly, we are forced back to the problem of vulnerability and resiliency. Consider just one solution.

That 0.30 solution

If adverse events are important causes in a theory of depression, they must be strongly associated with symptoms—more adversity, more symptoms; less adversity, fewer symptoms. To assume that such external events can have a strong impact on behavior is sensible enough. Who hasn't made such an assumption after observing abused children or stressed adults? But an assumption that one thing necessarily *causes* another is questionable on at least two grounds.

One problem is that an association, for example, between stress and symptoms, may be weaker and therefore less important than it seems. We typically measure degree of association in terms of correlations. For example, height and weight are highly correlated (correlations over 0.90), while IQ and physical attractiveness are poorly correlated (less than 0.20). According to many studies, measures of life events and personal adjustment are correlated at most 0.30, but often less. That at-best 0.30 correlation between stress and symptoms means that there's a lot more to symptoms than stress. But what?

To answer this question, we must raise a second question about one thing (stress) being an important cause of another (symptoms): Could this causal assumption sometimes be false? Surely it is false when an apparent cause turns out to be an *effect*—for example, when stress is the effect of symptoms such as the anxiety, irritability, sadness, or withdrawal that sabotage the capacity for love and work, diminish self-esteem, and alienate others. Dr. Ruth Westheimer supposedly once declared Johnny Carson to be "single-handedly responsible for Americans' lousy sex lives. People are watching him instead of having sex." Maybe this is true for some, but for others the reverse is surely true: lousy sex lives created opportunities to watch Johnny. The connection between Johnny-watching and lousy sex is like the connection between life events and symptoms. Either may be explained by the other—*or not.* That is, two things may be connected without one causing the other, as we shall see in the next chapter.

Whatever it means, the stress-symptom correlation is modest, rarely cracking the 0.30 barrier. Alas, trying to get to the bottom of the problem sometimes seems like digging for a pony we hope to find at the bottom of a barn full of horse manure. Sometimes our 0.30 solution seems like no solution at all. Why don't we get bigger correlations? The answer involves something so subtle it rarely gets noticed, yet so important it makes all the difference.

Correlations are like bikinis

Sometimes it helps to reduce a problem to its simplest form, as in the following diagram with two rows and two columns. The two rows represent positive versus negative environment; the two columns, positive versus negative behavior. A correlation is represented by the boldfaced co-occurrences of the shaded cells making up the *diagonal:* the *top-left* (+ +) and the *bottom-right* (− −). The more that observations fall in these cells—the more that they are on the diagonal—the stronger will be the correlation.

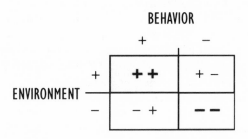

In a "just world," positive behavior will be related to positive environment (+ +), negative behavior to negative environment (− −). In the real world, however, co-occurrences often happen *off the diagonal,* with good parents having awful kids, awful parents lovely kids, well-mannered people committing suicide or mass murder, criminals doing good deeds, decent people getting screwed, bad guys getting the loot. The major point: Keep your eyes on those "off-diagonal" events, those + − and − +

combinations. To see why, look at the next diagram showing an environment-depression connection for 100 hypothetical people who represent the real world, where at any time severe depression affects about 1 in 20. The diagram shows how depression (5 cases) versus nondepression (95 cases) relates to negative and positive environments. (Again we shade the diagonal to represent just-world co-occurrences.) At first glance, the numbers might not seem all that interesting, but look closer. Notice that 78 percent of all the cases are on the diagonal (75 nondepressives plus 3 depressives). Sure enough, environment and behavior are correlated, but in what sense?

		BEHAVIOR		
		Not Depressed	Depressed	
ENVIRONMENT	Positive	**75**	2	77
	Negative	20	**3**	23
		95	5	Totals

Look at the numbers, starting from the 5 cases of depression and moving "back" to environment. In 3 of the 5 cases—a big 60 percent—we find negative environment, which supports the idea that negative environment is an important cause of depression. Now start from the 23 instances of negative environment and look "forward" to depression. Of the 23, only 3 are associated with depression—a measly 13 percent. This suggests that negative environment is *not* an important cause of depression. It may be that negative environments have a lot to do with *some* depressions, but little or nothing to do with others. We don't know, but one thing is clear: A correlation will suggest different things, depending on how we look. Looking at very asymmetrical correlations only from one perspective is like looking at things *only* through the usual end of the binoculars. Looking in the usual way, we see things up close and personal, but they are disjointed and out of context. Shouldn't we occasionally turn the binoculars around to get a more stable sense of the big picture?

Think of depression this way. Assuming that there really is a cause-effect relation in the correlation, the straightforward question, "Does adversity cause depression?" directs us to start out with the cause (adversity) and then to look for the effect (depression). However, the question we often ask reverses all this. We ask, "Is depression *caused by* adversity?" In other words, we start with the effect (depression) and work backwards to the cause (adversity). You might call it a *back-asked* approach, with the tail of effect wagging the causal dog. Given the asymmetry in correlations, as evident in the diagram, we can wind up barking up the wrong tree. That should give us pause.

How often does our hankering for plausible stories divert our attention from the truth? How often do we pay biased attention to occasional *co-occurrences*—adversity and depression, poverty and crime—while ignoring mere *occurrences*—depression *without* adversity, poverty *without* crime? To the lottery winner, that earlier hunch about that lottery ticket proved to be correct. Really? How many nonwinners had the same hunch, and what percentage of prior winners had no hunch? Consuming baking soda to counteract stomach distress proved deadly to the person whose stomach exploded. Really? How many people consume as much or more baking soda with no such ill effect, and what percentage of stomach explosions involved no prior use of baking soda? A premonitional dream about planes crashing proved true when the actual plane crash occurred, yet each night how many people dream about crashes that never occur? A small number of policemen at a mall might explain why a shoot-up could occur. Yet, how many malls with less police protection never have a shoot-up? How many with more police ever had one? Taking that antidepressant may trigger some suicides, yet how many depressed people taking even larger doses of the drug do not commit suicide but might have without it?

As author Arthur Koestler has said, most correlations by promising more than they usually deliver are like bikinis—skimpy, distracting, and misleading. What they reveal is suggestive, what they hide, vital. A healthy respect for "off-diagonal" occurrences serves us in two ways. First, it helps guard against overestimating the magnitude, causality, and utility of correlations. Second, it facilitates locating clues to the vulnerabilities and resiliencies of human nature.

The reason we don't get bigger correlations may therefore

have something to do with the nature of liability—in particular, the possibility that there are two kinds of liability. With one kind of liability, only some people are reactive to events; only *they* make the correlation happen. Perhaps reactivity depends on the fit between an event and personality. Rejection or bereavement is more likely to threaten highly dependent people with strong needs for acceptance and support. On the other hand, a business setback or physical disability is more likely to affect autonomous people with strong needs for independence and physical mobility. Ignoring such distinctions may cause us to underestimate the actual effect of stressful events on emotional symptoms [259]. Reactivity is only one kind of liability. Another kind of liability can cause symptoms to erupt spontaneously. For this reason alone, event-symptom correlations will be modest at best.

Valid but useless

We have seen how misleading correlations can be, especially when we ignore "off-diagonal" occurrences or look from only one perspective. Now it's time to see just how extreme the problem of misleading correlations can be. Let's say we want to explain an unusual problem or rare event, X. Just about anything can be an X, including many we've already mentioned: winning the state lottery, dying in a plane crash, some crazy person shooting up a mall, a stomach exploding. For the moment, let's stick with suicide as our X. How do we explain it? With things that go along with X, of course. In the case of suicide, these correlates would include loneliness, hopelessness, adversity, and the like. Such correlates we will call Y. Trouble is, sometimes an attempt to explain X events with Y correlates is not just inadequate, it's disastrous. The reason is a rather curious statistical fact of life called the *base-rate problem*.

The base rate of something is merely its rate of occurrence in the population. The lower its base rate—the lower its prior probability—the less confident you should be in predicting X. Base rate and prior probability are thus different ways of talking about the same thing. A rare X such as suicide has a low base rate. In contrast, any relevant Y, such as being depressed, will typically have a relatively high base rate. The base-rate problem comes with trying to explain rare events, such as suicide, by invoking relatively frequent occurrences, such as depression. Trouble is, the typical, easy explanation (Y) may be *worse than useless*. To appreciate why, let's try to predict suicide.

We know that suicide (X) is correlated with factors like depression and hopelessness (Y). We are therefore rightly tempted to *explain* suicide in terms of those factors. But remember, when X is rare while Y is common, the correlation is largely *one way*. Thus, if you start with X (suicide), you frequently find some Y (hopelessness). However, if you start with some Y, you rarely find X. It seems the very things (Y) that *characterize* X cannot be used to *predict* X. In other words, a Y may be characteristic of X, but X is not typical of that Y. Now you see it, now you don't—the rabbit seems to vanish back into the hat. Take a closer look at what turns out to be statistical sleight of hand.

Select a sample of young suicides, and what do you find? Over 90 percent will have had at least one, but probably many, of the following (Y) characteristics: male, divorced, depressive disorder, suicidal thoughts, prior suicide attempts. Because these are more characteristic of suicide than nonsuicide, they are justifiably considered valid correlates, or indicators of the suicidal disposition. The two circles in the first figure show this. Each circle represents a hypothetical population, one of suicides, the other of nonsuicides. Each has a dark area representing the percentage scoring "suicidal" on a test composed of valid indicators (Y characteristics). Clearly, a relatively high percentage of people who commit suicide will have scored "suicidal." Given the big difference in those dark areas, the test is obviously valid.

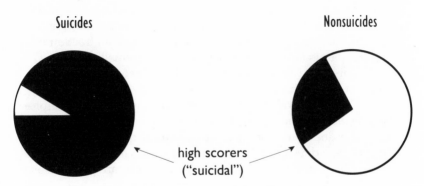

Suicides   Nonsuicides

high scorers
("suicidal")

So far so good, you might be thinking—like the guy in mid-flight after jumping from the Brooklyn Bridge. But there's a catch that, unlike the case of the jumper, may not be obvious. To see it, start with people who commit suicide, and you find that most of them scored "suicidal." However, start with people who score "suicidal," and ask if most of them later commit suicide. What if we selected high scorers and then waited a year? Consulting those circles suggests one answer, but it would be the wrong answer. The correct answer is that we would discover very few suicides, maybe even none. This is no exaggeration.

Consider just one study of people whose risk for suicide was presumably elevated for any of the following reasons: They had prior attempts, they had mild symptoms (warning signals), or they were related to depressed or suicidal people. You might say that, with these people, suicide had everything going for it. Nevertheless, such valid correlates alone or in combination correctly predicted *none* of the 46 suicides that occurred during a follow-up of 1,906 subjects. The authors admitted that valid correlates did not permit meaningful suicide prediction, even with high-risk inpatients [129]. In short, their predictive value was near ziltch. What's going on?

You've watched magicians. You know that they distract your attention with irrelevant flourishes so you won't recognize the hidden clue that demystifies the trick. Here's that clue. The two circles in the last figure were drawn the same size. That helped keep things simple—it focused attention on the validity of suicide indicators—but only by distracting attention from an essential fact: The population of suicides is miniscule compared to the nonsuicide population. Resizing the circles, as in the next figure, immediately reveals that most of the total dark (suicidal) area is in the *non*suicide circle; most people labeled suicidal are part of the *nonsuicide* population. In effect, a small fraction of a big number is larger than a big fraction of a small number. (To test yourself on this point about valid indicators vis-à-vis base rate, see the "Who Is Alvin?" Appendix note.)

The principle is clear: A valid indicator may be useless for predicting *any* low base-rate phenomenon. This principle can help us make decisions, for example, whether to use sophisticated machines to detect bombs placed by terrorists in airliner luggage [292]. Okay, assume that each year 100 bombs are placed. Also

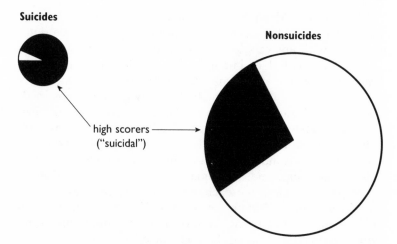

Suicides

Nonsuicides

high scorers ───────▶
("suicidal")

assume that the bomb-detecting machines are incredibly good overall: 99 percent of their decisions are accurate—there is only a 1 percent error. Finally, assume that all bombs are detected. That means that all of the 1 percent error is of the *false-alarm* kind, where a "bomb" is detected in innocent luggage. With 10 *billion* pieces of luggage passing through the detectors each year, our incredibly good machines will give us 100 *million* false alarms—1 percent of 10 billion. That's almost 28,000 each day, or almost 1,200 an hour.

Thus, perspective can make all the difference in evaluating a diagnostic test. In our example, there is a big difference between the perspectives of the test *designer* and the test *user*. The test designer cares about the difference in percentages, such as those shown in the first figure. The reason is that those differences indicate that the test is valid; it does capture important differences between two kinds of people. The test user, too, cares about test validity but also about differences in base rates, as shown in the second figure. The reason is that base rates indicate whether the test is useful—whether it can be used to diagnose a person and predict what that person will do. Let's say our test designer provides us with a test of 0.99 *overall* accuracy—sounds great. However, that test may yield a measly 0.000001 (one in a million) *diagnostic* accuracy—sounds hopeless. Again, it's not that valid correlates are not valid; it's just that sometimes they are not useful.

Well, if they don't predict, then in what sense do they explain? What's the point of looking for correlates if we don't wind up with answers to important questions, like why *some* people kill themselves but most don't. After all, we already know why people kill themselves—they are depressed, hopeless, or insane. But we want to know why most depressed, hopeless, or insane people do *not* kill themselves. It's not just a question about suicide, but about all sorts of abnormalities. Schizophrenia, a relatively rare event, is modestly associated with intrusive or indifferent mothering, ambiguous or conflict-ridden parenting, and such qualities. That is, the families of schizophrenics have these characteristics more than families chosen at random—but not much more. However, families with such characteristics *rarely* produce a schizophrenic offspring, which means that, finding those characteristics, you should *not* predict schizophrenia. These rather common qualities are therefore valid correlates only in a statistical sense; they have near-*zero* practical or theoretical value. In other words, though valid, though celebrated in textbooks, they don't explain—they certainly don't predict—schizophrenia. We might very well ask, what good is a theory that seems to explain so much, yet predicts so little, or as Shakespeare wrote: "If you can look into the seeds of time, and say which grain will grow and which will not, speak then to me. . . ."

A fable

Once upon a time, an earnest fellow wanted to explain that rarest of phenomena, the California redwoods (X). So, he went to the California redwood forest and made many observations about sunlight, soil, rainfall, and other correlates. Combining all these valid predictors (Ys), he came up with a Y theory to explain how redwoods came to be. He then began to test his Y theory, and lo, in other redwood stands he found the same sorts of correlates. Soon, Y theory was all the rage. Then it came to pass that a question was asked by a well-meaning lad who, in another era, might have wondered about a certain emperor's new clothes. Would creating all those Y conditions *produce* redwoods? Alas, no. Apparently, a critical element was missing:

redwood seeds, carriers of the requisite blueprint. Moral of the story: Theories can be too heavy on Y, too light on 'cause.

It's not redwoods, of course, but human phenomena that concern us here. We want to understand mental illness, but also creative genius, stellar athleticism, heroic courage. All too often, such extraordinary phenomena are ignored, or worse, represented in vacuous theories based largely on correlational observations that start with back-asked questions. It is nothing less than reverse alchemy that turns the gold of human experience into leaden explanation. Such theorizing trivializes or falsifies the extraordinary, and, given the continuities, the ordinary too. How often do we miss the subtle yet all important generative element while invoking social conditions, rearing, educational opportunity, and all that? Social learning theories may explain why we do this or that in this or that situation. They cannot explain a Mozart, a Jackie Robinson, a Helen Keller, or a manic-depressive. Then why, given the continuities of the human landscape, should we assume they can explain the average Joe?

14

BLUEPRINT SPECIAL

Popular theorizing about mental illness is sometimes just high-falutin' storytelling. We explain liability to depression or suicide by invoking deficiencies of mothering or other aspects of rearing during early childhood. What kind of explanations are these? How do we know if so-called causes are really causes or effects—or something else? In fact, how do we know when such theorizing merely denies our uncertainty and suspicion that we really don't know answers that we feel we ought to know? Perhaps much of our storytelling—what we like to think of as scientific theorizing—merely defends against the intolerable idea that depression, suicide, or other unfortunate developments often arise from chance factors, in other words, bad luck including the largely unpredictable roll of the genetic dice. With regard to the latter, consider the following imaginary scenario based on a true story [1; 207].

Beth is a young woman being treated for a severe personality disorder that her psychotherapist attributes to an upbringing that was too lenient, undisciplined, and emotionally distant—call it the Beth explanation. Sounds reasonable enough—never mind that that most kids exposed to the same kind of rearing do not develop mental illness—but here's the problem. Across town, Amy is being treated for the same personality disorder which, according to *her* psychotherapist, comes from just the opposite kind of rearing, one that was too strict, rejecting, and intrusive—call it the Amy explanation. Same mental illness, different explanations, both good stories—except for one fact: Beth and Amy are genetically identical twins separated early in life and reared apart. This simple fact raises a provocative idea: Perhaps the liability to certain kinds of mental illness has little to do with a particular kind of rearing, and much to do with a strong genetic potential that will flower in almost any environment. Call this the BethAmy explanation. How often, in the rush to embrace Beth explanations with no thought to Amy alternatives, do we miss a deeper (BethAmy) truth?

Common cause

A connection between one factor (rearing) and another (mental illness) might be causal, just as it seems. It might be a matter of parents affecting kids—for example, abusive or indifferent parents causing their children to develop neurotic or antisocial disorder. But it might be the reverse, with kids affecting parents (and thus their rearing). You only have to imagine what it must be like for the parents of hyperactive or psychopathic or suicidal children to appreciate how rearing can be the effect more than the cause of disorder. Yet, the connection might be otherwise— not causal in the usual sense of parents and children influencing each other. Drinking lemonade and going swimming are correlated—an increase or decrease in the frequency of occurrence of either one goes along with an increase or decrease in the frequency of occurrence of the other. But no matter how high the correlation, no one believes that lemonade drinking causes swimming or that swimming causes lemonade drinking. Obviously, both activities have a common cause, namely the weather. Then what about more complicated and controversial connections where common causes may not be all that obvious—for example, the correlation between poverty and crime, or the resemblance of parents and children?

No doubt there is a correlation between poverty and crime, but how strong is it and what does it mean? Poverty contributes to crime, no doubt, by spurring the criminal-minded to action. But crime contributes to poverty, given that not many criminal-minded people stay in school, keep a job, preserve property, or save for a rainy day. Despite the few who do get rich, criminals—at least the run-of-the-mill ones—generally have a relatively high poverty rate; they are also likely to come from poor neighborhoods. So, start with criminality and you may easily imagine poverty as a major cause. However, start with poverty, and the impression may be different, for the simple reason that most poor people are not criminals; just ask law-abiding citizens who are, or who grew up, poor. Moreover, within the common environment of even the poorest of family settings, only one of many siblings may become a criminal.

Such observations suggest an explanation for any poverty-crime connection that goes beyond one causing the other, namely that they share a common cause. That is, abusive or broken families, or certain genes found in the relatives of certain families can promote crime *and* poverty, in the same sense as summer heat promotes lemonade drinking and swimming. Such common environmental causes readily come to mind if we take the society-at-large, or *between-family*, perspective. But what about those striking individual differences we notice *within* families? Taking the *within-family* perspective more readily impresses us with the causal significance of antisocial personality and impulse-control problems specific to certain family *members*. Clearly, perspective will influence the direction of our explanations. Focus on society, and the bias will be toward obvious environmental factors, such as socioeconomic status, that differ greatly between families. Focus on family setting, and the bias will be toward obvious psychological factors, such as personality disorder, that differ among family members despite a relatively common environment.

In the spirit of these remarks, consider two ideas, one mentioned earlier about the seemingly negative effect of parental loss, the other about the seemingly positive effect of family rituals. The idea that early maternal loss enhances the liability to adult depression seems sensible enough. But the causal connection between loss and depression may sometimes be illusory. ·Major depression is a heritable disorder associated with suicide. Therefore, if the parental death is due to suicide, it may be a marker of a liability that is transmitted genetically to the child; genes, not loss, would be the primary cause. In this scenario, parental death and offspring depression are merely different expressions of a common heritable liability.

The second idea starts with an observation: Adults claiming to be emotionally healthier than others tend to report having experienced while growing up certain family rituals like eating dinner together or reading stories and having cookies and milk at bedtime. Apparently, even alcoholism is somewhat less likely in the offspring of alcoholics if family life included such rituals. It would seem that rituals suppress liability—but they might not. Rather, they might *express* something healthy about parents. An expressive hypothesis would hold that family ritual and relative mental health may be different expressions of a common genetic influence on the behavior of parents and the development of their offspring.

What causes what?

The expressive hypothesis may seem less satisfying than the idea that family ritual influences behavior. Popular media thrive less on unvarnished truth than on upbeat and trendy formulas designed to improve something or other. People want to feel that they have some control over important aspects of their lives, in particular, their children's development. That this development might stem less from rearing and more from a biased roll of the family genetic dice makes people uncomfortable if not anxious. Perhaps that is why, recently, you could find the expressive hypothesis buried in a four-line paragraph on the second page of a newspaper article [131]. There it was, expressed in innocuous language easily overlooked or forgotten because of the unremitting causal message of the title and surrounding paragraphs. To wit: perhaps family rituals are merely the outward signs of an already strong family.

We can apply our common-cause approach in a slightly different way to the question of the development of personality and liability to mental illness. Consider the connection between adult personality and childhood experience with TV shows. Aggressiveness during adolescence is indeed related to violent TV-watching at age eight. The correlation is about 0.30—no surprise in that—but in males only. What is the meaning of this male-only 0.30? Does it tell us the extent to which early exposure to violent TV programs *facilitates* adolescent aggressiveness?

Remember, the meaning of all correlations is ambiguous—developmental correlations are no exception. Early exposure to TV violence may have little impact on personality development; rather, certain personalities may simply be attracted to violent programs. In sum, exposure may be an *unnecessary* cause; aggressive kids don't need TV to be mean. It may be an *insufficient* cause; nice kids are immune to TV nastiness. It may be *no cause at all*, but rather an effect; violent TV is selected by aggressive kids or kids destined to become aggressive for other reasons. Doing more studies will make the correlations more reliable, but no less ambiguous.

Perhaps an experimental approach would reveal what causes what. We could randomly assign kids to a TV-violence or neutral condition and see what happens. In the laboratory, exposure to TV violence does promote rough and boisterous ("aggressive") behavior. This is most evident when the children see an adult model acting aggressively. But these findings can't tell us if such experiences, accumulating over time, help to condition an abnormal predisposition to act aggressively. It is more likely that a few *naturally* aggressive kids are responsible for most of the experimental effects—that the social environment, represented by the experimental manipulation, merely *brings out* an aggressiveness that would eventually emerge in almost any environment. In sum, what looks like an environmental cause may be a developmentally early expression of the problem—like the bud of a future flower.

Two unknowns

With questions about development, it seems we are often victims of Catch-22. Correlations may be relevant but ambiguous; experimental effects may be unambiguous but irrelevant. Yet there are ways out of this paradox. To appreciate this, consider how we might tackle the question of where child abuse comes from.

Newspapers report yet another story about a child abuser who was abused as a child. The strong impression left with the reader is that the earlier conditions *create* the potential for the abusive behavior that comes later. Perhaps the impression is inspired by feelings that the world is both symmetrical (like breeds like) and just (sins of the fathers, and all that). Perhaps it is reinforced by clinical studies of adults with personality problems who often report having been abused as children.

But remember how the impression you get depends on which end of the binoculars you look through—whether you start from behavior and look for causes, or start with presumed causes and look for behavioral effects. A lot also depends on how willing you are to consider "off-diagonal" events—people *not* abused as children who nevertheless grow up to be abusers, and abused children who do *not* become abusive adults. Asking about these may seem insensitive, even impertinent, yet we must if we are to know what causes what—and to what degree. Asking does not deny that many abusers probably *were* abused as children, or that abuse suffered during childhood *can* adversely affect a person's development, sometimes to the point of serious dysfunction. Rather, asking reminds us that there is much more to find out—that the truth often lies beyond the easy answers.

Newspaper stories leave us with affectively charged impressions and untested assumptions about what causes what—at best, these represent ambiguous correlations posing as explanations. We need more and we need better—specifically, definitive evidence of, for example, the extent to which the abusive disposition stems from having or not having been abused as a child. We can find out if we are clear about one very important thing. Parent-child resemblance is like an equation—the parents on one side, the offspring on the other. The equation has two unknowns—heredity and rearing—the two ways that parents give of themselves. We want to know which of these two parental gifts is the more powerful. But with one equation and two unknowns, no solution is possible.

Not to worry, because, as you will recall, with adopted children we get what amounts to two equations. One is the resemblance of adoptees and their *biological* parents, who represent genetic influence. The other is the resemblance of adoptees and their *adoptive* parents, who represent rearing. The importance of these two influences is given by the relative size of the parent-child resemblances as measured by correlations. That, in a nutshell, is the rationale for studying adoptees.

A study of abuse among adoptees could help settle the question of the relative impact of having been abused, but no such study exists. So, let's imagine one that uses two groups of new-borns adopted away at birth. One group is made up of the adopted-away offspring of known child abusers, the other group of the adopted-away offspring of nonabusers. All the adoptees are reared by normal parents in abuse-free homes. When they reach adulthood, the adoptees become parents, but what kind? We can imagine two scenarios, each supporting a different hypothesis.

In the first scenario, the adoptees of both groups have a comparable and low rate of abusing their own children. This happy outcome—abusive behavior eliminated by healthy rearing—suggests, indirectly, that abusive rearing explains the abuser disposition. In the second scenario, however, only the adoptees born of abuser parents have a high rate of abusing their own children—a rate comparable to that usually observed for adults abused by their natural parents. This outcome suggests that the abuser disposition expresses a genetic liability—perhaps operating through some brain instability that causes a violent reaction to certain kinds of frustration. The point of our imaginary experiment is *not* that one inference is correct and the other false. Rather, the point is that each can be tested against the other to estimate the *relative importance* of heredity and rearing. To see how this is done, let's exchange our hypothetical study of child abuse for a real-world study of manic-depression.

The adoption method is two-way. You can start with biological parents, and look "forward" to their adopted-away offspring. We did as much with our hypothetical study of abuse by adoptees. You can also start with adoptees and look "back" to their relatives—both the biological and the adoptive. Mendlewicz and Rainer took this second approach with bipolars and normals, some of whom were adoptees [226]. The investigators then located the biological and adoptive parents who could be assessed for psychiatric impairment. Elevated rates of bipolar and unipolar illness were found for the *biological* parents of bipolars, regardless of whether the parents raised their child. On the other hand, relatively lower rates were found for the *adoptive* parents of bipolars and normals. The difference in rates implicates a hereditary liability to bipolar illness. The high heritability implied by such findings is further suggested by the similarly high concordance rates for identical twins reared together (70 percent) and identical twins reared apart (67 percent) [254].

All in the family?

A genetic influence on liability is all the more important if it helps us to understand the origins of personality. So, let's ask two questions, one about why family members tend to resemble each other, and another about why they can be so different. These may seem like two different questions, but family resemblance and difference are really two aspects of the same thing: human variation. So, studying one side of the coin will tell you about the other side.

First question: What promotes family resemblance for traits like intelligence, extraversion, or liability to manic-depression? Simple answer: genetic and environmental commonality—specifically, the genes that first-degree relatives have in common and their shared environment, mostly within the family setting. Second question: What promotes differences among family members? Simple answer: genetic and environmental differences—specifically, genes not shared and the unshared environment, mostly outside the family setting. Of course, the trick is to find out *how much* heredity and environment determine the resemblances or differences between any two people.

To see how the trick is done, we reconsider twin resemblance measured by correlation. Genetically identical twins come from a *single* fertilized egg, or *zygote.* That is why they are sometimes called *monozygotic*—MZ for short. Fraternal twins, like any two siblings, originate from *two* separately fertilized eggs. That is why they are sometimes called *dizygotic*—DZ for short. Identical twins have *all* their genes in common. Fraternal twins, like any first-degree relatives, share only half their genes. The key question is this: Why is there a big resemblance for identical-twin pairs? Does it mostly come from their identical genes or mostly from their shared environment?

A great way to answer this question is to compare the resemblances of identical twins reared together with those of identical twins reared apart. We measure these resemblances in terms of correlations, and we look for *reliable differences,* whatever the numbers. For identical twins reared together, resemblance comes from their identical genes plus shared environment. For identical twins reared apart, however, any resemblance must come mainly from their identical genes; in other words, the correlation that measures identical-twins-reared-apart resemblance also estimates heritability. It is therefore easy to estimate the influence of the shared environment. Just take the correlation of identical twins reared together *(identical genes + shared environment)*, and subtract the correlation of identical twins reared apart *(identical genes)*. The remainder is *shared environment* alone.

Whether reared together or apart, identical twins display extraordinary resemblance. Therefore, subtracting the one correlation from the other often yields a small number. How small? Consider twin resemblance for intelligence as estimated by IQ correlations from the well-known Minnesota study of twins reared apart [44]. For 48 pairs of identical twins *reared together*, the correlation was 0.88. This is about as high as it gets, given that the correlation for individuals tested on two occasions—the resemblance of individuals with *themselves*—is 0.87. For 40 pairs of identical twins *reared apart*, the correlation—the heritability estimate—was 0.69. Actually that 0.69 is the *lowest* of five such estimates from American and European studies (correlations of 0.69, 0.71, 0.75, 0.75, and 0.78), averaging 0.75; so, using the 0.69 means *underestimating* heritability.

With resemblance estimated for identical twins reared together (0.88) and identical twins reared apart (0.69), it's easy to estimate the influence of the shared environment: just subtract. So, from the 0.88, which represents *genes + shared environment*, simply subtract the 0.69 which represents *genes* only. The resulting 0.19 is small. Yet, given those other identical-twin-apart estimates suggesting a heritability of 0.75 rather than 0.69, the 0.19 may actually *overestimate* the power of shared environments to forge resemblance. Another estimate comes from genetically *unrelated* siblings reared together, that is, either two adoptees or one natural child and an adoptee. All resemblance (positive correlations) between adoptees and other family members must of course be entirely environmental. *The actual resemblance is roughly zero.*

It seems incredible that this resemblance of family members might have *nothing* to do with sharing an environment during the formative years, but that is what the most definitive evidence suggests. For argument's sake, however, let's use that 0.19 correlation from the Minnesota research to represent the assumption that there is at least a small *shared-environment* influence. That 0.19 and 0.69 estimate for *gene* influence represent the two, mostly within-family, influences that promote resemblance. They add up to 0.88, which is simply the correlation of identical twins reared together. The only other thing to consider is the influence that promotes *differences,* namely the *nonshared-environment* influence. Easy: Just subtract the 0.88, representing *genes + shared environment* influence, from 1.00, representing *all* influences. The result is 0.12, also a remarkably small number.

What does it all mean? It means that we have a pretty good idea—we certainly know how to find out—about what promotes resemblance and differences among people. For intelligence as measured by IQ tests, the mix of influences seems to include a big genetic one and two little environmental ones: the unshared and the shared (within-family) influence, *the latter possibly being zero.* For personality traits, the mix is a little different. There's a substantial genetic influence (0.40 to 0.50), a tiny shared-environment influence that is probably less than 0.10—*it may very well be zero*—and a substantial nonshared-environmental influence (roughly 0.45).

On average, then, the evidence seems to boil down to this: *People are similar mainly to the extent that they share genes, but different mainly to the extent that they differ genetically and live in different environments.* That statement may be a bit simplistic; for one thing, it doesn't deal with extremely abusive or crazy environments that, without relief, can distort or sabotage human potential. Nevertheless, it does capture the nature of the evidence regarding what is generally true.

The implications are enormous, but here we need only be reminded by psychologist Sandra Scarr of what in all likelihood we already knew: "Feeding a well-nourished but short child more and more will not give him the stature of a basketball player. Feeding a below-average intellect more and more information will not make her brilliant. Exposing a shy child to socially demanding events will not make him feel less shy. The child with a below-average intellect and the shy child may gain some specific skills and helpful knowledge of how to behave in specific situations, but their enduring intellectual and personality characteristics will not be fundamentally changed" [279]. But of this too Scarr reminds us: The evidence on heritability does *not* mean rearing is unimportant to individual development, for, *on the contrary, children need parents in order to develop normally.* Rather, the evidence suggests that rearing *brings out* personality and intellectual potential, it does not stamp them in according to parental behavior and expectations. So far so good, you may be thinking, but here's the rub: To the extent that rearing acts to bring out rather than to stamp in an individual's potential, development *doesn't require a particular kind of rearing, which means it doesn't require a particular set of parents* [279]. And that is more than a little something to think about. (For more on heritability, see Appendix note, "Estimating Genetic Influence on Traits.")

The clay *is* the potter

It is clearer now than ever that identical-twin resemblance is more than a matter of having been treated alike. On average, identical twins reared together are no less alike if they or their parents believe that they are fraternal twins. Likewise, fraternal twins are no more alike if they or their parents believe that they are identicals. Actual genetic overlap, not rearing or physical appearance, seems to make the bigger contribution to resemblance for IQ and personality traits [176; 202]. Clearly, the resemblance of identical twins reared apart tells us that identical twins reared together are treated more alike because they are *already* more alike, and further, *that this similarity of treatment has little or no effect on shaping resemblance.* In other words, similar people have similar effects on their environments, whether they live with the same or different people. There's nothing mysterious in the idea that friendly people elicit friendly responses, unfriendly people unfriendly responses—except for one little thing. The usual concept of environment as something imposed from outside is unsatisfactory; it is not even a half-truth, and it obscures more than it illuminates.

The truth is that we actively *create* environments by *making* them happen, and by *selecting* them ready made—what psychologists Scarr and McCartney call "niche-picking." We create our environment through our storyteller instinct. We storytellers usually have an abundant supply of what we need—stories that we can relate to, stories that make sense to us as human beings and as individuals. The reasons are obvious: If not already surrounded by *our kind* of storytellers, we seek them out in life and in the media. If they prove reluctant or inadequate, and if goading does no good, *we make up our own stories*, in our observations, fantasies, dreams, and in our rationalizations.

Gifted children reared in dull surroundings seek what they need by inventing games or imaginary companions, or by discovering what their less gifted peers will require training to learn. Exotic yet instructive examples abound of mostly self-taught scientific geniuses achieving immortal greatness despite the most ordinary—even neglectful or abusive—childhood environments. The father of astronomer Johannes Kepler was a small-town innkeeper and a drunk whose sorry circumstances forced the boy to spend endless hours at drudge work. The father of mathematician Carl Gauss was a small-time, no-account bricklayer, indifferent if not hostile to his son's talents. Jean-Jacques Rousseau grew up poor and socially rootless, his mother having died and his father having deserted him during his infancy. Yet Rousseau became one of the best-known and most influential philosophers of the eighteenth century. Examples abound of extraordinary genius arising out of ordinary, even abysmal circumstances—children of butchers, bakers, and candlestick makers becoming intellectual or artistic giants. Such exceptions to the rule of parent-child resemblance disprove the misleading and degrading notion that we are mostly products of our environment.

Compared to their peers, gifted children grow up to be bigger, healthier, happier, more accomplished, more responsible, less neurotic or delinquent, and longer-lived. Stunning exceptions to this rule feed popular misconceptions about precocious children being awkward, introverted, unhappy—qualities that are usually the effects of social mismanagement more than signs of inherent abnormality. The fact is, geniuses are what they seem—superior. Moreover, this superiority shines through despite disadvantage. Against seemingly impossible odds, the genius of Kepler, Gauss and others became increasingly manifest in their extraordinary capability, mastery of material, and inventiveness. Despite ordinary or even deprived childhood circumstances, they forged more suitable ones, richer ones created by application of intelligence and inventive imagination to sometimes paltry raw material. Various objects were transformed into a collection, books were borrowed and mastered, mathematical tricks were worked out, word games were invented. Thus it is with gifted children who do in their extraordinary way what all children do more normally. Stunning examples of "off-diagonal" achievement are not exceptions but crystal clarifications of a rule of nature easily obscured in ordinary circumstances. Children are not just so much clay to be molded by parental potters. To a large extent, it would seem, the clay *is* the potter.

We create environments, often by transforming ready-made environments that we have actively selected to fit our dispositions, styles, and competencies. The talented gravitate toward like-minded people with whom they can then create intellectually and aesthetically stimulating conditions. Kindred souls seek each other out for romance and procreation in a process called assortive mating. Neurotics embrace likewise troubled partners with whom they create conflict-ridden, painfully unhappy relationships. Psychopaths gravitate toward similarly antisocial companions and exploitable victims with whom they create antisocial situations. Never mind their proclamations of having learned their lesson, changed for the better, or experienced born-again epiphany. Simply put, environments are *effects* as much as causes.

Given the high heritability of traits, the creation of environments must reflect *genetic* ways of being. To that extent, genetically related people will wind up in similar environments. The love, care, and intellectual stimulation, or abusiveness, negligence, and intellectual sterility that characterize a child's environment reflect genetic influence running through the family. Parental genes are thus the common biological *and educational* source of personality development. It is therefore wrong in every sense of the word—incorrect, deceptive, and harmful—to think of the environment created by parents as being not biological or not genetic. It is also wrong to think of the environment as merely something "out there" causing effects. Obviously, the behavior of parents, the quality of the environment, and the personality of offspring can facilitate, inhibit, or disrupt each other. Not so obvious is how much talent, personality, and liability evolve from inside out rather than accumulate from outside in—how much of what we call intelligence and personality comes from within, eventually developing a life of its own. In a sense, what comes from within *is* life, assimilating what is sympathetic, resisting what is alien.

And yet, nongenetic influences surely are important for explaining potential and behavior. That is clear from identical-twin differences that can't be chalked up merely to faulty measurement. From the beginning, uterine and postnatal environments are always somewhat different, even for identical twins. Psychological development depends on how the genetic blueprint is translated. An incompetent builder can mess things up even with a good blueprint while a skillful builder can compensate even for a bad blueprint. So, different builders with the same blueprint will produce somewhat different houses. Likewise, different environments, even with a genetic blueprint common to identical twins, will produce somewhat different results. Even highly heritable qualities will come out a little different—weight, handedness, direction of hair whorls, and the like, but also brain function, intelligence, ability, personality, and liability to mental illness.

Conventional wisdom tells the story of the power of imposed social learning over the unique directions of individual development, for example about how deficiencies and liabilities come mostly from what we can see: abusive fathers, wicked-witch mothers, lousy neighborhoods, and anything else we can imagine remediating. Unconventional wisdom tells a different story, about extraordinary resemblance for identical twins reared apart, which implies that human development unfolds mostly out of what we *don't* see. And therein lies a more compelling story, one rooted in definitive facts and intuitive truths about the human heart.

PART FOUR

IDEOLOGY AND ANTIDOTE

While you live, tell the truth and
shame the devil

—WILLIAM SHAKESPEARE
King Henry IV, Part 1, Act III, scene 1

15

ARE WE MYTHTAKEN?

Most people have some kind of theory for bizarre, dysfunctional, and dysphoric behavior, recognizing in these qualities the abnormal effects of brain disease or social disadvantage, bad genes or bad character. Whatever their theory, for them mental illness is real enough. Not so for others who, seeing deviance rather than disorder, call for tolerance and understanding rather than treatment or isolation. For them, mental illness is a myth cooked up by modern medicine men called psychiatrists. Taking a look at the counterintuitive view that mental illness is mere myth can tell us much about evidence and ideology, and more generally, about the psychological nature of explanation. But first, a little history.

Hysterical notions

From the beginning of recorded history, observers have recognized the outward expression of disease in abnormal behaviors from the manic-depressive to the epileptic. For example, the ancient Greek physician Hippocrates (460–370 B.C.E.) said, "If you will cut open the head [of farm animals with epileptic-like disease], you will find the brain humid, full of sweat, and having a bad smell. And in this way you see that it is not a god that injures the body, but disease. And so it is with man." This comment is from a 2,400-year-old treatise debunking those con-jurers and charlatans who argued that epilepsy is a spiritual ill-ness ("sacred" disease) rather than medical disease.

This rather modern view was nevertheless freighted with what are now mere historical curiosities, for example, the expla-nation for why some women constantly complain about such things as persisting pain, dizziness, weakness, trouble swal-lowing. The Hippocratic answer was that these were the symp-toms of bodily disruptions caused by a wandering uterus—*hystera*, in ancient Greek, whence our term *hysteria*. The Hippo-cratic solution to depressive illness was a bit less fantastic: an imbalance of four fundamental bodily fluids, or *humors* that make up each individual's temperament chemistry.

One of the bodily humors, black bile (*melaine chole*, in Greek), was said to be cold, dry, thick, and sour. An overabundance of black bile was said to cause many things—convulsion, insanity, blindness—the most pertinent being melancholia (black humor), which meant a kind of delusional madness that proba-bly included some of what we now call manic and schizophrenic disorder. If too much black bile made you *melancholic*, too much yellow bile made you *choleric* (angry, irritable). Too much phlegm made you excessively *phlegmatic* (easygoing, calm), but too much blood made you excessively *sanguine* (hopeful, confi-dent). In Hippocrates' terms, then, personality and behavior, both normal and abnormal, were expressions of the amount and balance of substances in body and brain.

Humoral theory was developed by an ancient Greek who lived around 450 B.C.E. Empedocles believed in four basic cosmic ele-ments, each with two properties, as shown in the table below. Being products of the cosmos, human temperament should reflect cosmic properties. Hence, the four bodily humors of Hippocra-tes corresponded to the four cosmic elements of Empedocles.

CLASSICAL GREEK MODEL OF HUMAN TEMPERAMENT

Element	Season	Property	Humor	Temperament
earth	autumn	cold, dry	black bile	melancholic
water	winter	cold, moist	phlegm	phlegmatic
air	spring	warm, moist	blood	sanguine
fire	summer	warm, dry	yellow bile	choleric

The Hippocratic tradition was remarkably durable. For centuries—right through the Middle Ages and into premodern times—physicians used its humoral notions, along with knowledge of the stars, to diagnose and treat disease. For example, in *The Canterbury Tales*, Chaucer (circa 1343–1400) speaks of "manye engendered of humour of malencolyk"—in other words, agitated depression caused by melancholy humor—and tells how physicians cared for medical and psychiatric patients by use of astrological signs and humoral theory. Such medieval theorizing was a curious mix of demonic and natural forces. The effects of spirits could combine with stress, diet, humors, and heredity. Scholars believed, for example, that if certain warm humors developed in the body, the devil or incubi might take possession of the victim. Or, invoking ancient astrological notions, they believed epilepsy to be caused by an overabundance of phlegm during the first quarter of the moon, blood during the second and third quarters, and black bile during the last. The planet Mars was believed to contribute to melancholia, and so on [343]. This curious mix of medico-astro-demonic notions included the following categories of mental illness: *insani* (bad heredity), *melancholici* (unbalanced humors), *lunatici* (lunar influence), and *obsessi* (demonic possession).

As late as the seventeenth century, scholars were still concocting theoretical stews made up of humoral and uterine notions mixed with astrology and demonology. But times were changing. Physics, astronomy, and physiology were advancing dramatically, and intellectual life was hurtling toward the Enlightenment. By the beginning of the eighteenth century, many ancient notions had passed into history. The wandering-uterus idea, for example, was eventually put to rest primarily by autopsies showing that the uterus of hysterical women remained in its normal place in the body. Thus did a little good science neutralize a lot of bad theory.

We moderns are no more immune than were the ancients to the lure of pseudoscientific notions. For example, many thinking people have worried about the influence of astrology. Dante consigned astrologers and soothsayers to the eighth circle of Hell where, with heads permanently rotated 180 degrees (Exorcist-style), they were compelled always to look backward while walking forward. Voltaire simply quipped that astrology is to

astronomy what superstition is to religion—the mad daughter
of a wise mother, and too long dominating the earth. Astrology
flourishes still, we might add, and despite the evidence that
astrologers do no better than chance when matching personality
profiles with astrological information. Moreover, it seems that
there is no correlation between birth dates and well-known scientific or political accomplishment [246]. Nevertheless, astrology is a thriving enterprise, as evident in the huge number of
newspapers that carry astrological predictions. The grip of
astrology is perhaps more compellingly evident in an extraordinary comment made in 1962 by the New York City Commis-
sioner of Markets in response to a petition submitted by an
organization of astrologers: he pledged to "investigate these
phonies claiming to be astrologers."

The first half of the twentieth century had its fair share of
false, even nutty, notions. One was that male susceptibility to
color blindness comes from insufficient color-related experiences during childhood. Another was that early psychological
trauma causes Tourette's syndrome (tics, twitching, grimacing,
explosive expletives). Still another was that conflict over toilet
training leads to obsessive-compulsive disorder. Such examples
represent a tendency to misrepresent the signs of disease as the
symptoms of bad rearing, and, in particular, of inadequate
mothering. Biological disorders as diverse as narcolepsy (sleep
attacks), hyperactivity, obesity, infantile autism, and manic-
depression were once theorized to come from bad parenting or
adverse social circumstances.

Consider the belief that the liability to schizophrenic illness
originates in intrusive, indifferent, or otherwise noxious
upbringing. Granted, the child of a schizophrenic mother is
more likely than most to experience such upbringing. It is even
true that the offspring of schizophrenic mothers have an elevated rate of schizophrenia—roughly 10 percent compared to
the less than 1 percent population rate. Trouble is, the elevated
rate of schizophrenia in offspring is roughly the same if the
father is the schizophrenic parent. Moreover, 90 percent of the
offspring of schizophrenics *never* develop schizophrenia, and 90
percent of schizophrenics have nonschizophrenic parents *most
of whom are normal*. For decades the so-called schizophrenogenic-
mother hypothesis prospered despite definitive evidence

against it. For example, children born of schizophrenics have that same 10 percent risk of becoming schizophrenic themselves *even when reared in adoptive homes*. And children born of nonschizophrenic parents have no excess risk *even when reared by a schizophrenic* [154; 328].

Wimps and warriors

Even when off base, the ancients were often in the right ballpark. Uterine theory was false, yet it anticipated a current view that hysteria may sometimes have a medical explanation. Humoral notions were false, yet they anticipated modern theories about depression that invoke neurochemical imbalances and hormone abnormalities. What the ancients lacked in technology and scientific knowledge they made up in common sense and astuteness. For example, Hippocrates considered epilepsy to be hereditary—manic-depression, too. For centuries, people have understood that diseases of the mental as well as medical kind run in families, sometimes skipping generations. They assumed them to be hereditary, though they did not know the genetic mechanism. They also knew that inbreeding magnifies the influence of such diseases, and that a vulnerability may show up in different kinds of symptoms. Such ideas are represented in clergyman/librarian Robert Burton's classic, *The Anatomy of Melancholy:*

> And where the complexion and constitution of the father are corrupt, there (saith Roger Bacon) the complexion and constitution of the son must needs be corrupt . . . [and] in manners and conditions of the mind, the habits of the fathers go forth with the children. [Furthermore] I need not therefore make any doubt of Melancholy, but that it is an hereditary disease. . . . And that which is more to be wondered at, it skips in some families the father, and goes to the son, or takes every other, & sometimes every third in a lineal descent, and doth not always produce the same, but some like, and a symbolizing disease. [And] for these reasons belike the Church and Commonwealth, human and divine laws, have conspired to avoid hereditary diseases, forbidding such [consanguineous] marriages as are any whit allied. . . .

By the end of the nineteenth century, mental illness was becoming a thoroughly modern concept, in large part because of two scientific developments: neurology, with its implied brain-behavior mechanisms, and evolution, with its implied genetic mechanisms. In evolutionary theory, adaptation is a numbers game popularly, if misleadingly, called *survival of the fittest*. Big winners produce the most offspring to carry their genes into the future. The fittest individuals are thus not necessarily the strongest; they might be the cleverest, for example, in knowing how to retreat from overwhelming threat. Clearly, the fitness concept can accommodate wimps as well as warriors, poets as well as politicians. Therefore, only when it affects genetic reproduction (number of offspring) does mental illness become a failure of adaptation—*maladaptation*. But, mental illness can be thought of as maladaptive in more than this narrow Darwinian sense.

All creatures instinctively defend their physical integrity through hide-and-seek and attack-and-escape behaviors. Humans display this principle in the domain of personality where *ego* integrity is defended through *mental* adjustments, for example, projecting blame and denying weakness, even mortality. With humans, then, survival of the fittest can be thought of as a dissemination of *personal* as well as genetic influence. Winners in the adaptation game have the strongest personalities—that is, extraordinary talent, temperament, charisma, or chutzpah—allowing them to achieve psychological control through admiration, affection, intimidation, or deceit. Ego adaptation through self-promotion means balancing selfishness and altruism, self-expression and self-denial, all guided by the ethical principles of accommodation that are intrinsic to the personality or imposed from outside. We recognize the value of fitting in and doing the right thing, of give and take and tit for tat, and the maladaptation of callous indifference or outright withdrawal, of mindless selfishness or unmitigated immorality.

Telltale signs

Severe mental illness is maladaptive in two ways. Given the Darwinian criterion of survivability, it is maladaptive in striking early enough to affect reproduction; and given the medical criterion of health, it is maladaptive in causing sufficient dysfunction to indicate, or strongly imply, disease. Age-old medical assumptions about the biological basis of mental illness—the notion of mental disease—became increasingly confirmed after the mid-nineteenth century, with the appearance of new discoveries about brain mechanisms, for example, in the specific area of the left frontal lobe that controls speech. For thirty years, a seemingly intelligent and mentally normal man with no detectible paralysis of the larynx or speech muscles had nevertheless been unable to speak. In 1861, the man died, and during an autopsy, the physician Paul Broca discovered a lesion in the lower-front part of the left cerebral hemisphere, the so-called speech area now known as Broca's area. Scientific discoveries were complemented by works of science fiction, such as Mary Shelley's gothic tale of Dr. Victor Frankenstein, physician turned occult scientist, whose personal deficiencies became manifest in a monstrous creation. Robert Louis Stevenson created the tragic tale of Dr. Jekyll. Through brain-altering drugs, a noble gentleman of good intentions became Hyde-bound to ambition and monstrous self-destruction. In these powerful stories of the dark side of human creativity is a new urgency toward exploring brain function.

Two things are increasingly obvious as we learn more about brain, behavior, and disease: First, psychiatric symptoms can indicate mental disease (*neuro*pathology) rather than just a sick environment (*eco*pathology). Second, the categorical separation of medical and mental diseases is increasingly artificial, and surely misleading when not actually false. Even without evidence of a gross lesion—no "hole" in the brain—we may still suspect brain disease, sometimes as a simple matter of logic. If brain damage can produce psychiatric disorder, at least some psychiatric disorder must involve brain abnormality. For example, damage to the front of the left hemisphere can cause anxious depression, while damage to the right hemisphere can cause apathy or indifference, the exact location being less critical. (See the "Brain Hemisphere Control" Appendix note.)

These days, however, we need not rely on mere logic or highly indirect sorts of evidence. Powerful EEGs, X-ray scans, and autopsy methods can yield undeniable evidence of brain abnormality that can explain some abnormal behaviors, and not just obviously neurological disorders such as Down's syndrome (formerly called "mongolism") and Alzheimer's disease. Evidence keeps popping up, such as anatomical anomalies or chemical imbalances found in patients with severe mental illnesses [330]. In addition, certain drugs have relatively specific effects on certain symptoms; lithium carbonate, for example, works astonishingly well with manic-depression, but not with other kinds of depression. Sometimes the suspected brain abnormality becomes manifest upon closer inspection, perhaps after some time. A minor depression can prove to be the early stage of a manic-depressive illness, a schizophrenic breakdown, or Alzheimer's disease. An agitated depression might even signal severe vitamin B deficiency (pellagra), a disease treatable through simple changes in diet.

Ironically, even hysteria, the most psychological of psychological disorders, may indicate a brain abnormality. Hysteria is diagnosed for diverse and ever-changing "medical," yet medically inexplicable, complaints about pain, loss of function, and odd sensations, usually offered in a dramatic, theatrical, or deceptive manner. The disorder is assumed to be *psychogenic*—caused by inner conflict or morbid imagination. Examiners sometimes act as if they were saying: This person looks sick, but I can't find anything medically wrong. Problem: Ambiguity, doubt. Maybe it's all in the person's head. Solution: Neurosis rather than pathophysiology. Yet, not only is hysteria associated with elevated rates of brain abnormality, brain abnormality observed in neurological patients can produce classic hysteria symptoms, so much so that some patients are initially misdiagnosed as "neurotic" [139; 293]. If people with brain damage can look this neurotic, then at least some people with hysterical complaints may have a medical disease. Hysteria suggests that the boundary between neurological and psychiatric disorders can be ambiguous—likewise, any boundary between disease and discomfort or dysfunction and deception. Calling something psychogenic—saying it's all in the head—may be taking the easy way out of a difficult situation.

Of course, evidence of high heritability for an abnormality is reason enough for suspecting brain abnormality. The evidence may be anything from the strictly anecdotal (the Castlereagh-Fitzroy story) to the near-definitive, in particular, the studies of adoptees. Granted, for none of the major mental disorders has research identified the "smoking gun" of abnormal DNA. It is nevertheless likely that such a gun will be found, given the findings of twin and adoption research.

Myth of MIM

The mental illness concept typically implies two assumptions about abnormal behavior. Assume a *neural* mechanism, and mental illness is mental disease. But assume a *mental* mechanism, such as debilitating inner conflict or negative self-concept—what then? Does mental illness still imply mental disease? Perhaps, but only if the inferred mental mechanism represents a discoverable brain abnormality. Otherwise it is disease only in the metaphorical sense of being *like* disease. Yet, mental illness need not be reduced to mechanism, neurological or metaphorical. Rather, it can mean dis-ease, an existential condition variously described as a state of being sick at heart, constricted, weighed down, alienated, empty, disconnected, demoralized [273; 274]. Well, some people just don't buy any of it; they reject the metaphors and even the neurological assumptions implied by conventional mental illness concepts [306; 307].

To appreciate the objection, consider two opposite views on deviant behavior conventionally identified as mental illness. The *mental disease* approach adopted in this book recognizes psychological abnormality in many kinds of deviant behavior; moreover, it seeks evidence of biological mechanism, allowing inferences about brain abnormality even from indirect evidence (high heritability). For example, a chronic pattern of moderately eccentric, delusional, and reclusive symptoms might be recognized as *schizotypal personality disorder,* that is, a heritable personality disorder of the schizophrenic kind. (People with this disorder, as well as their biological relatives, have an elevated risk for the highly heritable schizophrenic disorder.) In contrast, the *anti-mental disease* view sees little or no psychological abnormality in such deviant behavior. Moreover, this view is either indifferent or hostile to evidence of biological mechanism. In this contrarian view, so-called "mental illness" is redefined as a purely *social problem,* a problem of the pernicious mislabeling of alternative lifestyles.

A less radical anti-mental disease view can accommodate evidence that some deviant behavior *is* abnormal—dysfunctional, harmful, maladaptive—but it denies that brain abnormality is involved. Rather, it asserts that abnormal behavior arises mostly from a "sick" environment that victimizes otherwise normal people. So, without independent evidence of psychopathology, deviant behavior is not justifiably considered abnormal in this view, even with evidence of an underlying brain deviation. For example, one could accept the behavior-genetic and neurological evidence that homosexuality involves biological causality [24; 58; 199], yet still view it as an alternative lifestyle. That an intolerant society can turn homosexuality into a problem of living is another matter.

With *clearly observable* brain abnormality, the contrarians say, you have neurological disease. Otherwise, they argue, no scientific, medical, or ethical justification exists for using illness terminology to characterize unusual behavior. In other words, the invalid use of illness creates an identity (deviance equals illness) from mere resemblance of behaviors devalued by society. In this psychiatric version of the spirit made flesh, a social problem of acting sick has become a medical problem of being sick. In this transformation of metaphor into medical disease, deviance is reborn as pathology, becoming a modern myth—a *m*ental *i*llness *m*yth, or *MIM*.

Can this be so? Mental illness may be a flawed concept, but surely it is not a myth in the classic sense. For one thing, it lacks myths, fantastic qualities, and narrative structure. For another, it doesn't deal with ultimate questions, including how the world got started, the reason for traditions, and what happens after death. The idea of mental illness is neither ill-founded, uncritically held, nor unverifiable—indeed, just the opposite. It is scientific because it is testable and because it has increasingly moved us toward truths about abnormal behavior and, by extension, toward truths about normal behavior as well [86; 135]. (See the "Shadows on the Wall" Appendix note.)

Science is devoted to interesting and testable ideas, but this is only half the story. The other half is that science, in its use of metaphor and logic, is an art not entirely incompatible with mythmaking. At least initially, scientific notions may be more like guiding fictions than rational ideas. Sometimes, resonating with intuition, they have the right feel, the feel of being on the right track. Most times, they are dictated by the equations or by the data, though the implications of equations or experiments may sometimes seem inconceivable or even impossible because they require that contradictory things both be true. Einstein supposedly said that if quantum mechanics is right, then the world is crazy. "Well," says one researcher, "Einstein was right. The world *is* crazy" [159].

Science does not always involve direct evidence, something tangible revealed by X-ray or autopsy. Often, it is about testing ideas against evidence that may be fragmentary or indirect. To illustrate this important point, let's take IQ scores. A 120 on an IQ test is somewhat ambiguous, but not the *difference* between 120 and 160. People who score 160 know more, learn faster, and are "brighter" than people who score 120. Consider the prevalence of suicide. Although flawed and ambiguous, the statistic can still be useful to investigate psychological, environmental, *and even biological* causation. A 5 percent suicide prevalence may be flawed (inaccurate), and its meaning—is it "high" or low"?—may be ambiguous. Nevertheless, *differences* or *changes* in that estimate may be neither flawed nor ambiguous. A 2 percent rate is better than a 5 percent rate; a decrease from 5 to 2 percent is better than an increase from 5 to 8 percent. Even measures that are inadequate for *describing prevalence* may be more than adequate for *testing theory*, for example, the heritability of suicide liability, given elevated suicide rates in the biological, but not adoptive, relatives of suicides. The bottom line is that the inadequacy of our measurements (prevalence rates) and conceptualizations (mental illness) need not prevent us from making scientific progress in explaining important problems like abnormal behavior.

Says evolutionist Stephen Gould: "All science is intelligent inference: excessive literalism is delusion, not a humble bowing to evidence" [141]. Thus, genetic research has not uncovered "smart DNA," yet there is compelling indirect evidence that genetic differences contribute substantially to differences in measured intelligence (IQ). Of just two examples, the best known is surely twin and adoption data that point to the heritability of IQ, somewhere in the vicinity of 0.7. Less well known is the increasing evidence of brain *differences* corresponding to IQ differences [217]. Compared to their less intelligent counterparts, bright people appear to have larger, "faster," and apparently more efficient brains—larger in size measured from PET scans; faster in conduction velocity, or speed at which electrical impulses travel in the nervous system; and more efficient as evident in the reliability of discrete brain waves, or *evoked potentials*, elicited by simple sensory stimuli such as clicks or lights.

Evidence of heritable brain differences in intelligence can be ignored or denied, but to no good end, as we will see. For now, one key point is surely clear: Science is about testing inferences. Physicists don't have to see an atomic particle to infer its existence from the indirect evidence of tracks in a cloud chamber. Paleontologists don't have to see a dinosaur species—even its bones—to infer its existence from the indirect evidence of fossilized footprints. Likewise, psychopathologists don't have to see a biological abnormality—a "hole" in the brain or abnormal DNA—to infer disease from indirect evidence, such as identical-twin versus fraternal-twin concordance rates for mental illness. While no abnormal gene has yet been found for schizophrenia, manic-depression, or any of the other "big" psychiatric disorders, reliable evidence of high heritability points to such genes. In the face of such evidence, what does it mean to treat mental illnesses as myths? It means, paraphrasing geneticist Seymour Kety, believing in myths that have a strong genetic component [179].

A brain is a physical thing, a mind is no thing. Being abstract, mind has no weight—no matter. Strictly speaking, then, we can have brain disease (neurological abnormality) but not *mind* disease. What, then, about *mental* disease? People use the term "mental" to mean thinking, feeling, and behavior, that is, psychological properties of brain function, and not some vague ethereal stuff [233]. In short, mental illness means abnormalities of these psychological properties, and mental disease means brain abnormality that can explain those psychological abnormalities.

The MIM view is sometimes promoted with evidence that, just like medical illness, mental illness can be faked. Fakery has been pulled off by criminal malingerers working their insanity defense. It has even been accomplished by role-playing college students doing social psychology research. Under false pretense, normal people complaining of hallucination—voices saying "empty," "hollow," "thud"—have gained entry into mental hospitals as mental patients [265]. More dramatic was the case of Ken Bianchi, the so-called Hillside Strangler. By simulating multiple personality, he convinced some of the court-appointed psychiatrists of his insanity. But does fakability make mental illness merely a ploy, or schizophrenia or multiple personality less real? Does faking constipation or headache prove that these are bogus problems? Does a good impressionist's Nixon deny the real McCoy? Does learning to quack deny real ducks? The issue is not fakability or even laboratory simulations. Rather, the issue is how mental disorders, Nixons, ducks, and other interesting phenomena come about naturally [63].

Ironically, the MIM perspective has itself become a kind of myth—call it the myth of MIM [101; 233]. Now, like the witches of Oz, a myth can be good or bad, clarifying a truth or obscuring it. MIM is good myth in raising consciousness about the plight of psychiatric patients and the abuse of psychiatric power, given the public's frequently unsympathetic attitude, for even when sympathetic, people are unnerved by the mentally ill and relieved to be rid of them. On the other hand, MIM is bad myth when it is anti-science, that is, when it ignores or minimizes solid evidence such as the heritability of schizophrenia or manic-depression. Anti-science myth is bunk. "Bunk has its uses, though," quips biologist Peter Medawar: "It is fun sometimes to be bunkrapt." Indeed, but consider this serious point: Rejecting the argument that mental illness is a myth—even more, embracing the hypothesis that many mental illnesses indicate *disease*—need not indicate a satisfaction with medical approaches to the remediation of abnormal behavior. A closer look at the so-called medical model for treating abnormal behavior will enable us to appreciate better the conflict between the sociology of mental illness and the science of psychopathology.

16

THE BUICK STOPS HERE

If abnormal behavior is mostly a problem of living in an intolerant society, then remedial efforts are properly social, legal, and/ or political, but not medical. If abnormal behavior is fundamentally a social problem requiring the power of education and the force of law, then economic advantages in pursuing proper remediation shift from one profession (psychiatry) to others (psychology, social work, law). Clearly, it pays for professionals to battle over definitions that will preserve if not expand their domain, but to what end? In particular, what happens to the mentally ill caught up in large institutions where the psychological welfare of clients and the job satisfaction of employees or volunteers can so easily become secondary to the life of the organization?

Losing the baby with the bathwater

As a hybrid of biological science and healing art, medicine has scientific, social, and therapeutic aspects [287]. The scientific aspect is about disease and its amelioration. The social aspect is about public health policy, for example, prevention, education, and judicial questions of right to privacy and competence. The therapeutic aspect is about clinical treatment and doctor-patient relationships. Especially pertinent is the physician's power to make people endure scary or humiliating procedures. This power comes from unique sources of authority: scientific status based on knowledge about disease, moral status based on compassion of the healer, and sheer charisma, a carryover from the days when the knowledge seemed even more mysterious, and the healing function was priestlike.

If mental illness is a myth, then not much abnormal behavior is legitimately treated as medical. Yet, medicine in its psychiatric form has expanded the concept of disease (pathology) to include *mental* disease (psychopathology), which the critics think of as more metaphorical than material. Psychiatrists are physicians. They assess the symptoms of patients. They diagnose disorders based on known or suspected pathology. They use drug treatments and other therapeutic approaches. Even nonmedical professions—clinical psychology and social work, in particular—have adopted a medical model, at least the professional, if not the genetic, neurological, and pharmacological aspects.

In the MIM view, medical models in psychiatry create two problems beyond their false pretensions: false labeling and false therapy. Labeling behavior "sick" is the first step down a slippery slope to the loss of personal freedom and human dignity. Being a patient means being an invalid. Being an invalid—being psychosocially in*valid*—means being incorrect, erroneous, unacceptable. Unlike disease, mental illness is an inherent quality of the person, not something concrete and specifiable. Having no clear locus, there seems to be no obvious way to fix the problem or even to determine what its exact nature might be. Thus stigmatized, the so-called mentally ill are disliked, feared, degraded. At some point in history, being labeled "sick" might have been preferable to being labeled sinful or possessed—better an asylum than prison or the stake. Not any more, say the MIM standard bearers. Maybe not even back then, when, falsely accused by a nasty neighbor or scheming spouse, a person might be carted off to awful confinement on slimmest pretext.

In the MIM view, medical models mean inadequate treatment of real disease compounded by the inappropriate, even harmful, application of treatment for fake disease. The latter is possible on a wide scale for this important reason: the inordinate power of psychiatry reinforced by government. Government has two kinds of authority to coerce. One, police power, protects society from the antisocial individual. The other, what lawyers call *parens patriae*, is the power of a guardian to protect the immature, the mentally retarded, or the insane. Government's delegation of *parens patriae* powers is especially irksome to psychiatry's severest critics.

Too often, mental institutions are little more than awful places of incarceration where victims are intimidated, discredited, and finally, dehumanized. Maverick psychiatric professionals and former patients have even argued that psychiatry is the most abusive institution in America. Its victims are brutalized with bogus therapies, including powerful mind-altering and body-damaging drugs. Moreover, they are deprived of freedom, privacy, dignity, and civil rights. Private psychiatric hospitals are no exception to the rule of abuse of power and misuse of patients. Galvanized by the profit motive, they do inhospitable things. They keep patients longer than necessary. They deliver deficient, unjustifiable, or even dangerous treatment. They even make phoney diagnoses to fit the requirements of insurance companies rather than the facts of the case [178].

Thus it has been throughout history. Mental institutions run by psychiatrists have been instrumental in punishing people who acted differently, spoke out, owed money, or who were just plain inconvenient to a spouse or authorities. In his now classic essay, *On Liberty* (1858), philosopher John Stuart Mill noted sarcastically that when it was proposed to burn atheists, charitable people used to suggest putting them in a madhouse instead. Best known are horror stories about snake-pit institutions that warehoused the cast-off remnants of society. There, lost souls languished, naked and malnourished, in various states of amnesia, catatonia, or lunacy, wasting away in vomit, urine, and excrement. Attended, they endured the misguided if not homicidal application of crippling drugs, electric shock, or psychosurgery [248]. Less gruesome stories are told, from the usually shocking to the occasionally amusing—for example, about the twilight zone of government psychiatry, where innocent remarks and unconventional behavior are mistaken for incompetence or psychopathology. In fact, there are many stories of neglect, bungling, cruelty, but also of care and compassion. Yet how different is all this from the stories about other necessary institutions, including the political, the religious, the penal, and the military? Do we empty the jails because of the failures of the correctional system, or the hospitals because of the failures of the medical profession?

Society seems to have failed the mentally ill outside as well as inside the institutions. Starting in the 1960s, mental hospitals in the United States were depopulated from well over 500,000 inmates to about 150,000. Massive deinstitutionalization began when two important developments came together. One was the discovery of new drugs with powerful therapeutic effects. The other was a civil rights crusade in psychiatry spurred by MIM criticism. Increasingly, incarceration was permissible only for people who posed a danger to self or others—not for those who exhibited bizarre or otherwise socially offensive behavior that *might* indicate danger. With deinstitutionalization came increasing numbers of homeless people living in shelters or on the streets—perhaps as many as 400,000 nationwide.

Ironically, deinstitutionalization did as much as anything else to reinforce the misery of mental illness and the public perception of its reality [20; 104]. Anyone who walks the city streets or watches "60 Minutes" or "20/20" on American TV appreciates that a large percentage of the homeless are mentally ill. For example, 40 to 50 percent of the adult homeless of Baltimore have a severe and debilitating mental disorder, such as schizophrenia or dementia. The homeless also have markedly elevated rates of other symptoms. For example, up to 50 percent suffer from severe anxiety, while three-quarters of the men and over one-third of the women abuse drugs, mostly alcohol. Is it not gratuitous to say that they have a problem of living? Concerned observers wonder if the halfway houses or streets are really freer than institutions. Additional safeguards have been formulated, for example, to protect against involuntary and/or indefinite incarceration without psychiatric treatment and judicial review. There is even the right to refuse effective treatment. Such safeguards, however, can also prevent mentally ill persons from getting into hospitals where they can get help.

So, have we loaded the mentally ill with rights only to witness them burdened with drugs, confusion, and despair? The mentally ill are now armed with more rights than benefits. They are therefore as likely to be victimized by exclusion from, as entrapment by, the mental health system [161; 230]. Free societies must debate tough ethical questions regarding conflicts between individuals and society over rights and obligations. Is there a right to be ill, to be free even from well-intentioned applications of efficacious therapies? To what extent does freedom assume some minimal degree of competence and responsibility?

Unfortunately for the debate, being objective counts less than devotion to being philanthropic, righteous, and fair—and being philanthropic, righteous, and fair is hard to beat. How nice to counter conventional wisdom with the pronouncement that psychological dysfunction is merely an alternative lifestyle or problem of living (philanthropy). Yet, how does that square with evidence regarding mental disease or with the desirability of helping people to be happier or less disabled? How noble to condemn psychiatric authority (righteousness). Yet, does this not confound bureaucratic stupidity and willful cruelty with the inadequacies of institutions and the bungling of even well-meaning individuals? How satisfying to play down biological determination, especially the genetic kind that gives some an inherent advantage over others (fairness). Yet, how does this square with the evidence? With outright denial of mental illness, it would seem that we have what psychoanalyst Erich Fromm once described as ideology "around which one rallies and emotes. Productive research is replaced by intellectual propaganda, and the very people who pride themselves on having freed themselves from religion and dogmatism have unwittingly landed in just another denomination."

MIM criticism of psychiatry is thus a curious mix. Some of it is good, but some is not, to the extent that it denies genuine scientific, therapeutic, and humanitarian advances. Is the medical model, then, like an old Buick that once looked good but never ran right and ought now to be junked? Or is it rather like democracy, a poor, even corrupt, enterprise that nevertheless may be better than any *realistic* alternative? Perhaps, the real problem with the medical model is not application, but misapplication—the artless and overextended imposition of a *pseudo*medical model. Misapplication represents an abandonment of the basic values of openness to scientific data, commitment to the patient's benefit, concern about suffering, and valuing what works. But this is a key point: Even if the medical model were 100 percent inadequate, with caregivers incompetent, their political allies corrupt, and the people assigned diagnostic labels mere victims of a system—and even if it were all swept away in principle and practice—mental illness would remain to be explained, much of it as mental disease.

It is one thing to catalogue abuse and seek reform, quite another to argue that mental illness is more myth than hypothesis. Such arguments may be clever, even dazzling, but do they enlighten? They may stir us, but what will we feel in the long run when the evidence is out? The best bet is that they must fail because they can't make whole a political half-truth about the sociology of victims that denies the biology of behavior, that throws out the scientific baby of psychopathology with the political bathwater of mental illness. Seeking real reform requires courage and humanity. But calling mental illness a myth, evidence and common sense notwithstanding, is like the false philanthropy of the bird, described by Indian poet Tagore, who "thinks it is an act of kindness to give the fish a lift in the air [309]."

Shadow and substance

Central to the MIM argument is the contention that psychiatric patients are victims of erroneous labeling, that their behavior should not be called "illness" nor explained in terms of "disease." This serious charge is not without foundation. The mislabeling of behavior is easy to slip into when even those with the best of intentions look with limited or biased perspective. Are psychiatric patients, then, the victims of false labeling? One person's truth in labeling is not necessarily another's. Surely evidence, not mere argumentation, should be the final arbiter of truth. That is why a scientific rather than dogmatic approach is essential, as we will see in the next chapter. For now, consider more closely the question of erroneous labeling.

In medicine and psychiatry, the term *positive* means something undesirable as detected by a test—the AIDS HIV antibody detected by a blood test, for example. A *false positive* is a false alarm, for example, diagnosing a normal person schizophrenic. With very strict criteria, we can minimize such errors, but at the risk of making the opposite error. A *false negative*, or miss, is a failure to recognize illness, for example, calling a schizophrenic person normal. Neither type of error, *per se*, is worse than the other. It all depends on what you are trying to do. Which would be worse: falsely detecting, or failing to detect, the potential, say, to perform well at a job requiring special skills—or to commit suicide?

Denying evidence of mental disease because we hate how psychiatric professionals have treated mental patients can mean missing the significance of symptoms, especially mild ones that seem innocent enough. Mild depressions are common. Usually, they are nothing at all, like innocuous coughs or harmless moles. Yet we have seen that they may be early warning signs, weak expressions of a serious yet undisclosed disease such as manic-depression, Alzheimer's, brain tumor, or diabetes. Recall how colleagues misdiagnosed Castlereagh's suicidal depression as a symptom of overwork.

Up to twice as many psychiatric patients as normals have discoverable, even treatable, medical diseases [325]. Anxiety, depression, and psychosis can be aggravated, even caused, by diseases such as diabetes, hypertension, and arthritis [145]. Yet, many diseases go undetected, sometimes by physicians who refer patients for psychological treatment. For example, a patient was initially diagnosed with depressive disorder based on classic symptoms involving mood, sleep, energy, appetite, and thinking. She had been in psychotherapy and was taking antidepressant medication with which she had tried to kill herself by overdosing. Careful examination revealed hypothyroidism, a disease of the thyroid gland that causes hormone deficiency. During thyroid-replacement therapy, her depression gradually disappeared [127]. Sometimes a psychiatric disorder comes from too much rather than too little thyroid. Hyperthyroidism can cause nervousness, anxiety, and many physical symptoms, including fatigue, rapid heartbeat, breathing difficulties, and weakness. Severe untreated cases may include psychosis, manic-depressive mood swings, even dementia.

The question is simply this: How many troubled people have a medical problem that makes them seek psychiatric counseling for depression or some other emotional problem? How often does that treatment wind up focusing on character or upbringing? In the old days, people with obsessions and compulsions were treated as survivors of infantile trauma associated with their toilet training. Likewise, people with narcolepsy, a disorder of excessive sleepiness and sleep attacks, were treated as having a character deficiency. The fact is, toilet training has no causal connection to obsessive-compulsive disorder, and character flaws do not explain narcolepsy. Yet how many other false theories are still applied to the symptoms of disease? For example, women have been misdiagnosed as "hysterics" for complaining about what, in fact, is *microvascular angina*, pain caused by abnormally small arteries of the heart [22; 249].

CAT Scan: Normal   CAT Scan: Alzheimer's Dementia

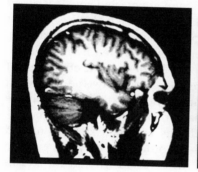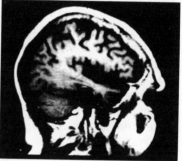

About 40 percent of people with Alzheimer's disease are depressed, half of them with a diagnosable disorder, no doubt misleading when the more fundamental (and lethal) disease is missed [338]. The computer-assisted X-rays, or CAT scans, shown here illustrate this point. Each gives an inside view: the one on the left is of a normal brain, the abnormal one on the right was taken from a patient with Alzheimer's disease who nevertheless was initially diagnosed with depressive disorder. Note the loss of tissue (dark fissures and other areas), giving the shrunken brain a prunelike quality. The simple point is that psychiatric labeling can be wrong in fabricating pathology, but also in denying it.

Genetic bogeyman

Denial of biological causality extends beyond brain and body to the more remote plane of genetic blueprints. It's not so much

266 / THE BUICK STOPS HERE

the denial that genes play a role in anomalous dysfunctions, special talents, or genius, for who would argue that Down's syndrome is not genetic, or that genius like Mozart's is the product of good mothering or excellent schools? No, it is more a denial that genetic differences explain psychological differences in the vast middle range of intelligence and liabilities. Such denial can make otherwise perfectly sensible, even brilliant people say things that may seem right but are just plain wrong.

Heritability is a major bogeyman of MIM mythology, which puts the MIM position at odds with what most people appreciate, deep down, anyway—that human differences are substantially heritable. The phrase "all men are created equal" is about equity, not equality; it is a legal principle of equal protection, not a biological principle of equal physiology—the truth of which is epitomized in the pithy comment once offered by mathematician Leo Szilard: "I'm all in favor of the democratic principle that one idiot is as good as one genius, but I draw the line when someone takes the next step and concludes that two idiots are better than one genius." The sentiment behind this comment is reiterated by geneticist Theodosius Dobzhansky who opined that "all men should be equal—in order that they can grow to be different"; and by Will and Ariel Durant who, in *The Lessons of History*, concluded that there is great danger of tyranny in denying human inequalities. Nature, they say, ignores the egalitarian sentiments expressed in documents such as the American Declaration of Independence and the French Revolutionary Declaration of the Rights of Man. Rather, Nature dictates that "we are all born unfree and unequal: subject to our physical and psychological heredity . . . diversely endowed in health and strength, in mental capacity and qualities of character." Except in our utopias, the Durants continue, equality and freedom are opposed, such that where one flourishes, the other must fade. "Leave men free, and their natural inequalities will multiply . . . only the man who is below average in economic ability desires equality; those who are conscious of superior ability desire freedom. . . . Utopias of equality are biologically doomed, and the best that the amiable philosopher can hope for is an approximate equality of legal justice and educational opportunity" [90].

For standard-bearers of MIM, the wonderland of evidence must seem curiouser and curiouser. How odd that genetically identical people reared apart are remarkably alike while genetically unrelated people reared together are remarkably unalike. Is this not stunning *scientific* evidence of what psychologists have called self-actualization—that becoming a person(ality) involves the ripening of unique genetic potential? What better antidote to antihereditarian social theorizing? And yet, the antidote often fails to take hold because its concepts and causal mechanisms are not (a) *tangible*—capable of being seen, imagined, felt; (b) *personal*—relevant to the self; (c) *social*—involving familiar characters of family and community easily caste in stories of good guys and bad, perpetrators and victims; (d) *remediable*—capable of being understood as an educational problem to be solved socially. Lacking these personally satisfying qualities, genetic explanations are at a disadvantage.

Just as heritability implies something neurological, heritable abnormality implies the possibility of mental disease. Yet this logic, like the evidence, may be resisted—for one thing, because heritability seems vaguely reprehensible. One feels that since racists use genetic explanations people who invoke genetic explanations are playing a dangerous, racist game. At best, heritability suggests that life is a stacked deck or an uneven playing field. Worse, it seems to saddle some people with disadvantages that can't be overcome. In short, there is a nastiness about heritability that gives nice folks pause.

Heritability also seems exculpatory, used to excuse the irresponsible, incompetent, or antisocial acts of people who may seem irrational but surely know what they are up to. Well, not necessarily. True, a person with a heritable tendency to be irritable and impulsive does have a tougher time, but with the exception of unusual cases involving clear-cut insanity or incompetence, a person can be held responsible for personal behavior. With constant vigilance and heroic effort, even the toughest challenges from within—the compulsions, addictions, impulses, delusions of mental illness—can be mastered to varying degrees. Heredity may thus be a matter of courage as much as selfishness. With mental illness, it complicates—it does not beg—questions regarding the cause and culpability of actions.

In the MIM view, people who seem irrational and therefore not culpable are actually rational in pursuing their own objectives. It therefore follows that they ought to be held to the same standards as everyone else. In short, a bogus condition ought not to be invoked as a defense in criminal cases. Granted, mental illness rarely excuses criminal behavior since, in most cases, it little affects knowledge of right and wrong. Even most psychotics are legally sane, with a capacity to appreciate a criminal act or its consequences. Courts nowadays rarely absolve a person because of mental illness, mitigating though it may be. While mental illness complicates the problem of assessing intent, comprehension, and therefore responsibility for an antisocial lifestyle or criminal behavior, the insanity defense comes up in less than 1 percent of cases and is successful in only a fraction of these, perhaps no more than 25 percent. Moreover, in such cases, incarceration is often longer, and subsequent offenses less likely than with comparable crimes not involving an insanity plea [60; 261].

Heritability seems too arbitrary, implying that we are merely outcomes of chance and fate—chance from the roll of genetic dice, fate from the determinate influence of the resulting genetic blueprint. If chance and fate make victims of the mentally ill, it is better to think of them as victims of external circumstances. At least these are changeable through education and politics, or so it would seem. Heritability also seems to dehumanize, reducing individual differences to something mechanical and statistical. It seems forever bound up with probabilities, concordance rates, population rates, and maybe worse, biological mechanisms that seem to require special scientific sophistication to comprehend.

With questions of rearing and the social environment, just about anyone—any good storyteller—can be a theorist; with biological mechanisms, most people feel theoretically disenfranchised, excluded from the explanation game. Images of patients victimized by physicians or children traumatized by parents compel our attention and are remembered because they are concrete and, sadly, because they are often true. Moreover, they are good stories, having villains, victims, heroes, and manifest cause-effect connections; they appeal to our deepest storyteller instinct. Against these stories, how can heritability—or any scientific concept—compete? The often remote and lifeless data and concepts of science simply promote a glazing of the eyes.

And yet, to those of us who are even remotely familiar with

the evidence, the biological basis of the human spirit becomes increasingly evident, meaningful—*even comforting*. Mrs. Meant-Well must have been comforted by advice columnist Ann Landers' ringing defense of decent, well-meaning parents. You know them—trashed by outrageous fortune and freighted with guilt about outcomes for which they may have little or no personal responsibility. In responding to the letter of an evidently distraught and frustrated parent, the columnist wrote: "I have come to believe in the genetic factor which has been ignored by many behavioral 'experts' " [195]. But the genetic factor tends to get lost or diluted in social theorizing about human behavior and educational rhetoric about children. For example, the celebratory declaration that all kids are gifted and talented is a triviality, for what creature great or small is not in some sense "gifted and talented"? To use the same words for the touching efforts of the mentally retarded and the timeless creations of the genius sabotages meaning and insults intelligence; it is the moral equivalent of equating the speech of parrots and people.

Two things are wrong with this misuse of language, one having to do with how words are used to construe meaning, the other with how they are used to promote ideology. With respect to language and meaning, physicist and cosmologist Steven Weinberg in *Dreams of a Final Theory* warns that "we ought to respect the way that [words] have been used historically, and we ought especially to preserve distinctions that prevent the meanings of words from merging with the meanings of other words" [321]. With respect to ideology, social critic Allan Bloom warns that the misuse of language is an anti-elitist smoke screen of false philanthropy whereby language is corrupted and concepts trivialized in the effort to promote some social agenda. "Words that were meant to describe and encourage Beethoven and Goethe are now applied to every schoolchild. It is in the nature of democracy to deny no one access to good things. If those things are not really accessible to all, then the tendency is to deny the fact—simply to proclaim, for example, that what is not art *is* art" [37]—likewise, to proclaim what is not myth *is* myth.

Anti-hereditarian rhetoric tends to muddle vital distinctions, for example, between-group and individual differences, and social and nonsocial environmental influences. Criticism of the twin/adoption research on heritability—like criticism of the medical treatment of mental disease—sometimes seems less motivated by an interest in better methods to uncover the facts of mental illness than in an effort to strengthen ideology. At worst, it gives the impression of masking a suspicion that genetic differences *do* contribute to individual and group differences, including liability to mental illness. (See the Appendix note, "Coming to Terms with the Genetic Bogeyman.")

Some people find MIM arguments delightfully counterintuitive and fashionably counter-cultural. Others consider them more like what one observer called "fiction that thinks it's sleek and fashionable when it's really just dangerously thin" [264]. Mostly antiscientific siren song, MIM arguments work by preying on our subjectivity and lack of information. Calling mental illness a myth is provocative, no doubt, yet even dazzling arguments can obscure the simplest truths. The mental illness concept is not false because it has promoted cruel and stupid behavior. Psychiatric abuse is real, and the plight of patients is serious indeed. But these melancholy facts of life say more about the abuse of people, mentally ill or not, than about the reality of the mental illness. And the reality of mental illness is less a matter of ideology than scientific inquiry. But what does that mean?

17

GREAT OCEAN OF TRUTH

How, then, shall we proceed with the toughest questions about ourselves and the causes of our behavior? Novelist John Irving says, "It's a no-win argument—that business of what we are born with and what our environment does to us. And it's a boring argument, because it simplifies the mysteries that attend both our birth and our growth" [160]. He is completely right in the sense that the argument is *statistical*, applying to the general rather than to the individual and thus oversimplifying human experience, making it less real, less poignant. Moreover, Irving is even mostly right when the usual evidence comes from correlational studies that confound cause and effect, nature and nurture. With correlations and their attendant ambiguities, there is always room for uncertainty, misunderstanding, and the ideological arguments that feed on both. Nevertheless, Irving is dead wrong on at least one account. With twins and adoptees, we *can* move beyond sterile debate to estimate how much nature and nurture matter. We *can* turn otherwise no-win arguments into testable hypotheses and objective explanations—if we have what it takes.

What if 'tweren't brillig?

What it takes is science-mindedness, a special combination of analytical, intuitive, and skeptical attitudes. Science-mind-

edness means always being on the lookout for a better explanation, always asking how *else* something might be, which means
expecting that one's ideas are likely to prove wrong. That is the
reason for paying attention to "off-diagonal" events that fail to
fit expectations. Science-mindedness is thus a critical, but also
creative, facility for discovering connections in things that seem
unconnected. It is both a willingness to speculate about hypothetical mechanisms, but more, an ability to come up with ways
to test their validity.

In this search beyond the horizon and beneath the surface
of appearances—in this going beyond the information given, as
psychologist Jerome Bruner put it—lies a strong intellectual element that may seem alien to many people, but need not be.
Science-mindedness is, after all, common sense at its best, a
mixture of accurate observation and merciless logic. But more,
science-mindedness can be thought of as one of many expressions of a storyteller instinct that we all share. Granted, it is an
especially responsible and creative expression—responsible in
the sense of being constrained by skepticism and objective evidence, creative in the sense of producing novel, even beautiful
ideas. It is therefore the best antidote to irrationality and ideology that we have, whether we are scientists or laymen.

For now, consider the combative element of science-mindedness as expressed in the disposition to analyze critically and
to suspect the worst. Breaking things down to see if they survive close scrutiny means transcending two powerful tendencies—really two sides of a self-centered coin. One is the
tendency to accept that which is self-serving, whatever the truth
of the matter. The other is to reject what is alien—as if being true
to yourself requires resisting everything else. As physiologist
Wilfred Trotter noted: "The mind likes a strange idea as little as
the body likes a strange protein and resists it with similar
energy. . . . If we watch ourselves honestly we shall often find
that we have begun to argue against a new idea even before it
has been completely stated."

This conservatism—call it the parochial side of human
nature—aims for sameness and safety while promoting intoler-
ance of change. The adventurous side—call it Pandoran—is
curiosity and willingness to experiment, at least to question conventional wisdom. The parochial side has always lived in ambiv-

alent association with the Pandoran, sensing that forbidden knowledge can bring only sadness and despair. This natural apprehension is part of our cultural tradition. The Garden of Eden story, for example, is about the melancholy effects of curiosity—lost innocence and security. Today we recognize it as the cost of at least trying to satisfy a hunger for the fruits of a deeper knowledge—of process and causation—beyond mere labels we attach to things. Yet curiosity, the Pandoran element of our nature, forever persists, beginning spontaneously in childhood with endless dreaming and asking, "Why?" and continuing into adulthood with the combative "yeah, but" and the creative "what if?"

For over 100 years we have delighted in Lewis Carroll's neologistic poem, "Jabberwocky." We have accepted that " 'twas brillig and the slithy toves did gyre and gimble in the wabe," but did we ever wonder, well, what if 'tweren't brillig? What would the slithy toves do, then? Would they become less slithy, or slithy in less obvious ways? Would they revert to their recognizable slithiness when conditions once again became more brillig? Perhaps they would be as slithy as ever regardless of brilligness. In other words, we tend to accept rather than question what we've always known, especially if it makes sense or at least pleases us. But the problem is obvious: What if what we assume to be true isn't? We assume that rearing explains the development of this or that characteristic, but what if that's incorrect or at best, a half-truth? What if, for example, as evidence suggests, the quality of rearing has nothing to do with the risk of becoming a manic-depressive, a schizophrenic, a psychopath? That is, what if the important thing were not the suboptimal rearing you can see, but a genetic factor you can't see?

Where genetic differences make all the difference, how can identical twins ever be discordant? We asked and answered this question almost at the outset (Chapter 2), but consider the question in its proper historical context. Margot Fischer's was the classic study of identical twins discordant for schizophrenia [105]. Turning the tables, she thought of identical-twin discordance not as an end of the trail for the genetic hypothesis, but a beginning of the road. Specifically, she shifted attention from the twins to their offspring. She discovered that the offspring of the seemingly normal twins and the offspring of their manifestly ill co-twins had the same elevated rates of disorder. In other words, schizophrenia is highly heritable, manic-depression perhaps even more so, but as a genetically transmittable liability that need not show up in manifestly abnormal behavior. Fischer had gone past the cover to the pages of the book, beyond what is obvious to what is not. The key to origins of mental illness might lie hidden beyond the light shed by illness behavior and by conventional wisdom on concordance rates. It seems Fischer was able to see things in a different light.

The truth in the falsifiable

Science-mindedness involves the familiar instinct of curiosity but also a somewhat alien principle that even beautiful theories should succumb to ugly facts (T. H. Huxley)—that we "get a clearer perception and livelier impression of truth produced by its collision with error" (J. S. Mill). We may be embarrassed by the errors we commit, but they are vehicles to carry us to knowledge and truth. Perhaps, then, the idea of learning through mistakes is not so alien, for isn't falling down the way we all began our learning as toddlers—from the ground up, as it were?

Scientific development has sometimes taken advantage of the detailed observations and know-how of devoted investigators with honestly held but erroneous theories—even of super-scientists including Newton and Kepler who dabbled in alchemy or mystical theorizing. The work of alchemists, astrologers, and phrenologists once provided a rich source of information for the sciences of chemistry, astronomy, and neurology. Likewise, the writings of MIM mythologists have galvanized psychopathologists to clarify a scientifically defensible concept of mental illness.

Here's an example of how an erroneous theory nevertheless promoted scientific discovery. During the late 1940s, Australian psychiatrist John Cade theorized that mania is caused by a toxic substance excreted in urine. Accordingly, he experimented on guinea pigs with samples of concentrated urine from manics, schizophrenics, and others. The samples had similar toxic effects, though somewhat greater for the manic sample. Cade suspected urea, a major constituent of urine, but the three samples did not differ in this substance. He then noted that urea's toxicity is reduced by creatine (a crystalline nitrogenous substance), yet once again, the three samples did not differ. A lesser man might have dropped the matter, but Cade pressed on. Perhaps, he thought, manic illness occurs when creatine's normally protective effect is diminished by yet another factor—maybe uric acid. To make it soluble for injections, he mixed uric acid with the relatively light metal, lithium. The resulting salt, lithium urate, had the unexpected effect of *reducing* urea's toxicity and more, it sedated the animals. The effectiveness of another salt, lithium carbonate, proved that, indeed, the key ingredient was lithium. Cade tried lithium carbonate on himself with no major effect, then on manics with great success. The rest, as they say, is history, with a false theory leading the way to a true treatment.

True or false, a scientific idea is not just opinion or hunch, though it may start out that way. Rather, it must be *falsifiable*— not necessarily false, but if false, capable of being disproved. Susceptibility to disproof is enshrined in the *principle of falsifiability*. The cliché "They're just theories" is therefore inappropriate when applied to theories that are falsifiable or sustained by the verification of their predictions [296]. We can treat falsifiability as a moral principle to be embraced by *anyone*, layman or professional, with healthy skepticism, but also with a willingness to be proven wrong.

Darwin admitted that all of his initially good ideas were reformed or abandoned. Chemist Sir Humphrey Davy once admitted that his most important discoveries arose out of earlier failures. "The world little knows," said physicist Michael Faraday, "how many of the thoughts and theories which have passed through the mind of a scientific investigator have been crushed in silence and secrecy by his own severe criticism and adverse examinations; that in the most successful instances not a tenth of the suggestions, the hopes, the wishes, the preliminary conclusions have been realized." In a sense, then, the evolution of scientific ideas is like the evolution of species. A few survive, but most are dead ends that, like fossils in geological strata, are preserved in the historical record. The aim of science, according to philosopher Karl Popper, "is not to save the lives of untenable [ideas] but, on the contrary, to select the one which is by comparison the fittest, by exposing them all to the fiercest struggle for survival" [252]. An obvious example is the survival of a strong genetic hypothesis put through nontrivial tests, the most spectacular of which involve comparing the resemblance of genetically identical siblings reared apart with that of genetically unrelated siblings reared together. Despite the flaws of any one study, collectively they have come close to falsifying definitively a popular assumption about the paramount influence of rearing.

Like moral sensitivity or artistic sensibility, science-mindedness is one of many attitudes that make experience meaningful. Exclusive devotion to the principle of falsifiability will work best with some problems addressed in some contexts, for example, questions of mechanism tested in the laboratory. It will do less well with—it may be positively destructive to—other problems addressed in other contexts, for example, questions of meaning and value. Social critic Jacques Barzun drives home the point. "No scientist could survive half an hour outside his laboratory if he tried to apply his habitual tests to his common experiences—analyzing, measuring, questioning such things as his neighbor's truthfulness, his tradesman's honesty, his wife's fidelity" [27].

In the competitive day-to-day world of science, devotion to falsifying erroneous ideas is probably like devotion to God, with good intentions outnumbering good deeds. Scientists have clay feet just like everybody else; they are vulnerable, egocentric, materialistic, personally biased. Reluctant to consider that their ideas may be simple-minded and probably wrong, some use tests that favor rather than threaten their theory. But at the same time, a lot of time is spent applying the principle of falsifiability to the *other* guy's ideas. Since those other guys have the same intention, there is plenty of scrutiny, skepticism, and error correction to make the enterprise work.

Fearful of being scooped or not funded, scientists may lose sight of principle, focusing on what's fashionable or profitable and cutting corners in a mad rush to produce and publish. Moreover, the idea that they must identify and admit their errors can be forgotten when scientific questions become political issues. The idealized view of science is clearly contradicted by the all-too-human tendencies of professional scientists to resist new, innovative ideas while tolerating mediocre work

[27]. Then there is that darkest side to the enterprise, the moral equivalent of sinning against the First Commandment: cooking or completely faking the numbers [156]. Nevertheless, the principle of falsifiability usually prevails, and the fakery of liars, self-promoters, and ideologues is eventually discovered.

The scientific community thus differs from political and religious communities in relying on logic and evidence more than deception and coercion. In this view, science-mindedness is really quite noble. It represents freedom—the freedom to question, to explore, to make mistakes. With this freedom comes responsibility to tell the truth. Freedom is the hallmark of civilized society based on tolerance, and this means that, in theory anyway, the scientific community is held together by a power of virtue [201]. In a word, adopting the principle of falsifiability reflects a special kind of *con*science, an ability to transcend naive credulity, irrationality, and self-serving prejudice. Here, then, in science-mindedness, is something truly unique to humans, for what other creature, including those with language and a sense of humor, is able to cast doubt on its own abstractions?

Having our cake and eating it too

Suspicious of insensate abstraction and dispassionate analysis, most people nevertheless have trouble getting beyond the off-putting sense that science is just plain elitist. Of course, the objection is to a *certain kind* of elitism. After all, we appreciate the kind that serves our interests and is not thrown in our face. We have no problem with the elitism of athletics, says sociobiologist Edward O. Wilson, because athletes are the incarnations of our ideal self, serving as heroic representatives in the universal and eternal conflict of self (us) against non-self (them). In the clash of athletes and in the excitement of slogans, banners, and ideologies, spectators instinctively sense tribal struggle, anticipate the thrill of beating the hell out of those other guys [333].

It is different when it comes to the intellectual elitism that fails to flatter the ego or stimulate the id. Alienation from disciplined mental work is more than indifference. It is, says Barzun, an active, instinctive, sentiment that, sensing intellect as the enemy of life, requires that the bright and knowledgeable kid, like any "deviant," be treated mercilessly by his happily ordinary fellows. The antipathy stems from a deep-rooted suspicion that, free of vigorous action and practical results, the life of the mind is no life at all. Who but a scientist can appreciate the comment of an ancient Greek philosopher indicating that he would rather discover a single causal connection than win the throne of Persia, or the comment of a contemporary scientist: "It seems to me that, just as the Church did in former times, science offers a safe niche where you can spend a quiet life classifying spiders, away from . . . the world of telegrams and anger" [247].

There is another element of the anti-elitism directed toward science-mindedness, something Historian W. J. Cash in *The Mind of the South* describes as a kind of swashbuckling primitivity. In his view, the average guy "is a child-man [in whom] that primitive stuff of humanity lies very close to the surface . . . he likes naively to play, to expand his ego, his senses, his emotions . . . he will prefer the extravagant, the flashing, and the brightly colored—in a word . . . he displays the whole catalogue of qualities we mean by romanticism and hedonism." Such a person will surely not bother with theoretical and abstract aspects of knowledge. Do we not recognize a stamp of something universal, a simian preference for the palpable over the intangible, the cunning and clever over the conscientious and intellective? It is one thing to admire the stunning achievements of science that bring power, comfort, and excitement. It is quite another to appreciate the *process* of science-mindedness that need not be directed at anything of practical or emotional significance.

No wonder science-mindedness for popular consumption usually requires some sort of transformation to make it palatable. In one such transformation, the process of science-mindedness is de-emphasized in favor of the activities of the scientist (Jacques Cousteau) and the results and products of investigation (Thomas Edison); here is science-mindedness with a human face and an evident use. In a different transformation, the process of science-mindedness remains the focus, but as a caricature designed to reinforce the human element—for example, *Star Trek*'s Spock, who is admired for his computer-like brilliance but cared about for his repressed human side, his tragic flaw. Too often, caricatures of science-mindedness are negative, as evident in legions of bespectacled eggheads, absent-minded professors, and mad scientists that populate movies and TV.

Roughly 20 percent of TV scientists commit felonies, suggesting that, along with corporate executives and lawyers, scientists are the most dangerous group in TV land [114]. Silly or sanguinary, such cheap caricatures hardly represent the real thing. Rather, they express an ambivalent mix of envy, apprehension, and alienation.

Moreover, science-mindedness has always seemed alien when associated with discoveries that have threatened people's sense of place and purpose, and their illusions of innocence, freedom, immortality, and grace. Copernican science replaced a self-evident geocentric universe with the alien image of an insignificant planet careening through mostly empty universe. With Newtonian science, heaven and humanity lost metaphysical luster and became just so much machinery. The Einsteinian era brought relativity and quantum theory, which eroded the illusion of a self-evident Newtonian world, the basics being probabilistic, uncertain, and ultimately unknowable. As the physical world yielded up its secrets, humans became less central in the ultimate scheme of things. Personal imagery was giving way to theories, pointing to what Weinberg calls "chilling impersonality in the laws of nature." All this while the post-Freudian revolution was overturning illusions about our rationality and conscious self-determination.

People therefore may sense science-mindedness to be a not entirely happy step beyond the objectivity of adulthood that is itself a step beyond an earlier, more subjective stage. For some, it is a melancholy development, this exchange of a toy land of pre-logical experience for more logical terrain, diminishing as it does our ability to experience the world with the immediacy and intensity that came to us easily during the "magic years" of our childhood [111]. In *The World in the Evening*, novelist Christopher Isherwood speaks wistfully of a window with a multicolored design of grapes and leaves through which he would peer as a child. He muses about "changing the scene, at will, from colour-mood to colour-mood and experiencing the pure pleasure of sensations that need no analysis. . . . How had red felt, at the age of four? What had blue meant? Why was yellow? Perhaps if I could somehow know that, now, I should understand everything else that had happened to me in the interval. But I should never know. The whole organ of cognition had changed, and I had nothing left to know with. If I looked through that window now, I should see nothing but a lot of adjectives."

Adult reason and spirituality transcend the child-eye view. Likewise, science-mindedness, as other high-minded intellectual capacities, transcends adult mentality. We gain much with each transcendence, yet loss also sometimes seems evident, perhaps more so with science-mindedness than with esthetic-mindedness or other sophisticated ways of thinking. Consider, for example, the near-death experience of being in a tunnel with light-suffused loved ones, angelic chaperones, and religious personages. It is meaningful, but can it be satisfying to characterize this compelling experience as merely the hallucinatory effect of aberrant neural activity in a dying brain? The application of science-mindedness to human experience has surely yielded a lot, but not without a lingering sense that, as Wordsworth wrote, "there hath passed away a glory from the earth."

There is, then, a feeling in some that science-mindedness distorts, even sabotages, human experience—like "a basilisk which kills what it sees," as C. S. Lewis put it. Yet hear the counterargument. Science-mindedness has intellectual, but also intuitive, esthetic, passionate—even spiritual—facets. A synonymy of truth and beauty is felt by many philosophers and poets, but by many scientists too [62]. "Beauty is truth, truth beauty," wrote Keats in a poetic evocation of Plato's idea that we delight in the beauty *and sense of inevitability* that comes with truthful recognition—cognition that recreates through the medium of personal consciousness what the human soul instinctively knows.

No wonder scientists sometimes admit to applying to their equations and theories not just the objective criteria of falsifiability, but the *esthetic* criteria of simplicity and harmony, and the subjective criteria of beguilement and awe. Thus, while they are like most people with an ability to appreciate things the old-fashioned way, scientists are nevertheless unlike most people in one important way: They can discover new meaning, beauty, and spirituality in technical and mathematical abstractions that leave the rest of us cold; they can thrill as much to a mathematical equation as to a Mozart symphony. Physiologist and anthropologist Jared Diamond has likened doing jungle anthropology to experiencing Bach's choral prelude for organ on the Lord's

Prayer. For him, the complexity of the rhythms, voices, and themes is, in a way, God's voice in the luxuriant complexity of nature. Not exactly what you'd expect a scientist to say, but there it is. And listen to Nobel Prize-winning ethologist Konrad Lorenz who, in *On Aggression*, says: "The rainbow is no less beautiful because we have learned to understand the laws of light refraction to which it owes its existence, and the beauty and symmetry of design, color, and movement in our fishes must excite our admiration even more when we know that their purpose is preservation of the species that they adorn." Maybe we can really have our cake and eat it too—the beauty and mystery of things along with their analysis.

Playing at work

Science-mindedness is creative, which means that it is intuitive, affective, and fun. The scientist takes much pleasure discovering nature's hidden potentials [55; 262]. The objective is to see connections in diversity, and to transform the complex and ambiguous into meaningful and beautiful form—to discover in theory the truth of the matter. And in this process, Louis Pasteur said, chance favors the prepared mind to transform observations and imaginative insights into testable hypotheses. A mind is prepared by intuition and instruction. Intuition comes from personal experience inspired and shaped by the genetic blueprint; intuition leads to a discovery of evidence. Instruction comes through tutelage and other forms of formal education; instruction is an imposition of evidence.

For the trained scientist, tutelage and experience yield a more formal kind of preparedness, the knowledge of theory and data that serves as foundation for what comes next. Newton's work on universal gravity represented and extended earlier and extant notions, in particular the inverse square law regarding the effect of distance on the gravitational attraction of two bodies. Darwin's evolutionary theory evolved out of similar if not identical notions about how speciation arises, including natural selection. Freud's psychoanalytic theory was a synthesis of psychiatric concepts often misattributed to him—including unconscious thought, infantile sexuality, childhood trauma, and repressed frustration. The Watson-Crick double helix model

282 / GREAT OCEAN OF TRUTH

represented a restructuring of then-current ideas about DNA.

In effect, there is an interconnected and progressive quality to scientific knowledge. Nevertheless, there is the other side of scientific progress, where more chaos and therefore less predictability are the rule. It is progress through flashes of insight, shifts of perspective, whole-cloth invention, sheer serendipity. Serendipity refers to discoveries based on accident exploited by sagacity, though it is the accident part that usually sticks in people's imagination. Serendipity can be a lucky event, sometimes coming from mistakes, screw-ups, misunderstandings—a light left on, a flame not turned down, a glass jar left opened [165].

Occasionally, a lucky finding appears, whole cloth as it were. James Wright was a General Electric engineer researching synthetic rubber during World War II. For some reason, he combined boric acid and silicone oil. Result: Goofy stuff that bounced—no good for truck tires, and no good to anyone in or outside the scientific community. No good, that is, until the early 1950s when, marketed in egg-shaped containers, it became Silly Putty. More typically, the lucky finding does not simply appear ready-formed. It may not even be so much a finding as a lead. The meaning of this lead may have to be *discovered* by a mind prepared to recognize and exploit something others have ignored or misunderstood.

There are many interesting stories of how, quite serendipitously, researchers discovered antidepressant, antipsychotic, and other biological treatments for mental illness. Back in the late 1940s, for example, psychiatric researchers discovered the tranquilizing side effects of weak or otherwise unmarketable antihistamines. Thus, out of research to develop antihistamines came the serendipitous discovery of major tranquilizers such as chlorpromazine (Thorazine) that revolutionized psychiatric treatment in the 1950s. For the prepared mind, anything can be a source of discovery and delight. One investigator's dross—a bad idea, a side effect—turns out to be another's gold. It takes something special to recognize the gold because, like the panned variety, it is easily overlooked for lacking luster. Sometimes, however, even those who have that something special don't have it in every instance. The great nineteenth-century microbiologist Alexander Fleming followed up on a chance observation. The activity of a colony of staphylococcus bacteria had become blocked by an impurity inadvertently allowed to contaminate the culture. So it was that Fleming discovered penicillin, but someone else was to discover its therapeutic value.

Science-mindedness means continuous improvement of what is known, but also discontinuous improvement through sudden, unexpected discoveries of connections between previously unconnected observations. It is the latter that Steven Weinberg attributes to the greatest scientists when they play the role of *magician* rather than *sage*—magician whose deep insight comes in a flash, compared to the sage whose conclusions come through orderly thinking that follows known principles. Whether through chance or magic, the effect is zig-zaggy more than smooth progression. Our instinctive capacity for flashes of insight can be appreciated by seeing apes suddenly realize that one thing can be taken for something else. A branch sticking out of a tree can be broken off and used to retrieve food just out of reach. Such apish versions of necessity as mother of invention suggest something important. Much of our creative thinking, as with the more pedestrian kind, is done unconsciously and nonverbally, then presented, whole cloth as it were, for systematic and orderly evaluation and revision, after the fact.

The scientific mind is prepared by mastering prior knowledge, and by having an intuitive feel and facility for the essence of certain things. This facility is often manifested with a flash of insight in the imagery of fantasy and dreams. Intuitive facility is surely mysterious, but perhaps less so when we can recognize it in something mundane, for example, the common yet miraculous language-learning capability displayed by children. That it is instinctive is evident right from the beginning. The biased head turning of infants indicates a natural preference for linguistic over other sounds. All two-year-olds exercise a special readiness to solve linguistic problems presented by speech sounds that would otherwise be mere noise. This readiness enables us to learn incredibly quickly despite the subtlety and complexity of language. It makes us attend to or seek out information to which we are attuned. It is species knowledge—what Socrates would have called soul—that in each of us becomes personal competence.

Giftedness is then a mere exaggeration of, and devotion to, what the rest of us do more modestly in discovering and mastering the world (adaptation) and in becoming unique persons (self-actualization). Those gifted in language have what some might consider more than their fair share of the human readiness. So it is with poets, artists, philosophers, scientists, and some of the rest of us. Genius is an uncanny ability to cut through distracting appearances to objective reality and to psychological truth. Perhaps it is like a neuropsychological master key that fits the reciprocal shape of things out there. Like Mozart with the music of the sensual world, Einstein was in tune with the mathematics of the physical world, so much so that his intuitions, eventually confirmed, outpaced the evidence of the day [251].

Great scientists sometimes seem to proceed on the right path despite seeming evidence that they are wrong; they *know* they are right, and they stick to their guns [185]. Ironically, this attitude makes them somewhat insensitive to the principle of falsifiability. Here is a vision of the great scientist as artist and seer— likewise the great mathematician whose work is later recognized by physicists as a beautiful embodiment in theory of some deep aspect of the real world, beautiful in the sense of being both valid and "perfect" [321]. Less divine mortals must rely on a more sobering mixture of inspiration and falsification. In contrast, the gifted scientist seems able to feel and articulate the truth of the matter. Exalted ability to get to the heart of a problem is probably characteristic of artists, mechanics, poets, musicians, athletes, and physicians—psychologists too, but only those few with an uncanny gift for insight into the darkest regions of mental life [157].

Science-mindedness means being prepared by education and personal experience. It means having a feel for and devotion to problem solving in an area intuitively appreciated. It also means being *playful*. What else would you call the germ painting of Sir Alexander Fleming? A veritable Matisse of microbes, Fleming placed different-colored microorganisms on a petri dish, then "painted" them by manipulating temperature, pH, antibacterial agents, and the like [262]. It's not that others couldn't do this. It's that no one thought of doing it. But what kind of mind thinks of such things?

Science-mindedness is playfulness in the behavioral sense of painting with microbes, but also in the mental sense of playing with ideas, in dreams, for example. At times, our dreams may express a truth that we cannot get at during wakefulness. It might be a personal truth—for example, a "nonsensical" dream depicting a good friend behaving indifferently or badly—yet that later proves to be insightful. It might be an objective truth. The great nineteenth-century chemist Friedrich August Kekulé dreamed of a snake revolving with its tail in its mouth. A bit of nonsense? Not really. Kekulé recognized in the image a symbolic answer to a question that had preoccupied him for a long time: the structure of the benzene molecule. The answer suggested by the dream image: ring-like.* (For more on dream insight, see Appendix note, "Solutions in the Dream.")

Many scientists enjoy metaphor, allusion, word-play. Any kind of playfulness may spark testable hypotheses while providing endless amusement. Fleming believed that his scientific work was play, moreover, that he was playing when he discovered penicillin. Newton, on his deathbed, supposedly revealed that he had been "like a boy playing on the sea-shore, and diverting myself in now and then finding a smoother pebble or prettier shell than ordinary, whilst the great ocean of truth lay all undiscovered before me." Clearly, scientific playing is like the play of children with serious learning to do [189]. Children are naive empiricists; scientists are sophisticated empiricists. Both discover the world in their play: children in their diversions and games, and scientists in their theories and research. In the hands of the gifted scientist, then, work is serious child's play.

There seems to be a fit between the prepared and playful characteristics of the scientist, and the structured and accidental characteristics of the environment. In the environment, things seem just to happen, some potentially more interesting or useful than others. There are chance as well as systematic events that the nonscientist may experience as Lady Luck or the hand of

---

*At about the same time of Kekulé's discovery, English chemist Archibald S. Couper (1831–1892) independently hit upon the solution, though, for complicated reasons, he never got much credit. The most famous examples of simultaneous discovery in science are calculus, co-discovered by Newton and Leibnitz, and natural selection, co-discovered by Darwin and Wallace. Others include the airplane, telescope, telephone, telegraph, photography, sunspots, and the elements oxygen and nitrogen.

providence. A playful imagination, especially an educated and experienced one, constantly *generates* such accidents. It doesn't just exploit those that occur by chance.

Unlike other disciplines, however, science subjects the products of preparedness and playfulness to an *empirical* form of critical evaluation. It thus represents a powerful combination of logic and imagination that can transform hypotheses into real-world models and machinery [46]. Through it all runs a quality of persistence driven by pleasure and suffering. Many scientists (including Pasteur, Pavlov, Einstein, and Feynman) have described their work as joyful, exciting, passionate. Others have admitted experiencing enduring doubt. Nevertheless, they persisted. Tenaciously sticking to a problem despite the arguments of colleagues or the failure of specific hypotheses makes that much sweeter the joy of discovery, not to mention beating the odds. Einstein says that "the years of searching in the dark for a truth that one feels, but cannot express, the intense desire and the alternations of confidence and misgiving, until one breaks through to clarity and understanding, are known only to him who has himself experienced them."

Knowledge hard won comes from the effort to achieve not just facts but an interconnected knowledge that facilitates new ideas [223]. Sometimes, to convince others, such knowledge requires doing outrageous things. Joseph Goldberger finally convinced a reluctant medical community what they had long resisted: that the depression, diarrhea, dermatitis, dizziness, running sores, and vomiting of pellagra are caused by inadequate diet, not by poor sanitation [296]. First, he disproved their theory by showing that he didn't develop pellagra after injecting himself with the blood of pellagra victims—not even after eating their nose secretions and consuming little pellagra balls made of flour, their urine and feces, and scrapings from their sores. Second, he all but proved his theory by showing that subjects developed pellagra if given a high carbohydrate/low protein diet, but not if given a balanced diet. What more impressive example of science-mindedness in action. Here are keen observation and experimental rigor, yes, and persistence and courage—and more. Maybe we should call it chutzpah born of a capacity for imagination that can soar yet remained focused—

that can transcend the irrationality and egocentricity of mental illness and even normal experience.

Castlereagh at his window

So there it is—science-mindedness at its critical, creative, and courageous best, directed toward falsifiable ideas and serving as antidote to both ideology and irrationality. In this sense, it is surely an antithesis to mental illness. We might very well wonder what would be the effect on the life of individuals, families, and societies were the science-mindedness of human nature more reliable and finely tuned. (We might ask the same question about other high qualities such as the moral or esthetic sense.) Would we merely have better reasons, methods, and explanations for doing what we do and being what we are? Or would we be happier, with more compassion and less mental illness?

As it is, perhaps most times all we need is a little information to clarify the muddle and a little courage to focus the will. A little knowledge may be a dangerous thing, but only if misused by charlatans and ideologues to promote half-truths or outright lies. Otherwise, a little knowledge can edify, reassure, and even delight. We may not be experts, but a little knowledge about Mozart and his music makes the concert that much more enjoyable. And what about the effect of a little knowledge of the human landscape with its mountainous terrain which, while not always avoidable, may yet be managed? Might such knowledge, conveyed clearly and with humanity, comfort the distressed; might it even make the difference between life and death?

For a time, I was haunted by an image of Lord Castlereagh at his window, bathed in morning light, yet lost in the darkness of delusion and despair. With courage and determination he had withstood setbacks, even failures, and the unrelenting criticism that comes with highest office. But in the end, his powers and confidence seemed to melt away, leaving him alone, unprotected, and unloved. A nineteenth-century biographer sadly noted that while "his wisdom and resolution had won for his country security and independence, and glory, all these services were forgotten, and he became, beyond all other individuals, the object of the most intemperate abuse." Even after the suicide, attacks on his character continued, like this scurrilous doggerel coughed up by Lord Byron:

> Posterity will ne'er survey
> A nobler grave than this:
> Here lie the bones of Castlereagh:
> Stop, traveler, and piss!

To those who consider Castlereagh a hero, Byron's mockery seems gratuitous if not callous. Therefore let him remediate this injustice with proper application of his own words (from "The Dying Gladiator"). For a brief instant, Castlereagh is again at his window, dying in the arms of Bankhead. Like an ancient Greek chorus, Byron speaks:

> He leans upon his hand—his manly brow
> Consents to death, but conquers agony;
> And his drooped head sinks gradually low;
> And through his side the last drops, ebbing slow
> From the red gash, fall heavy, one by one,
> Like the first of a thundershower; and now
> The arena swims around him—he is gone
> Ere ceased the inhuman shout which hailed the
> wretch who won.

With his life's work, Castlereagh had won his place in history. With suicide, he had won his release from pain—but, it seems, without any real understanding of himself or the biological nature of his suffering. Knowing what we now know, would Castlereagh have endured, accepting life out of the power that comes with knowledge; or would he have sought relief even sooner, rejecting life out of a heightened sense of its absurdity? Knowledge is power, indeed, but to what end?

Envoi

With an appreciation of science-mindedness, we end a journey that began in the domain of mental illness. There, we found people buffeted by feelings of joy and sadness, stretched to the limits of hope and despair, and forced to confront, sometimes delusionally, the deepest questions of life and self. And in the interplay of the vulnerabilities and resiliency that characterize liability, we confronted not only mental illness, but also heightened creativity, deeper insights into the human condition, courage, and the capacity to heal.

In the heritability of intelligence, personality, and liability, we found good evidence that the external environment affects our development, not just through demands imposed by society to shape our behavior, but through opportunities exploited by us to fulfill our potential. And in the heritability of so many qualities, including the will to live, we found that the freedom to be ourselves may be a freedom from social influence, but not from biological influence.

In the domain of personality dynamics and everyday problem solving, we found that any serious inquiry into such questions can be distorted or derailed by subjectivity and irrationality. Yet these obstacles to discovering the truth can be circumvented— in principle, anyway. For questions about meaning, value, and existence, answers may be found through introspection that draws on intuition, common sense, and logic shaped by personal experience. For questions about the mechanisms of behavior, answers can be found in the domain of science-mindedness. There, free of ideological drag lines, rational and intuitive ideas can be tested in the crucible of falsification and transformed by the spirit of creativity.

In all three domains of our odyssey—in mental illness, conventional normalcy, and science-mindedness—we discovered conflict and inconsistency at the heart of human nature, but this may not be so bad. Vulnerability yet resiliency, irrationality yet objectivity, anxiety yet courage, selfishness yet altruism, destructiveness yet creativity: all these qualities make us inventive, unpredictable, full of surprises. Human qualities, good and bad, unfold as a ripening of potential beneath the outward show. Our potential can be developed, delayed, or denied, yet it endures. Shakespeare said it most poetically—"if it be not to come, it will be now; if it be not now, yet it will come; the readiness is all." The readiness of human nature inspires travel in a landscape shared with other human beings. To the extent that we are genetically unique, readiness will inspire travel along distinct paths. To the extent that we are genetically the same, readiness will inspire travel along common paths. Thus are we unique and alone, yet similar and connected to like-minded travelers. The evolution of our readiness connects us to other species, and to the rhythms of the planet. Ultimately, it connects us to the stars.

APPENDIX

CHAPTER 3

TAKING STOCK

A. GETTING ESTIMATES

Estimates of mental disorders in the community come from large-scale *epidemiology* research (*epi:* about; *demio:* from *demos*, or people). A celebrated example is the Epidemiologic Catchment Area (ECA) study of over 18,000 people in five representative sites—New Haven, Baltimore, St. Louis, Durham (North Carolina), and Los Angeles—which was funded by the National Institutes of Mental Health [257].

The heart of the research is a questionnaire with over 250 items designed to enable diagnosis of specific mental illnesses. For example, the 27-item section on depression starts with this question: "In your lifetime, have you ever had two weeks or more during which you felt sad, blue, depressed, or when you lost all interest and pleasure in things you usually cared about or enjoyed?" Later come questions about appetite and sleep (too much or too little), fatigue, energy (slowness or restlessness), libido (sexual indifference), thinking (poor concentration), feelings about the self (worthless, guilty, sinful), and inclinations toward suicide. For each section of the questionnaire, the interviewer determines symptom severity and duration, and whether these are related to the use of drugs or treatment for a medical condition. The result is that, apparently, about a third of the adult U.S. population currently has, or at some time has had, a significant psychological disorder, most typically involving anxiety, depression, or substance abuse.

No estimate is etched in stone. Each depends on which behaviors are considered definitive and how liberal or conservative are the criteria [75; 123; 323]. For example, depressive disorder will be rarer if the diagnosis requires ten rather than five symptoms, or two or more episodes rather than one. Estimates derived from any one study will surely depend on many factors. One is the diagnostic instrument or assessment procedures used by investigators; another is the interviewer, in particular, how well-trained, intuitive, and aggressive the interviewer is in pursuing pertinent information. A third factor is whether the information is acquired first- or second-hand. In one study of depressive disorder, interviews of informant-relatives yielded a prevalence estimate of about 17 percent, while direct assessment of family members yielded a noticeably higher estimate of about 25 percent [318].

B. Coming to terms

Estimates of a mental illness are expressed in *rates*, percentages of a group or population affected by a disorder during some specified period of time, or "window," for example, six months. There are several different kinds of rates.

Incidence rate refers to *new* cases only—first-time cases that begin during the designated time period—divided by all people in the reference group who have not yet had the disorder (and are thus at risk). Depending on the study, the reference group might be identical co-twins, all first-degree relatives, or the entire population.

Prevalence rate refers to *all currently active* cases—new ones (incidence cases) plus old (recurrent) ones—divided by the entire population (reference group). The time frame typically is a narrow "window," say one month.

Notice that incidence and prevalence refer to something tangible—more or less current illness we can "see" in the relatively narrow "window." With the next two measures, we extend our assessment, first to the less tangible (distant past illness), then to the intangible (future illness).

Lifetime prevalence rate includes all current cases (prevalence) *plus past cases*—divided by the entire population (reference group). With lifetime prevalence, we extend the temporal "window" all the way back, as in: "Did you *ever* have this disorder?"

Morbidity risk (a different kind of rate) refers to all current or past cases (lifetime prevalence) *plus estimated future cases*—that is, people who have ever been ill, but also never-ill people who are *expected to be ill*. To estimate morbidity risk, you divide lifetime prevalence (numerator), not by the entire population, but by a "reduced denominator"—a denominator reduced by the degree that the population has not yet passed through the risk period. For example, while all older adults who are through the risk period might be weighted fully (1.0), young adults only partly through the risk period would be weighted only 0.5; children, since they are not yet into the risk period, would not be counted, that is, they would be weighted 0.0. Using this "reduced denominator" yields an estimate (morbidity risk) that is larger than lifetime prevalence. The estimate is, in theory, what the investigators would eventually have arrived at had they waited till everyone in their group(s) died.

CHAPTER 4

ANATOMY OF A SYNDROME

Abnormal behavior is usually described in terms of symptoms—roughly speaking, the psychological units of a *disorder*—used here in the descriptive sense of syndrome, or collection of symptoms, rather than in the theoretical sense of disease.* Like a disorder, a symptom can refer to something directly observable (complaint about pain) or indirectly observable (a behavioral deficit); no theoretical meaning need be attached to it. The table shows how depressive symptoms can be described in terms of observability (objective versus subjective) and change from normal, that is, excesses ("positive" symptoms) or deficiencies ("negative").

Observability of the Symptoms	Nature of the Symptoms	
	Excessive	*Deficient*
Objective (expressed)	agitated, insomniac tearful, avoidant	inactive, unresponsive, anorexic, forgetful
Subjective (felt)	angry, frustrated, anxious	anergic, anhedonic,† apathetic, hopeless, demoralized

*The *drome* part of the term comes from a Greek word meaning running or course, as in "hippodrome" (a course where horses run) or palindrome (a running of words that mean the same thing read either forward or in reverse order, for example, "A Toyota," or "A man, a plan, a canal, Panama.").

† Anergic referring to lacking energy; anhedonic referring to the lost ability to experience pleasure.

On the other hand, as we said, a symptom can signify something hidden below the behavioral surface, an inferred state. There may be little apparent connection between a symptom—for example, irritability, constipation, or insomnia—and the hypothesized psychopathology (depressive state). Furthermore, symptoms are not just a passive expression of psychopathology. They are also an active expression of a person trying to cope. Symptoms such as unresponsiveness, paranoid delusions, and social withdrawal protect the depression-wracked self against fearful and painful threats from the disorder and from society [300].

HORMONES AND DEPRESSION

A. HYPOTHALAMUS-PITUITARY AXIS (HPA) AND DEPRESSION

The best-known example of a hormone abnormality in depression involves the hormone cortisol, whose level in the blood normally goes up under stress but remains abnormally high in severe depression. The culprit seems to be a collection of brain structures called the *hypothalamus* plus other brain structures—collectively, the *limbic cortex*—that control the hypothalamus. (The hypothalamus and limbic cortex together make up the so-called *limbic system*, which organizes needs and emotions, integrating them with learning and memory.) The cortisol abnormality is simplified with the help of the diagram at the top of the facing page.

The diagram shows the so-called *HPA* system in which the Hypothalamus deep in the center of the brain controls the Pituitary ("master gland"), which in turn controls the Adrenal cortex. Control at each link is hormonal. In the HP link, for example, the hypothalamus produces *corticotrophic releasing hormone*, or *CRF*. This hormone mobilizes a specific part of the pituitary to produce ACTH: adrenocorticotrophic hormone—from *adreno*: adrenal; *cortico*: cortex; *trophic*: facilitating. The *feedback* link from *A to H* represents the blood-borne cortisol that is fed

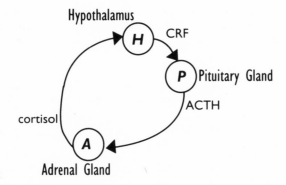

Hypothalamus

H   CRF

P Pituitary Gland

ACTH

cortisol

A

Adrenal Gland

back to the brain, enabling the hypothalamus to keep tabs on the serum inventory of cortisol.

Notice that this is a *negative* feedback system. When cortisol increases, the hypothalamus *reduces* its signal to the pituitary. When cortisol consequently decreases, the hypothalamus *increases* its signal to the pituitary. The hypothalamus is thus like a room heater governed by a thermostat—increasing heat deactivates the heater; cooler room temperature is fed back and activates the heater; increasing heat is fed back and inactivates the heater, and so on. Negative feedback will normally keep cortisol levels under control, allowing only small fluctuations around a "setpoint." Actually, this setpoint isn't rigidly set, but shifts in circadian fashion, being lowest at the beginning of sleep, highest at the end. (The connection between such circadian rhythms and depression is discussed in Chapter 5.)

In many severely depressed patients, the hypothalamus seems to become insensitive to cortisol. Like a partially deaf person who talks too loudly, the hypothalamus sends its hormonal signal to the pituitary with unrelenting regularity. The effect is a "high-flat" pattern—too much cortisol with too little circadian rhythmicity. This last observation about a high-flat pattern is yet another reason that investigators suspect a circadian abnormality in at least some depressions. A flat rhythm is unstable, that is, capable of shifting with respect to other biological rhythms or to the light-dark cycle of the external world—which suggests a mechanism for depression (see Chapter 5).

Hypothalamic insensitivity to cortisol feedback can be observed by challenging the HPA system with a dose of synthetic cortisol called *dexamethasone* (pronounced: deksa MEHtha sone). Dexamethasone is administered orally before sleep (11 P.M.). The next day, plasma levels of cortisol are assessed (at 8 A.M. and 4 P.M.). The hypothalamus of a normal HPA system should react to the synthetic cortisol by reducing its activating message to the pituitary, in turn causing a reduction of cortisol. Initially, cortisol levels should drop, then gradually return to normal. This "suppression" pattern explains why the procedure is called the *dexamethasone suppression test,* or *DST.* Twenty to 40 percent of severely depressed people—50 to 90 percent of cortisol-hypersecreter depressives—show an abnormal pattern on the DST. Cortisol suppression is weak and quickly reversed, returning to normal (or high) baseline levels, which is why the abnormality, usually called "nonsuppression," is more accurately called "early escape from weak suppression."

There appears to be a strong, *negative* relation between levels of cortisol and levels of specific neurotransmitters (e.g., norepinephrine)—the more of one, the less of the other. This negative correlation implies some neural control mechanism for the HPA—in the hypothalamus itself, or perhaps "upstream" in other parts of the brain's limbic system, thus indirectly affecting depressive episodes. No one knows for sure. Something else is suggested by all this DST business. Apparently the depressions of "nonsuppressors" and "suppressors" may involve different mechanisms—different imbalances of serotonin, norepinephrine, acetylcholine, dopamine, and/or other neurotransmitters. That, of course, makes life complicated for researchers and patients alike. Nevertheless, our understanding of brain mechanisms grows with research on antidepressive drugs that have known effects on neurotransmitters. Moreover, there are excellent reviews—thorough and exhaustive—that provide the technical details and their scientific implications [134; 332].

B. POSTPARTUM AND PREMENSTRUAL DEPRESSION

There is much uncertainty regarding the role of hormones in postpartum depression, the kind of depression that attacks women after childbirth [125; 250]. Most instances are mild cases of the blues, tearful sadness lasting at most a day or two during the second or third week after the birth. The depression may be an intensification of something begun earlier but kept under control. Other postpartum depressions are moderate, but a few are severe and occasionally psychotic. Causes remain obscure though there is no lack of psychological speculation about the woman's self-doubts, resentments, ambivalence, or guilt over negative feelings toward the baby. The fact that depressions can occur in the new father or upon receiving an adopted baby supports the possibility that psychological factors are important, but that is easier said than clarified. Neither personality, age, nor even specific hormonal abnormalities have been clearly established as causes. The fact that the more severe depressions erupt in the first few weeks while the milder ones come later suggests that the former are more physiological, the latter more psychological.

Elevated liability to major affective disorder is associated with elevated liability to postpartum depression. Women who have ever had major depression have an elevated risk (20 to 25 percent), and the relatives of such women and of women suffering severe postpartum depression have *comparably* elevated rates for affective disorder. Women who have suffered from PMS-related depression are also at risk, so there may be a common affective vulnerability running through postpartum and premenstrual depressions.

PMS, found worldwide and experienced by up to 30 percent of American women, comes in the form of mostly minor symptoms: pain, water retention, inability to concentrate, depression, anxiety, or irritability [164; 270]. Arguably, a connection may exist between severe PMS and liability to affective disorder, but it is not clear whether PMS is a different expression or merely a byproduct of depressive disease [73; 144; 220]. While hormone treatments apparently have little or no effect, a still unknown hormonal abnormality is suggested by the fact that PMS is sometimes treated successfully with antibiotics designed to be used against ovarian infection [92]. In other cases, it can be normalized with so-called "ovariectomizing" drugs that block the cyclic release of menstrual hormones [236]. On the other hand, the importance of hormone abnormality is less clear—for example, where symptom relief is achieved with antidepressant or anti-anxiety drugs [148]. Another example is relief with so-called light therapy—doses of bright light given daily for two weeks [245]. One possibility is that the evening light may fool the brain into thinking it's still daytime, the effect of which is to normalize abnormal biorhythms. PMS, depression, and sleep are discussed briefly in Chapter 5.

Women are rightly concerned about the social stigma and emotional abuse that can come with a diagnostic concept that gives formal recognition even to an admittedly extreme, clinically significant form of PMS. It seems that premenstrual dysphoric disorder (formerly called late luteal phase dysphoric disorder) will for some time remain debatable—clinically, theoretically, and politically—that is, until its nature and treatment can be established scientifically.

CHAPTER 5

SLEEP RECORDING AND
REM DREAMING

A. SLEEP RECORDING

Sleep cycles are recognized in large part from patterned electrical signals coming from the brain, as indicated in the figure. These signals are actually tiny voltage fluctuations picked up by electrodes (indicated by dots [●] in the figure) attached to some part of the head and passed to a polygraph (multi-channel writer). The polygraph (A) amplifies the voltage fluctuations, transforming them into corresponding fluctuations of pens that scratch out a pattern on continuously moving paper from which stages of sleep can be inferred. So, for example, amplified signals from electrodes placed on the scalp (lower part of the figure) become a wiggly paper trail of brain waves, the EEG, or *electroencephalogram* (*encephalo* meaning head or brain; *gram* meaning written record).

Sleep Recording

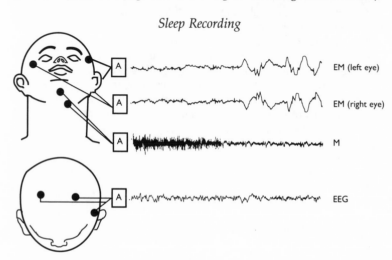

EEGS of Wakefulness and Sleep

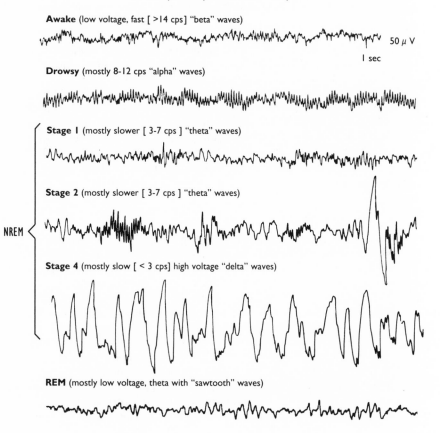

Awake (low voltage, fast [>14 cps] "beta" waves)

50 μ V

I sec

Drowsy (mostly 8-12 cps "alpha" waves)

Stage 1 (mostly slower [3-7 cps] "theta" waves)

Stage 2 (mostly slower [3-7 cps] "theta" waves)

NREM

Stage 4 (mostly slow [< 3 cps] high voltage "delta" waves)

REM (mostly low voltage, theta with "sawtooth" waves)

In this way, eye movement (EM) and chin-muscle tension (M) are recorded. The paper trail scratched out during a single night may be over a quarter mile long.

You can see in the figures that each EEG pattern differs in terms of *speed* and *amplitude*. Speed ("fast" versus "slow") is measured in *cycles per second*, or *cps*. Amplitude (high versus low voltage fluctuations) refers to the amount of pen excursion above and below the midline of the tracing.

The EEG of alert wakefulness (top line in the figure) is a low-voltage, fast (14+ cps) pattern called *beta*. The EEG of relaxed wakefulness (eyes closed, mind wandering) is a slower and more rhythmic low-voltage, moderately fast pattern called *alpha* (8 to 12 cps). Alpha usually alternates with beta but predominates just before sleep onset. If you become bored and glassy-eyed with all these details, you are probably producing lots of alpha. If you are too sleepy to read this, you are probably producing a different wave pattern.

With sleep, a person normally drifts through four stages of nonREM, or NREM, sleep, so-called because they lack the rapid eye movements of REM sleep. Each NREM stage, 1 through 4 shown in the figure (stage 3 not shown) is characterized by a unique EEG. About 90 minutes later, and then roughly every 90 minutes, the sleeping person enters REM sleep, a sample of which is shown at the bottom of the figure.

B. REM AND NREM SLEEP

In the early 1950s, researchers studying the sleep of infants noticed what turned out to be scanning-like eye movements. Along with a distinctive kind of EEG pattern, these eye movements were the outward sign of an inner state of intense brain activity—and perhaps dreaming. One could only speculate with infants, but with all others, dreaming was indeed what researchers discovered when subjects were abruptly awakened from REM sleep.

REM sleep was hypothesized to facilitate all kinds of psychologically important things: to exercise genetically coded neural programs (species-specific instincts), to consolidate memory traces of recent learning, and to facilitate emotional adjustment through personal problem solving [19; 68; 224]. These assumptions are modern expressions of older ideas, the best-known examples being Freud's theories about dreams as symbolically disguised expressions of, and attempts to gratify if not work through, unconscious needs. Does some dreaming represent a kind of symbolic self-indulgence, or is it an insightful, even creative, kind of thinking that accumulates over endless nights to enrich the knowledge base of our self? Does all this mental activity contribute to the development of personality? In other words, is this self-expressive process really self-*serving*? Is it an *egocentric* REMembering of things past that shapes our evolution into the future? If so, are we better off having dreamed—or worse off? Questions about dreaming are notoriously difficult to test, and no one has a definitive answer, though speculations abound [68].

NREM sleep was also hypothesized to serve all sorts of functions: to facilitate tissue repair through enhanced protein synthesis, to promote energy conservation through lower basal metabolism, and to enhance security by enabling avoidance of predators. Any theory of sleep function must explain very short sleepers, those rare birds who might very well be called the geniuses of sleep, who seem to do in one or two hours (some nights even less) what the rest of us need six or more hours to do. Moreover, they are efficient and well-adjusted people who tend to be relatively more active, extroverted, productive, better at handling stress, and seemingly better adjusted [149].

After awakening from Stage 2 sleep, especially later in the night, you might remember some kind of dreaming or maybe just disjointed thoughts [68; 109]. It is different with NREM Stages 3 and 4 sleep with their billowy *delta* brain waves. The delta pattern is physiologically and psychologically most distant from the beta pattern of alert wakefulness. Therefore, people in delta (especially Stage 4) sleep are least responsive to arousing stimuli, most confused upon awakening, and least likely to recall any conscious experience. For these reasons, delta sleep is "deep." Stage 4—the stage with the most continuous delta activity— has been likened to an existential void. In that void, thinking, consciousness, and personality seem to vanish. It is a kind of psychic "death" from which we are gently resurrected, repeatedly, every night.

CHAPTER 7

ALTRUISTIC SUICIDE

While focusing on the egoistic and anomic kinds of suicide, Durkheim discussed another—altruistic suicide—that, while occurring in all cultures, is part of the rituals of only some. Altruistic suicide is associated with the *excessive integration* that characterizes non-Western societies where individual dispositions and rights tend to be subordinated to social obligation, ritual, family, community, religion. Historically, non-Western suicide sometimes took on ritualistic forms. In *suttee*, for example, an Indian woman following a strong sense of obligation would join her husband on his funeral pyre. In *seppukku*, a Japanese man would deal with intense embarrassment and shame by self-disembowelment. Then there was suicide by freezing; an aged Eskimo would go out on the ice to relieve his family of the burden of caring for him.

One of the most ironic and touching stories of altruistic suicide is that of Joseph Meister. As a young boy, Meister had been repeatedly bitten by a rabid dog. Nevertheless, he was saved from certain death by Louis Pasteur's application of a new vaccine. Later, as official gatekeeper at the Pasteur Institute, Meister committed suicide in 1940 rather than agree to German demands that he open Pasteur's burial crypt [185].

In biblical times, and even today, people have committed "noble" suicide to defend against being raped, enslaved, or converted to an alien religion. Throughout Chinese history, high-placed women would hang themselves to preserve their honor when the siege of a city was broken and widespread rape was expected. Another type of suicide—call it "rational"—is universally recognized throughout history. It is suicide in the face of intolerable pain and progressive disease. Quite the opposite, what suicidologist Shneidman calls *egotic,* is a highly subjective, intellectualized kind of suicide seen in irrational and delusional psychotics [288].

SEROTONIN AND SUICIDE

Given the complexity of brain mechanisms, any proposed neurochemical abnormality is likely to be, at best, only a small part of the suicide story. Nevertheless, a good candidate is some mechanism volving the neurotransmitter serotonin. For one thing, hostile or violent behavior—attacks of anger in people with depression or committing suicide in a violent manner—is associated with evidence of low or otherwise abnormal serotonin function. Moreover, reducing or blocking serotonin functioning seems to enhance aggressiveness, perhaps in part by promoting hostile thoughts that further increase the risk of violent behavior. It is as though the capacity to apply psychological brakes were damaged [171].

Consider two other related observations regarding young and elderly suicides and/or serious suicide attempters. The first is *abnormally low*—sometimes abnormally high—levels of brain serotonin [18; 166]. The second is *abnormally high* numbers of serotonin receptors [212]. Receptors are microscopic structures embedded in the neural membrane whose chemical shape allows them to be occupied by specific neurotransmitter molecules.

Another bit of evidence from antidepressant drug responsiveness allows the following speculation about a serotonin mechanism [211]. Certain antidepressants such as fluoxetine (trade name: Prozac) work by reducing the ability of the presynaptic neuron to take back and store serotonin. The immediate effect of these so-called reuptake blockers is a buildup of serotonin and therefore increased neural activity. Then, during roughly two weeks, compensatory changes occur in pre- and postsynaptic neurons, some therapeutic—a more normal firing pattern restored—but some not. In a few people, the drugs may produce a worsening of symptoms and heightened risk for suicide. A chronic, even treatment-resistant, problem may then develop.

CHAPTER 9

EGO PROBLEMS

One problem seems to be too much blind impulse and selfish disposition (id) and too little adaptability (ego strength). The result is frustration, helplessness, egocentricity, dysphoria. To contain the id part of personality, the ego part employs *id-regulatory* defense mechanisms including those described in the table. These cognitive strategies inhibit and transform id tendencies, rendering them more benign and less manifestly antisocial [102; 115; 258; 280].

ID-REGULATORY DEFENSE MECHANISMS

Type	Explanation	Examples
Repression	Blocking personal consciousness of threatening impulses, ideas, or feelings associated with anxiety (e.g., harm, abandonment) or guilt (moral transgression)	Inability to perceive or recall threatening experiences or forbidden desires—in particular, those from early childhood; appearing to be naive or inhibited
Displacement	Impulses unconsciously felt toward one person expressed toward someone else	Anger at the boss taken out on the spouse
Reaction formation	Transforming unconscious impulses, feelings, or ideas into conscious but acceptable opposites, for example, anger into "affection" or erotic impulses into "aggression"	A mother's unconscious hostility toward her child is transformed into relentless "concern" about his well-being, including compulsive checking for dirt, broken glass, or other "dangers"

Undoing	Unconscious hostility turned into "good deeds"; this form of expiation is a moral version of reaction formation (indicating strong superego influence over ego defense)	Excessive helpfulness, even altruistic behavior with, people unconsciously hated
Isolation	Isolation of a feeling (anger) from its appropriate referent (parent) so that it is experienced only in a different context (when alone)	An unemotional talk with a boss (unconscious father figure) is followed some time later by inexplicable rage
Intellectualization	A form of isolation, a retreat from feelings to abstract concepts, principles, theories	An unconsciously frustrated patient calmly agrees with the therapist's hypothesis that he must be angry with his father and that this anger probably stems from his Oedipal conflicts

The imperious id is one problem; another problem, *ego deficiency*, is an inability to cope with impulses, needs, and external events—an *"existential"* problem, or insufficiency of being in the world coupled with a sense of the absurdity of existence and reality. A deficient ego is subjectively experienced in abiding feelings of inadequacy, unlovableness, vulnerability, emptiness, and unreality—of not being fully alive. Ego deficiency motivates the *ego-compensating* defenses described in the next table. The irony is that, while these defenses make things at least seem better by compensating for deficiencies, they also make things worse by promoting hypersensitive, emotionally volatile, impulsive, promiscuous, abusive, addictive, interpersonally chaotic, and self-destructive behaviors; all these are the familiar signatures of the classic "character-neurotic" disorder (or so-called "borderline" condition).

EGO-COMPENSATORY DEFENSE MECHANISMS

Type	Explanation	Examples
Primitive denial	Adopting insensitive, aloof, and/or grandiose pretense in fantasy and behavior to reinforce a sense of strength and importance	Believing that one has special "powers" or "talents;" denying the significance of otherwise evident deficiency or failure

EGO-COMPENSATORY DEFENSE MECHANISMS *(Continued)*

Type	Explanation	Examples
Primitive idealization	Overidentifying with people misperceived as omnipotent, omniscient, all loving, or all good, thereby securing an enhanced sense of security, importance, or power	Believing that the therapist has perfect insight; deifying and giving unquestioned allegiance to a cult leader
Primitive devaluation	Adopting a hostile, degrading, or unforgiving attitude that helps to bolster fragile self-esteem by minimizing others	Emphasizing other people's faults; mocking or minimizing their achievements, adopting a supercilious or disdainful attitude
Projection	Attributing "bad" aspects of oneself to others or situations without recognizing them in oneself	Misperceiving one's weakness as an "external threat"—paranoid suspiciousness, for example
Pseudovitality	Enhancing the sense of being alive by engaging excessively or irresponsibly in highly stimulating and emotionally arousing behaviors	Reckless sensation seeking; provocative, aggressive, or exhibitionistic behavior; self-mutilation or dramatic suicidal gestures.

The difference between the two psychoneurotic conditions, the conflict ridden and the inadequate ("borderline"), clarified in the following table, boils down to this: While the strong ego is being threatened (by frustration), the deficient ego is threatened by not being.

PSYCHOLOGICAL DIFFERENCES

Facet	Conflict ridden	Inadequate (borderline)
Clinical condition	Insecurity and anxiety with interpersonal relations marked by guilt and anger	Vulnerability and depersonalization; derealization; emptiness; interpersonal relations marked by hostility and a mixture of intense idealization and devaluation

Theoretical condition	Frustration of impulses, that is, deep conflict between the impulsive (id) and the expedient (ego) and moral (superego) aspects of personality	Defects in the capacity to organize and control impulses to master the world of objects and persons, and to organize experience into a coherent sense of self
Resulting symptoms	Phobic fear of animals; obsessive fear of dirt; hysteric amnesia for sexual experiences	Paranoid pseudosuperiority (e.g., litigious letter writing); hysteroid pseudovitality; sadomasochistic sensation seeking

CHAPTER 11

CAPITALIZING ON CHANCE

Imagine that you select two groups: a "bright" group composed of people with extraordinarily high IQ scores, and a "dull" group composed of people with extraordinarily low IQ scores. For each group, get the mean IQ. Each group mean will surely deviate from the expected value—the population mean, which is roughly 100. The mean of the "bright" group might be 130; the mean of the "dull" group might be 70. The really interesting finding is this: The next time the same IQ measurements are made on the same people—nothing special is done in the interim—each mean is now less deviant from the population mean. The "brights" now average 125, the "dulls," 75, with both numbers closer to the population mean. The apparent change is therefore called *regression toward the mean* [319].

Did people get less or more intelligent? No, and it's easy to see why. Nothing is perfect—surely not the measures nor the averages based on those measures. All measures—especially the deviant ones you initially observed—are unreliable to some extent because of chance. Starting with an oddball observation or selecting a deviant group means capitalizing on chance factors that involve environment and behavior, as well as errors of measurement.

Regression toward the mean is the law, a statistical fact of life that partly accounts for apparent change, for example, across generations on whatever measure you select and whichever direction you look. For example, the children of schizophrenics are, on average, less abnormal than their parents, and are infrequently schizophrenic (about 10 percent). Likewise, the parents of schizophrenic children are, on average, less abnormal than their children, and are even less frequently schizophrenic (5 to 8 percent). The children of parents with IQs of 130 are, on average, somewhat less bright than their parents. The parents of children with IQs of 130 are, on average, somewhat less bright than their children.

Incidentally, you might be wondering why extreme IQs don't disappear over the generations, with just about everyone of later generations ending up at the mean. The answer is simply that regression toward ordinary IQs is counterbalanced by the effects of the large population of ordinary parents who *occasionally* produce extraordinary children—just enough to replenish the small population of "extraordinaries." In other words, a small percentage of a large number (extraordinary offspring of ordinary folks) can equal a large percentage of a small number (more ordinary offspring of extraordinary folks).

We can change in two ways—deeply, enduringly from within, and superficially, unreliably from without. The one way is through a genetically guided unfolding of our nature reinforced by learning (biologically prepared learning); the other is through an environmentally shaped accommodation to external demands independent of preferred ways of being. Whether evident or obscure, change may be real *or it may be illusory* (as in regression toward the mean). There are no easy formulas for recognizing the difference. Nevertheless, making the distinction will surely move us closer to a clear-eyed understanding of human nature and self-actualization—the fulfillment of individual potential.

CHAPTER 13

WHO IS ALVIN?

Alvin is a nice person, thoughtful and considerate, yet a little awkward around people. Frankly, he would rather read a good book than go to a party. Some might even consider him shy but he doesn't think of himself this way. He collects coins, enjoys classical music, and likes to hike on his own. Question: Is Alvin a librarian or a teacher? Did you answer librarian? The description of Alvin is certainly consistent with the stereotype of librarian as bookish or introverted. Moreover, the probability that your stereotype-driven answer is correct depends on the stereotype's validity—how much more likely it fits librarians than teachers—but it depends on something else, too.

For the sake of making a point, let's start with validity and then get to the "something else." Suppose the description given above fits 80 percent of male librarians but only 20 percent of male teachers. This 80–20 difference represents the validity of the stereotype, meaning that Alvin is four times more likely to be a librarian than a teacher, *other things being equal.* Innocent phrase, that. Problem is, other things are *not* equal—remember the misleadingly equal circles representing suicidal and nonsuicidal populations? Fact is, there are far more male teachers than male librarians. So, ignoring the stereotype and going with prior probability, you should assume that Alvin is a *teacher* rather than a librarian.

Suppose that male teachers outnumbered male librarians 100 to 1; better yet, make it 1,000 to 10. Suppose we had an unbiased sample of 1,000 teachers plus 10 librarians that fairly represented this population ratio. This means that out of the 1,000 teachers, 200 fit the stereotype (20 percent) while out of the 10 librarians, 8 fit the stereotype (80 percent). There are twenty-five times more *teachers* than librarians despite the validity of the librarian stereotype. The main point is that basically a small percentage of a very large number (200) yields a bigger number than a large percentage of a small number (8). However true or false, stereotypes may be misleading.

It would have been different had we begun with the observation that Alvin is a librarian. Then, our valid stereotype plus an equal prior probability of introversion and extroversion (the population has an equal number of each) would have justified betting that Alvin is an introvert. However, we started with information about Alvin's introversion. In this case, our consideration of prior probability (as well as stereotype validity) should have made us bet that Alvin is a teacher. Moreover, we should bet this way even though we *feel* that he ought to be a librarian.

CHAPTER 14

ESTIMATING GENETIC INFLUENCE ON TRAITS

A. A CAUTIONARY NOTE

Like height or temperature, traits such as intelligence are assumed to be continuous (from low to high) and therefore measurable along a graded scale (e.g., IQ) like that of a ruler or thermometer. Graded measurement allows us to measure resemblances among people in terms of correlation, a zero correlation indicating no resemblance, a 1.00 correlation indicating perfect resemblance. (We won't be concerned here about negative correlation.) A positive correlation for IQ in parents and children, for example, would measure parent-child resemblance, that is, the degree to which, *on average*, bright parents tend to have bright children, dull parents to have dull children—the degree to which the IQ score of parents and children "go along," or predict one another.

Manifest psychological adjustment (from normal to abnormal) is assumed to be graded. Yet, for practical reasons, psychological adjustment is typically treated *categorically*. For our purposes, this "either-or-treatment" means two things: Behavior is either "normal" or "abnormal," and resemblance is measured by *concordance*, for example, the extent to which both members of a pair of identical or fraternal twins tend to be ill or not ill. (Concordance is thus categorical correlation.) But categorical resemblance (concordance) can be misleading, especially if we want to use observations on behavior (illness/wellness—a discontinuity) to theorize about potential (*liability to* illness—a continuum). So, to "put back" the continuity—for example, when estimating the heritability of liability (a continuum)—*concordance rates for illness must be transformed into special correlations.** The details of that transformation really

---

*These *intra-class correlations* estimate the *overlap* in the variability of twins and their co-twins (each twin pair being a "class"). Randomly select one member of each pair to comprise a sample of twins; that leaves a sample of their co-twins. An intra-class correlation estimates the extent to which

need not concern us if we will just remember one thing: Inferences about the relative influence of genes (heritability) made on the basis of concordance rates simply won't do though, alas, they are done all the time in the media.

B. Environmental influence through the lens of adoption research

Heritability is estimated from the resemblance of people whose genetic relation can range from 0 percent (adoptees) to 100 percent (identical twins).* Really good heritability estimates come from adoption studies. One adoption method—the rarest of all—measures the resemblance of reared-apart identical twins. Identicals reared apart have 100 percent genetic overlap but (ideally) no rearing overlap if, first, they are separated at birth *and*, second, their rearing environments, while differing in quality, are nevertheless roughly comparable on average. (This rearing-nonoverlap ideal need be only approximately true for the twin-apart method to work.) For identicals reared apart, then, any trait or diagnostic resemblance (correlation) must estimate heritability—call that influence, g, for *genetic* influence.

A second adoption method measures the resemblance of *singleton* (non-twin) adoptees and each of their *biological* relatives—parents or siblings, for example. Since the comparison is for people who share only *half* their genes, any resemblance (correlation) will represent only the *"half-influence" of genes*—$\frac{1}{2} g$. But $\frac{1}{2} g$ (or "half heritability") is meaningless. Therefore, to get g, we simply *double* the parent-child correlation, that is, $2(\frac{1}{2} g) = g$.

---

measures taken from the twins predict corresponding measures taken from the co-twins, and vice versa.

*It is said that identical twins share 100 percent of their genes while any two *first-degree* relatives share 50 percent, *second-degree* relatives share 25 percent, and so on. Actually, this sharing refers to *variable* genes, those promoting human differences, for example, in *color* of eyes. Most genes for which we are all identical are *invariant*, insuring universal traits such as *number* of eyes. Of all human genes, roughly 70 percent are invariant and 30 percent variable. Therefore, "50 percent overlap" for first-degree relatives means sharing half of that roughly 30 percent, or about 15 percent, which leaves roughly 15 percent *not* shared. That "little" percentage non-overlap explains the striking differences in physical and psychological qualities that distinguish its members.

Incidentally, rates of twinning vary throughout the world, with identical twinning apparently random, and fraternal twinning running in families. In North American whites, for example, twinning occurs in about 1 in 87 births, one-third of the cases being identical twins, one-third same-sex fraternal, one-third opposite-sex fraternal [117].

A Conceptual Model for Estimating Social and Nonsocial Environmental Influence

	OBSERVED RESEMBLANCE (correlation)	INFERRED INFLUENCE
STEP 1 (subtraction)	identical twins reared together	genes + shared environment: social & nonsocial
	−identical twins reared apart	**genes**
	difference #1	shared environment: social & nonsocial
	difference #1	shared environment: social & nonsocial
STEP 2 (subtraction)	−genetic unrelateds reared together	shared environment: **social**
	difference #2	shared environment: **nonsocial**

With the two adoption methods just described, you can, at least in principle, estimate the influence of social and nonsocial *environments,* as shown in the two-step diagram above.

Information from adoption research that uses twin or singleton adoptees can thus be used to estimate the relative importance of different kinds of environmental influence. Most people don't realize this, thinking that behavior-genetic methods are for estimating heritability only.

C. HERITABILITY DOESN'T ALWAYS ADD UP

With the two adoption methods just described you also get estimates of two kinds of heritability (g)—in a sense, one kind that "adds up" and one that doesn't. The *additive* kind involves relatively small genetic influences that accumulate in graded manner—the more genes, the bigger the effect. For example, the more genes you have for tallness, IQ, or anxiousness, the taller, smarter, or more anxious you tend to be. Think of a concert hall. The more instruments in the orchestra, the louder and richer the music tends to be; the more numerous the skilled players, the more pleasant the sound. Yet, no one player's contribution is essential to the effect of the music.

It's quite different with *nonadditive* genetic influence, where each gene makes a unique and essential contribution to a genetic *pattern*. It is that pattern, not merely the additive effect of individual genes, that determines the trait. Think of a radio. Assembling even most of the parts required by the schematic yields no music; take one part out of a functioning radio and it falls silent.

Nonadditive traits are an interesting part of the heritability story [206]. Consider, for example, the trait of social potency, the sense of being able to influence if not dominate others—a trait that probably represents some charismatic mixture of things like attractiveness, self-confidence, and assertiveness. On the one hand, socially potent parents typically transmit to their children less than the *complete* genetic pattern required to create the trait—thus, the absence of parent-child resemblance for potency. On the other hand, socially *non*potent parents might nevertheless, as "carriers," each transmit a different half of genes necessary for the trait. Combining in an offspring, the genes create the trait as if out of the blue—really out of the hidden genetic blueprint. Note that, again, but for an opposite reason, the effect is an absence of parent-child resemblance for potency.

In general, then, though heritable, *the nonadditive trait isn't familial;* it shows little or no tendency to run in families. You can see why for nonadditive traits there is little or no resemblance for the trait between siblings, including fraternal twins who, like a parent and child, share only 50 percent of their genes. No wonder fraternals show a less than 0.10 correlation (almost no resemblance) for potency even when, for identicals, the correlation is almost 0.70 [206; 207].

D. Estimating heritability

Identical twins reared apart are identical for *all* their genes, additive and nonadditive. Pairwise resemblance for such twins must therefore estimate *broad heritability*—that is, additive *and* nonadditive genetic influence. Most twin research on *broad* heritability compares the resemblance (in correlation) of *reared-together* identicals and fraternals. To estimate broad heritability, investigators just *double the difference* between the correlations of the identicals and fraternals. Here's why. The resemblance of identicals reared together reflects 100 percent genetic overlap (g) plus common environment (e). However, the resemblance of fraternals reared together reflects *50 percent genetic overlap* ($\frac{1}{2} g$) plus common environment (e). Subtracting fraternal-twin resemblance ($\frac{1}{2} g + e$) from identical-twin resemblance ($g + e$) leaves a difference of $\frac{1}{2} g$—genetic *half-influence.* Doubling this difference yields *g*—genetic influence (broad heritability).

Yes, but what does that doubling *really* mean? Remember that we are asking about the influence on psychological resemblance of genetic relatedness—of the *full range* of genetic relatedness you find in the population from 100 percent (identicals) to 0 percent (unrelateds), *not the restricted range* of relatedness you find within families from 100 percent (identical twins) to 50 percent (siblings including fraternal twins). Since fraternals are 50 percent related, the difference between them and identicals represents *only half the entire range* of genetic overlap that we want to investigate; that is why we must double the difference—to "put back" that half of the range that is missing. If that is confusing, imagine an experiment wherein we create pairs of *genetically unrelated* "twins." We do this by inserting a fertilized but genetically unrelated egg into the uterus of newly pregnant woman. The resulting births would involve genetically unrelated twins who would be reared together. Can you see why, even after subtracting the resemblance (correlation) of these genetically unrelated twins from the resemblance (correlation) of identical twins, we would *not* multiply by two?

Much behavior-genetic research yields estimates of only "narrow" (additive) heritability. Those estimates come from studying the resemblance of adults and their adopted-away offspring. Unlike identical twins reared apart, a parent and a reared-apart offspring are identical for only *half* their genes. This means that an offspring will inherit only half the genetic elements of a trait that a parent might display. With nonadditive traits, getting half the elements won't do the trick; the offspring—like a radio that is silent because it lacks all the necessary components—won't display the trait. In effect, the nonadditive parental *traits* will not be transmitted even though half the relevant *genes* are transmitted.

Now you can appreciate why any resemblance between a parent and that parent's adopted-away offspring must reflect *mostly additive* genes (narrow heritability). But note that, for any one parent, that additive-gene influence must be a *half*-influence, with the other parent contributing the other half-influence. It follows, then, that doubling a parent-child correlation yields a general estimate of how much a trait is determined by *mostly additive* genes. Now you can appreciate better why this estimate is called *narrow heritability.* Subtracting this estimate from the broad heritability estimate derived from reared-apart identical-twin correlations (resemblance) gives you a rough estimate of nonadditive gene influence.

E. The Long and the Short of It:
A Carving Lesson

All attempts to measure psychological qualities—especially when discrete categories such as diagnoses are used—will involve some error, and measurement error is *non*genetic, or "environmental." Therefore, not taking measurement error into consideration may mean—it usually does mean—overestimating environmental (underestimating genetic) influence. In this light, measurement error with identical twins is particularly interesting. Mistaking impermanent or trivial differences for meaningful differences in traits and liabilities can undermine theorizing about individual differences.

We can see how this might happen with a group of imaginary professionals who specialize in diagnosing what convention says is abnormal shortness. We'll call them *shortologists* (pronounced like the word "psychologists"). Shortologists classify people categorically as either abnormally short or not, drawing the line at four foot, six inches. People well below this line are easy to identify as short, but what about people in the ambiguous region slightly above, at, or below the four foot six cutoff point? For them, shortologists use special diagnostic measures to decide if they are to be classified (diagnosed) as short or not.

The shortological approach is practical for working with short people, but what about for investigating height? After all, shortness is merely one region of a height dimension that also includes mediums and talls. So how can studying short people provide clues about height? No problem, say the shortologists. Even though they work with people at the short end of the measurable dimension of height, they can still test hypotheses about the entire dimension. For example, to test the idea that height is highly heritable, they seek out short identical twins and measure their co-twins. To no one's surprise, they find that most short identicals have short co-twins. Nevertheless, some co-twins—up to 30 percent in some studies—turn out to be "not short." Question: How much of this discordance is real, and how much is the illusory effect of measurement error?

Remember, shortologists draw a line between the tallest short and all others including the shortest of those others. Drawing the line means that a pair of identicals is discordant *even if one twin is four foot five* ("short") and the other is four foot six ("other"). Yet no one thinks that four foot five short people are more likely to be called "short" or to have problems of living than four foot six "others." No one thinks that their offspring will differ much in height. And, despite any height discordance in identical twins that we may find, no one doubts that height is highly heritable. (In fact, over 90 percent of all the variation in height comes from genetic variation.) Yet some people *are* fooled by identical-twin discordance for mental illness. They are fooled into minimizing the importance of measurement error involved in categorizing, that is, placing people in or outside an illness category. The result is a bias toward underestimating genetic influence in liability, with a corresponding tendency to overemphasize the environment, especially the social environment.

We get into problems when, like shortologists, we draw lines across continuous dimensions from normal to abnormal. We wind up with seemingly useful categories, but do we gain more than we lose? Common knowledge indicates that to carve a turkey without making a mess, go for the joints. If, as one psychologist says, "classification is the art of carving nature at the joints, it should indeed imply that there is a joint there, that one is not sawing through bone" [172]. What about carving landscapes of disease into categories of illness? Alas, often it seems we are cutting through bone and making a mess. Categories should capture real-world facts. So we may very well ask about the real-world facts, for example, of manic and depressive behavior and of suicide. What are the relevant categories, and what do they reveal—indeed, what do they hide?

F. A FINAL OBSERVATION

You may be thinking that there are potential problems with adoption and twin approaches to estimating heritability. The biggest objection people usually have is with the twin method, in particular, the assumption of comparable e effects on identical-twin and fraternal-twin resemblance. After all, we know that identicals are treated more alike, so isn't there a big difference in e for identicals and fraternals? And doesn't that big difference make a difference? Apparently not; it seems that being treated more alike is the *effect* (not the cause) of their being alike, which says something in general about the cause of sibling resemblance, namely their genetic overlap.

In short, just as teaching need not engender long-term learning of what is taught, and just as propagandizing need not lead to true conversion, parenting need not shape personality development—certainly not to the extent that many people assume. It is one thing to expose people to environments, even to force their behavior to accommodate to external expectations and demands. It is quite another to achieve reliable effects of the kind intended. (All parents know this, though they sometimes forget.) The power of parenting is in bringing out the potential of the individual, a potential that is highly heritable. One could therefore argue that environment works best when, as a key, it unlocks potential through encouragement and example; and that it works worst when, as a sledge hammer, it smashes potential through abuse and trauma. Clearly, then, evidence of the high heritability of traits does not mean that parenting has no effects; on the contrary, it explains why parenting effects are guaranteed.

CHAPTER 15

BRAIN HEMISPHERE CONTROL

Developing a brain theory of depression is made all the more difficult because of unresolved questions about brain function, including how the two brain hemispheres contribute to moods and emotions [118; 180; 242]. Some researchers argue that the right hemisphere is specialized to express and comprehend both positive and negative affect. Others, even if they accept right-hemisphere dominance over affect, argue that the two hemispheres have a somewhat different affective "outlook"— the left hemisphere has a more positive, optimistic outlook, the right has a more negative, pessimistic outlook. This idea is supported by certain observations, for example, that electroconvulsant shock treatment (ECT) for depression works better when the electrodes are placed over the right rather than the left hemisphere (left-side ECT may produce anxiety and depression).

There are other clues. With left-hemisphere damage, either of two kinds of depressive reaction can occur. One is an acute and desperate protest-type reaction marked by anxiety, crying, and aggressiveness. The other, a more stable despondency, is characterized by discouragement, a sense of incapacity, and a feeling of loss. With right-hemisphere damage, *nondepressive* reactions can occur. One involves a peculiar kind of *indifference*, an inability to appreciate the fact that one is ill and disabled—*agnosognosia* is the technical term for this reaction. Another is a facetious and joking attitude. A third involves fantastic explanations, delusions, and hatred toward affected body parts. Over time, the agnosognosia and delusions diminish while a tendency to minimize or even joke about psychological disability becomes more apparent. It would seem, then, that a relative loss of left-hemisphere control has something to do with depression.

While it is simply too early to construct a credible neuropsychological theory of depression, the most interesting possibility is that depression reflects a pathological shift in the balance of metabolic and electrophysiological activity—relatively less left and more right activity, especially in frontal areas. The origin of this shift could be external or internal, psychological or physiological, genetic or learned [153]. During severe depression, the anterior left hemisphere is metabolically underactive *relative to the anterior right*, an asymmetry that seems to be reversed by treatment with antidepressant medication [214]. But the really interesting thing is that some kind of hemisphere imbalance may be more than just a characteristic of depression; it may be a biological marker of *liability*. An anterior left brain wave pattern suggesting *relatively* deficient activation may be detectable, not just in depressed subjects, but also in *nondepressed subjects who were previously depressed* [153]. The liability hypothesis would be strengthened were the pattern found in many of the clinically *never-depressed* first-degree relatives of depressed patients. Such a finding—it has yet to be reported—would suggest that some brain-based vulnerability is manifested, like a sinister promise fulfilled, at least in some kinds of clinical depressions.

Incidentally, the idea that depressed people have something wrong in the anterior part of their brain is the theoretical equivalent of old wine in a new bottle, the wine being at least 600 years old. In *The Canterbury Tales*, Chaucer describes a knight's pathological grief as located "biforen, in his celle fantastic," that is, in the anterior part of the brain where fantasy is bred.

SHADOWS ON THE WALL

Behavior becomes abnormal to the extent that it sabotages well-being and the capacity to function. The operative word is *extent* because abnormality is a matter of degree, like shades of gray or the depth of twilight. Then, how sad is too sad? Where does eccentricity cross the line to become the symptom of a psychological disorder? Another question about boundaries: Where does one disorder end and another begin? We explored that question with depressive illness, discovering distinctions within affective disorder (the manic versus nonmanic-depressive kind) and between affective and nonaffective (personality) disorder. Deciding where to draw the line always depends on personal experience, social convention, and scientific consensus—all, to some extent, artifacts of culture. Nevertheless, we have seen that categories of abnormality are *useful artifacts*—useful to diagnosticians, therapists, and scientific researchers, not to mention the people who suffer from mental illness.

Different perspectives can be taken on the problem of abnormal behavior, as evident in the table that begins on the next page. Depending on the nature of the behavior and the evidence, one or more of these perspectives will apply.

Commitment to a scientific perspective can be personal as well as intellectual. That is why scientific debates over differences in perspective can be intense, even nasty, though rarely violent unless transformed into matters of politics or religion. To appreciate the nature of scientific conflict, imagine that there are observers in a cave facing a wall upon which are cast shadows. (This cave metaphor is a mixture of Plato, who first philosophized about our shadow world, and psychologist Victor Frankl who put the cylinder-shadow metaphor into the psychiatric literature [112].)

The observers' job is to root out the truth behind the shadows—*circular* shadows suggesting that the unseen object probably is circular in nature. On a wall at right angle to the first, other observers see *rectangular* shadows suggesting that the unseen object probably is rectangular. Apparently, the unseen something is cylindrical, casting different-shaped shadows in the light of consideration. In a sense, psychiatric symptoms are like shadows of something unseen—behavioral representations of underlying disorder. Different symptoms can mean different disorders. However, if they mean different aspects of the same disorder, then focusing on one or the other would be inadequate. Yet, it sometimes happens that a "circularist" or "rectangularist" approach is taken even by people who give lip service to the importance of being "cylinderist."

"Circularist" theorizing might emphasize social causality—traumatic childhood experience and current aversive conditions. That could explain many things, for example, the dramatic increase of adolescent suicide during the last 30 years coming from social changes such as declines in family life, educational achievement, church attendance, and the like. "Rectangularist" theory with its emphasis on biological causality could also explain many things, for example, that regardless of overall rates, suicide is more likely in certain families, probably for genetic reasons. How else can we explain elevated rates of suicide only for the biological, *not adoptive*, relatives of suicides?

"Cylinderist" theorizing gives equal consideration, though not necessarily equal weight, to both views. Thus, a change in suicide rate reflects the effect of changing circumstances (circular factor) on an especially vulnerable group (rectangular factor). The advantage of being an equal-opportunity employer of ideas from different perspectives is

Perspective	Paradigm	Key Words	Major Assumptions	Pragmatics (What to Do)
Descriptive	Nosological	dimensions, categories, disorders, base rates, classification	Categories and dimensions of abnormality can be discovered by observing co-variation among symptoms, course, and treatment outcome. Types of abnormality, or *disorders*, can be defined reliably, organized meaningfully in *classification* systems, and assessed by *epidemiological* methods for their population prevalence, or *base rate*.	Classification systems can be improved: made more *reliable* (with better behavioral criteria) and *valid* (by incorporating new empirical knowledge). Thus, current criteria are *working definitions* that evolve in response to research evidence and clinical experience.
	Cultural	maladaptation, mental illness	Definitions of maladaptation and "mental illness" are *culture-specific*. Even universal abnormalities, such as depression, have culture-specific behavioral expressions (sick-role behavior) and social meanings (what is abnormal or "sick" in one culture may not be in another). Thus, regardless of possible underlying disease, abnormality and illness are, in part, *cultural* concepts.	Cultural changes may be encouraged to increase tolerance of behavioral and mental deviance (i.e., calling fewer things "abnormal" or "sick"). Efforts should be made to discover which abnormalities are culture specific (and why) and which, despite behavioral differences, are fundamentally the same, i.e., psychopathological *universals*.

Perspective	Paradigm	Key Words	Major Assumptions	Pragmatics (What to Do)
Environmental	Ecopathological	unpredictability, uncontrollability, stressor	Psychologically harmful aspects of the social and physical environment (e.g., abuse, neglect, conflicting demands, etc.) that produce abnormal behavior can be reduced to two basic factors: *unpredictability* and *uncontrollability*. Comparable *ecopathological* factors in the laboratory yield animal models of human disorders ("experimental neurosis").	Family and work environments can be made less confusing and more manageable to reduce the sources of stress and maladaptive learning (family therapy, community mental health movement). Humanitarian changes can also be encouraged in institutional settings (mental health reform movements).
Intrapsychic	Behavioral	conditioning, reinforcement	Abnormal behavior (including feelings and cognitions) is *learned* and maintained in response to stimuli and reinforcers just like normal behavior, that is, through normal learning mechanisms such as classical and instrumental *conditioning*. Thus, the primary causal and controlling factors are *environmental*.	Such behavior can be eliminated by conditioning techniques such as counterconditioning and behavioral reinforcement or punishment used by behavioral therapists.
	Cognitive	congnition, attribution, imagination	Abnormal behavior is controlled by what a person thinks. While typically rooted in external events, cognitions are somewhat *autonomous* (have a "life	Abnormal behavior can be eliminated by a therapeutic "re-education" of cognitions about self (e.g., negative self-image) and

Approach	Key Concepts	Nature of Abnormality	Therapeutic Change
		of their own"). This is even truer of dysfunctional cognitions (e.g., negative self-concept), all of which helps to explain why abnormal behavior is so *predictable* (repetitive) and so resistant to change ("defensive").	environment (e.g., suspicion, pessimism).
Social Learning (Cognitive/ Behavioral)	triadic reciprocity, expectations, attributions	Mutual influence exists among three factors: environment, behavior, and cognition/affect (the person[ality]). This *triadic reciprocity* means that abnormalities in any one factor influence, and are influenced by, abnormalities in another.	Therapeutic change can be obtained by changes produced in the environment or induced in behavior (e.g., assertiveness or competence training) as well as by "direct appeal" to the cognitions.
Psychodynamic	conflict, repression, infantile psychosexuality, defense mechanisms, symbolic self-expression	Fundamental *conflict* exists between selfish motivation (libidinal, aggressive, dependent, affiliative, instrumental) and social realities (e.g., punishment), especially during childhood. Repressed, conflict-ridden residues of early frustration ("psychic lesions") are converted *unconsciously* by defense mechanisms into somatic, emotional, and thinking abnormalities. Fundamental problem: impulse *inhibition*.	Therapeutic change requires confronting unconscious conflicts by psychoanalyzing personal behavior (e.g., interpreting dreams) and interpersonal behavior (e.g., analyzing the transference). The therapeutic model is, philosophically, both educational and "medical."

Perspective	Paradigm	Key Words	Major Assumptions	Pragmatics (What to Do)
	Humanist/Self-Psychological	blocked self-actualization, conditional positive regard, ego deficits	Abnormal behavior reflects *blocked potential* for unique *self-actualization* occurring when individuals learn, through abuse or *conditional positive regard*, to deny their own natural way of existing. The result: *alienation* from self (feeling "empty," meaningless, unreal) and *detachment* from others (indifferent, hostile, manipulative), and *compensatory* (as opposed to inhibitory) *defenses*. The effect: chaotic, destructive, infantile behavior. Fundamental problem: *ego-deficit*.	Therapeutic change requires *unconditional* positive regard to encourage the individual to get in touch with true feelings and ways of experiencing (positive self-acceptance), with the goal being the ability to appreciate the self and, eventually, others.
Physiological	Genetic	heritability, diathesis	Genetic factors cause some disorders and contribute to the *risk* of developing other disorders (diathesis).	Genetic counseling may be useful to prevent or reduce the risk of certain disorders.
	Neuropsychological	"bad wiring," lesions, chemical imbalance	Specific brain abnormalities—whether of genetic, somatic, or external origin—cause some disorders.	Medical treatment can alleviate "mental illness" (the psychological symptoms of brain abnormality).

acknowledged by theorists of both camps. However, this acknowledgment is often recognized in principle more than in practice. After all, how enthusiastic can one be about a viewpoint that seems alien or lacks the right feel. For many, the cylinderist view is therefore like the notion of brotherly love—earnestly articulated yet quickly abandoned when push comes to shove. Theorists of each camp may wind up talking past each other or getting into sterile arguments over unnecessary misunderstandings. They may stop talking to each other entirely—a dysphasia compounded by a kind of dyslexia that makes a person unable to read the handwriting on the wall.

CHAPTER 16

COMING TO TERMS
WITH THE BOGEYMAN

Solving problems by proclamation may work, but only for a while. Proclamations about the social origins of schizophrenia and manic-depression, for example, have fared rather poorly when tested against alternative assumptions about biological (in particular genetic) influence. Perhaps this development isn't too surprising, given that such abnormalities are readily perceived as illness stemming from disease. But what about other abnormal behaviors readily perceived as character flaws stemming from bad environment? With the problem of antisocial behavior and crime, can we yet ask the same questions and apply the same methods that have proved so useful with the problem of affective disorder and suicide? For example, can we adapt the same twin and adoption methods to estimate the heritability of antisocial traits or of liability to criminal acts? If the answer is yes we can but we should not, why the objection?

Consider the cancellation of a conference on genetic aspects of crime slated for October 1992. The cancellation occurred after the National Institutes of Health withdrew funds in response to strong objections raised against the idea—not to mention the ethics of pursuing the idea—that compared to rearing, community conditions, and situational factors, biology contributes a lot to the crime problem [132]. One anti-biology argument simply denies that genes are important to traits that dispose people to antisocial behavior and criminal acts; therefore, why waste time and money pursuing nonexistent "crime genes"? Another admits that genes might be involved—not "crime genes," but heritable traits that dispose toward criminal behavior. Nevertheless, it advises against their investigation on the grounds that results could prove embarrassing to certain groups. Whether psychologically naive or politically astute, such arguments promote more heat than light, mostly by denying or obscuring offensive explanations, ironically by promoting the widespread suspicion that there may be more than a little truth to what is being so vigorously denied.

To cast a cool light on a hot but muddled topic, let us start with the crime problem measured in terms of *crime rate*, the estimated number of crimes in a population during some period of time, say a year. What does this number mean? Ten crimes could come from one very active criminal doing all ten crimes, ten occasional criminals doing one crime each, or any other combination that adds up to ten. A crime rate therefore must literally be the product of two numbers: (1) *criminals* in a population—the *prevalence* of people who commit at least one crime; and (2) *crimes per criminal*—the *incidence* of crimes. Thus:

$$\underset{\text{(crime rate)}}{\underset{\text{PER POPULATION}}{\text{CRIMES}}} = \underset{\text{(prevalence of criminals)}}{\underset{\text{PER POPULATION}}{\text{CRIMINALS}}} \times \underset{\text{(incidence of crimes)}}{\underset{\text{PER CRIMINAL}}{\text{CRIMES}}}$$

Prevalence and incidence arise most likely from different causes or from a different mix of the same causes. Therefore, understanding the crime problem will be no simple matter, especially if prevalence and incidence are not distinguished. For example, with greater vigilance and less tolerance for criminal acts, we might see a decrease in the crime rate. But why? The lower rate might indicate a proportionally greater decrease in the incidence of crimes than in the prevalence of criminals. At least this is what we would predict from a biological theory of so-called *criminal-mindedness*—a misnomer for self-indulgent, imprudent, impulsive, deceitful, egocentric, and specifically antisocial traits whose strength and numbers constitute merely a *disposition* to criminal behavior. With biological theory, we would therefore expect that social and political changes would have the greatest impact on incidence (criminals would be more careful), less impact on prevalence (only those most at risk—the highly criminal-minded—would continue their criminal behavior), and least on liability (given that the biological sources of criminal-mindedness would remain little changed). Research relevant to such an assumption usually focuses on either the behavioral (criminal) or the psychological (criminal-minded) aspects of criminality.

Focusing on the behavioral aspect, investigators simply divide subjects into those with or without a criminal record. They may then further divide the criminals according to age at first arrest and repetitiveness of criminal activity, the assumption being that these represent degrees of criminal-mindedness. Focusing on the psychological aspect, investigators measure, for example, the severity of two major kinds of criminal-mindedness—the primary psychopathic and the unstable antisocial—that make up much of what is called antisocial personality. *Primary psychopathic* traits include callous lack of empathy, superficial charm, pathological egocentricity, and lack of remorse.

Unstable antisocial traits include impulsivity, low frustration tolerance, violence proneness, and inability to formulate realistic long-term plans.

Here's a likely scenario: biological and *nonsocial* environmental (e.g., prenatal) factors contribute to impulsivity, restlessness, imprudence, egocentricity, irresponsibility, and other traits. These, combining with either psychopathy or relatively low intelligence and muscular physique (strength and confidence), can dispose toward criminal behavior. Evidence on the heritability of any of these (and other) traits is hotly debated, as well it should be [137; 334]. Nevertheless, a genetic hypothesis for these traits is a reasonable bet, for one thing, given the evidence that they are associated with physiological abnormalities, such as "underarousal" (low resting heart rate and more high-amplitude/slow-wave EEG) that *predict* criminal behavior years before it becomes a problem [255]. No surprise, then, about reliably greater identical- than fraternal-twin resemblance on measures of criminality implying a substantial heritability—roughly 0.5—for at least some of the psychopathic and unstable traits that make up antisocial personality. That leaves a 0.5 to be explained environmentally, a question about social and nonsocial (e.g., uterine) influences, not to mention errors of measurement, that adoption research is particularly suited to answer.

We usually think of adoptive homes—surely the most carefully selected ones—as providing *better-than-average* quality of rearing and community. If that is true, and if the crime problem were strictly a matter of the quality of the social environment, adoptees from such homes should be relatively *less* criminal-minded, *whatever their biological background*. Yet, the evidence suggests otherwise. Adoptees generally score above-average on tests of antisocial attitudes that predispose to crime [331]. (Most adoptees are normal, of course, but enough score high on the relevant measures to elevate the average significantly.) Moreover, the highest measures of criminality—in particular, prevalence—are typically found for the adopted offspring, at least one of whose biological parents has a criminal record, compared to the adopted offspring, neither of whose biological parents has a criminal record [67].

Consider two more observations. First, there is a rare chromosomal variant of the male (XY) pattern, where each cell of the male has an extra Y chromosome. This XYY anomaly makes affected males prone to petty (nonviolent) criminality, probably out of a combination of low intelligence and poor judgment [336]. Given that such traits come from many genetic and nongenetic sources, not much of the crime problem will be explained by the XYY anomaly—true, but that is not the point. The point is that there may be other, perhaps many, as yet undetected genetic anomalies with similar or other antisocial effects, for example, genetic anomalies that, altering brain function, account for reckless impulsivity, inexplicable outbursts of violence, arson, or sexual brutality. Researchers have just reported evidence that such behavior in males can come from a defective gene that is located on the X chromosome and that codes the enzyme MAOA (see Brunner et al. reference in the Additional Sources). The more such biologically discontinuous syndromes exist, the less likely that crime can be merely a matter of "quality of environment." Is this point not worthy of investigation?

The second observation is that, although most criminals were once juvenile delinquents, most juvenile delinquents *don't* become criminals. Rather, they seem to outgrow their antisocial ways despite all that conditioning and all those bad habits and crime-ridden environments that supposedly explain why others continue their criminal ways. Wouldn't it be important to determine objectively what many people suspect— that biology makes *some* contribution to resiliency as well as to vulnerability, to courage as well as to capitulation, to character as well as to character disorder (psychopathy)? Surely it is more than just scientifically legitimate—surely it is *socially desirable*—to seek out and debate biological evidence relevant to such obviously important "off-diagonal" questions as: Why do *non-adopted* children from "good" family environments sometimes turn out "bad," and why do children—even juvenile delinquents—from "bad" families sometimes turn out "good"? The alternative to such inquiry—simply blaming the social environment for "bad" outcomes while crediting it for the "good"—seems as simpleminded as it is insulting.

Answers to questions about criminality cannot lie merely with education and social engineering that deny the antisocial and self-destructive elements of human nature. Such approaches are doomed to fail because, while pretending to remediate defects peculiar to modern society, they ignore the evidence of human biology and the lessons of history. As social critic James Burnham observes in *Suicide of the West:* "Only those who know very little about the history of mankind can suppose that cruelty, crime or weakness, mass slaughter or mass corruption, are exceptions from the normal human rule. A doctrine of human nature that paints a picture of what man might be that is in direct contradiction to what he has always and everywhere been may be a comfort to the spirit, but is not to be taken very seriously as a scientific hypothesis."

If, as we have seen, discomfort with "genetics" reflects concern most specifically about individuals (the heritability question), and most generally about mankind (the human nature question), it also reflects a more intermediate concern about groups. The group-differences bugaboo raised by the biological—in particular, the hereditarian—approach to criminality requires our attention, if only to clarify a vital distinction.

Objections even to talking about heritability are fueled by the suspi cion that documented genetic reasons for *individual* differences must implicate genetic influence over *group* differences. The fact is, however, that the truth or falsity of the suspicion will never be revealed by any heritability estimate. The simple reason is that a heritability estimate helps us understand individual differences *within some group or population;* it reveals nothing definitive regarding genetic influence either within any one individual or between any two groups [334]. Even if, hypothetically, individual differences in criminality were 100 percent genetic—that is, even if the heritability of criminality were 1.0—*group* differences could be 100 percent environmental. The same could be supposed for intelligence (IQ) or other traits.

Think of height. Height is highly heritable for Americans (probably around 0.9), but also for Pygmies, despite their much lower *average* height. Likewise, height is highly heritable for contemporary Japanese, but also for earlier generations whose average height was much less. The difference in the average height of Americans and Pygmies is *mostly genetic;* the average American has more "tall" genes than has the average Pygmy. However, the *change* in average height of Japanese is *mostly environmental*—modern diets that include more meat and dairy products. Clearly, the average height difference between Americans and Japanese two generations ago was *mostly environmental.* But again, such differences and changes in average height, whether mostly genetic or mostly environmental, exist *whatever the heritability of height* for each group. In sum, group differences might be mostly genetic (like the American-Pygmy difference), mostly environmental (like the American-Japanese difference generations ago), or something in between. With respect to criminality, and again, hypothetically to reinforce a key point: Even if *individual* differences within each group were 100 percent heritable, *group* differences could be 100 percent environmental or 100 percent genetic, or anything in between. Research, not ideology, would reveal the truth.

The anti-hereditarian argument applied to questions of criminality tends to promote two things: the belief that inconvenient ideas suppressed today will remain suppressed tomorrow, and a false philanthropy that denies some people the right to investigate while denying other people the right to know. The result is more research on shadow rather than substance—on correlates and effects rather than causes. Ironically, the effect of all this activity is the impediment of progress toward understanding how environments really work, first, early in life during personality development to supplement genetic potential, and later, during adulthood, to bring out that potential.

CHAPTER 17

SOLUTIONS IN THE DREAM

Was Kekulé's dream really a metaphorical solution (snake = benzine ring), or was it merely a fortuitous image that ignited the more rational thought of wakefulness (as well as the illusion that the dream was indeed the solution)? "Let us learn to dream, gentlemen!" Kekulé was supposed to have said. A provocative proclamation, especially for a scientist, but the truth is, we can't be sure what role dreaming plays in scientific solutions. Nevertheless, many people believe that everyday problems, especially personal problems, do lend themselves to solution.

My favorite dream solution involves a personal rather than scientific problem. The story starts with an engaging word game. On a piece of paper, each player writes a vertical column of capital letters from A to Z. Then someone reads out loud a random sentence or two from a book or magazine, and each person writes down all the letters in a vertical column to the right of the first, making each letter from the second column pair up with a letter from the first. This procedure yields 26 pairs of letters. The problem is to identify paired initials of famous people or story characters, for example, Tom Thumb, an OK solution for T. T. A limited time, say five minutes, is allowed for each game. For each identification, you get ten points from every player who fails to identify that pair. Examples: B. L. = Bert Lahr or Burt Lancaster or—you get the picture. You can really rack up points if you know Zena Bethune, Yves Montand, Xavier Cugat, ZaSu Pitts, and other Ugga Buggas. Some double-vowel pairs seem impossible, like U. U. and O. O. (Okay, Ozzy Osbourne, but what about U. U.?) Some pairs are easy, like A. A. But what about E. E.? It should be possible to get it, but one time it wasn't, and therein lies a tale.

One night, on a camping trip, the E. E. pair came up. No one in our party could get it. This is shameful for a psychologist familiar with Erik Erikson's work, but forget that. Anyway, my wife wakes me in the wee hours to relate a dream. The dream was about her former high school math teacher about whom she hadn't consciously thought for over 10 years. In the dream, he is arranging seats (letters?) in an auditorium—nice symbolism, but hardly worth the waking. Wait, she says, his name was Ewing. An E guy! And his first name? She couldn't recall, but some weeks later we got out her old yearbook, and Bingo! *Earl Ewing.* Good old Earl. Good old wife to come up with a subjectively meaningful solution—right(eous) if not objectively correct.

REFERENCES

1. Abrams, S. (1986). Disposition and environment. *The Psychoanalytic Study of the Child, 41*, 41–60.
2. Abramson, L. Y., Alloy, L. B., & Metalsky, G. I. (1988). The cognitive diathesis-stress theories of depression: Toward an adequate evaluation of the theories' validities. In L. B. Alloy (Ed.), *Cognitive processes in depression* (pp. 3–30). New York: Guilford.
3. Ackerman, J. S. (1987). Jonah. In R. Alter & F. Kermode (Eds.), *The literary guide to the Bible.* Cambridge, MA: Belknap (Harvard University Press).
4. Ackermann, R., & DeRubeis, R. J. (1991). Is depressive realism real? *Clinical Psychology Review, 11*, 565–84.
5. Adler, T. (1989). Shy monkeys are born, not made. *The APA Monitor,* August 1989, p. 5.
6. Akiskal, H. S. (1983). Dysthymic disorder: Psychopathology of proposed chronic depressive subtypes. *American Journal of Psychiatry, 140*, 11–20.
7. Akiskal, H. S., Bitar, A. H., Puzantian, V. R., Rosenthal, T. L., & Walker, P. W. (1978). The nosological status of neurotic depression: A prospective three- to four-year follow-up examination in light of the primary-secondary and unipolar-bipolar dichotomies. *Archives of General Psychiatry, 35*, 756–66.
8. Akiskal, H. S., Djenderdejian, A. H., Rosenthal, R. H., & Khani, M. K. (1977). Cyclothymic disorder: Validating criteria for inclusion in the bipolar affective group. *American Journal of Psychiatry, 134*, 1227–33.

9. Akiskal, H. S., Hirschfeld, R. M. A., & Yerevanian, B. I. (1983). The relationship of personality to affective disorders. *Archives of General Psychiatry, 40,* 801–10.
10. Alexander, V. (1991). *Words I never thought to speak.* New York: Lexington.
11. Allen, M. G. (1976). Twin studies of affective illness. *Archives of General Psychiatry, 33,* 1476–78.
12. Alloy, L. B., & Abramson, L. Y. (1988). Depressive realism: Four theoretical perspectives. In L. B. Alloy (Ed.), *Cognitive processes in depression* (pp. 223–65.) New York: Guilford.
13. Altman, K. L. (1991). Doctor writes about assisting patient's suicide. *Austin American-Statesman,* March 7, 1991, pp. A1, A9.
14. Alvarez, A. (1973). *The savage god: A study of suicide.* New York: Random House.
15. Andreasen, N. C. (1980). Mania and creativity. In R. H. Belmaker & H. M. van Praag (Eds.), *Mania: An evolving concept* (pp. 377–86). Jamaica, NY: Spectrum Publications.
16. Angst, J. (1973). Masked depression viewed from the cross-cultural standpoint. In P. Kielholz (Ed.), *Masked depression* (pp. 269–74). Berlin: Hans Huber.
17. Angyal, A. (1965). *Neurosis and treatment: A holistic theory.* New York: Viking.
18. Arato, M., Tothfalusi, L., & Banki, C. M. (1989). Serotonin and suicide. *Biological Psychiatry, 25,* 196A–97A.
19. Arkin, A. M., Antrobus, J. S., & Ellman, S. J. (1978). *The mind in sleep: Psychology and psychophysiology.* Hillsdale, NJ: Lawrence Erlbaum.
20. Arnhoff, F. N. (1975). Social consequences of policy toward mental illness. *Science, 188,* 1277–81.
21. Aschoff, J. (Ed.). (1981). *Handbook of behavioral neurobiology: Vol. 4. Biological rhythms.* New York: Plenum.
22. Associated Press (1990). Women's "false" pains tied to artery ailment. *Austin American-Statesman,* January 17, 1990, p. A4.
23. Avery, D. H., Bolte, M. A., Dager, S. R., Wilson, L. G., Weyer, M., Cox, G. B., & Dunner, D. L. (1993). Dawn simulation treatment with winter depression: A controlled study. *American Journal of Psychiatry, 150,* 113–17.
24. Bailey, J. M., & Pillard, R. C. (1991). A genetic study of male sexual orientation. *Archives of General Psychiatry, 48,* 1089–96.
25. Barchas, J. D., Elliott, G. R., Berger, P. A., Barchas, P. R., & Solomon, F. (1985). The ultimate stigma: Inadequate funding for research on mental and addictive disorders (editorial). *American Journal of Psychiatry, 142,* 838–39.

26. Barrett, J. E. (Ed.). (1979). *Stress and mental disorder.* New York: Raven.
27. Barzun, J. (1964). *Science: The glorious entertainment.* New York: Harper & Row.
28. Basolo, A. L. (1990). Female preference predates the evolution of the sword in swordtail fish. *Science, 250,* 808–10.
29. Bauer, M. S. (1990). Rapid cycling bipolar affective disorder. *Archives of General Psychiatry, 47,* 427–32.
30. Baumann, F. (1990). Liberal education and the natural bourgeoisie. *Academic Questions, 3* (Fall 1990), 54–58.
31. Baumeister, R. F. (1990). Suicide as escape from self. *Psychological Review, 97,* 90–113.
32. Beck, A. T. (1967). *Depression: Clinical, experimental, and theoretical aspects.* New York: Harper & Row (Hoeber Medical Division).
33. Beers, C. W. (1981 / 1907). *A mind that found itself.* Pittsburgh: University of Pittsburgh.
34. Benbow, C. P., & Stanley, J. C. (1980). Sex differences in mathematical ability: Fact or artifact? *Science, 210,* 1262–64.
35. Benbow, C. P., & Stanley, J. C. (1983). Sex differences in mathematical reasoning ability: More facts. *Science, 222,* 1029–31.
36. Bertelsen, A., & Gottesman, I. I. (1986). Offspring of twin pairs discordant for psychiatric illness (Abstract). *Acta Geneticae Medicae et Gemellologiae, 35* (Special issue on twin research), 82.
37. Bloom, A. (1987). *The closing of the American mind.* New York: Simon & Schuster.
38. Blumenthal, S. J. (1988). Suicide: A guide to risk factors, assessment, and treatment of suicidal patients. *The Medical Clinics of North America, 72* (Anxiety and Depression), 937–71.
39. Blumer, D. (1975). Temperal lobe epilepsy and its psychiatric significance. In D. F. Benson & D. Blumer (Eds.), *Psychiatric aspects of neurological disease* (pp. 171–97). New York: Grune & Stratton.
40. Blumer, D. (1982). Chronic pain as a psychobiologic phenomenon: The pain-prone disorder. In D. F. Benson & D. Blumer (Eds.), *Psychiatric aspects of neurologic disease* (pp. 179–94). New York: Grune & Stratton.
41. Bonime, W. (1962). *The clinical use of dreams.* New York: Basic Books.
42. Bortner, M., & Birch, H. G. (1970). Cognitive capacity and cognitive competence. *American Journal of Mental Deficiency, 74,* 735–44.
43. Bouchard, T., Lykken, D. T., McGue, M., Segal, N. L., & Tellegen, A. (1991). IQ and heredity: Response. *Science, 252,* 192.
44. Bouchard, T. J., Jr., Lykken, D. T., McGue, M., Segal, N. L., & Tellegen, A. (1990). Sources of human psychological differences: The Minnesota study of twins reared apart. *Science, 250,* 223–28.

45. Bouchard, T. J., Jr., & McGue, M. (1990). Genetic and rearing environmental influences on adult personality: An analysis of adopted twins reared apart. *Journal of Personality, 58*, 263–92.

46. Boulding, K. E. (1980). Science: Our common heritage. *Science, 207*, 831–36.

47. Bowers, K. S., & Kelly, P. (1979). Stress, disease, psychotherapy, and hypnosis. *Journal of Abnormal Psychology, 88*, 490–505.

48. Bowlby, J. (1960). Grief and mourning in infancy and early childhood. *Psychoanalytic Study of the Child, 15*, 9–52.

49. Bowlby, J. (1985). The role of childhood experience in cognitive disturbance. In M. J. Mahoney (Ed.), *Cognition and psychotherapy* (pp. 181–200). New York: Plenum.

50. Bowlby, J. (1990). *Charles Darwin: A new life*. New York: Norton.

51. Bracha, H. S., Torrey, E. F., Bigelow, L. B., Lohr, J. B., & Linington, B. B. (1991). Subtle signs of prenatal maldevelopment of the hand ectoderm in schizophrenia: A preliminary monozygotic twin study. *Biological Psychiatry, 30*, 719–25.

52. Bracha, H. S., Torrey, E. F., Gottesmann, I. I., Bigelow, L. B., & Cunniff, C. (1992). Second-trimester markers of fetal size in schizophrenia: A study of monozygotic twins. *American Journal of Psychiatry, 149*, 1355–61.

53. Breland, K., & Breland, M. (1961). The misbehavior of organisms. *American Psychologist, 16*, 661–64.

54. Brody, J. E. (1992). Doses of pineal gland hormone can reset the body's daily clock. *New York Times*, November 3, 1992, pp. B5, B8.

55. Bronowski, J. (1965). *Science and human values*. New York: Harper & Row.

56. Buckley, P. (1989). Fifty years after Freud: Dora, the Rat Man, and the Wolf-Man. *American Journal of Psychiatry, 146*, 1394–1403.

57. Burnham, J. (1985 / 1964). *Suicide of the west: An essay on the meaning and destiny of liberalism*. Washington, DC: Regnery Gateway.

58. Byne, W., & Parsons, B. (1993). Human sexual orientation: The biologic theories reappraised. *Archives of General Psychiatry, 50*, 228–239.

59. Cameron, M. (1965). Why psychosis. *Michigan Quarterly Review, 4* (Winter 1965), 14–18.

60. Carpenter, W. T. (1992). The insanity defense and mental illness (letter to the editor). *Science, 256*, 292.

61. Chance, S. (1992). *Stronger than death: When suicide touches your life*. New York: Norton.

62. Chandrasekhar, S. (1987). *Truth and beauty: Aesthetics and motivations in science*. Chicago: University of Chicago Press.

63. Chapman, L. J. (1969). Schizomimetic conditions and schizophrenia. *Journal of Consulting and Clinical Psychology, 33*, 646–50.

64. Chodoff, P., Friedman, S. B., & Hamburg, D. A. (1964). Stress, defenses and coping behavior: Observations of parents of children with malignant disease. *American Journal of Psychiatry, 120,* 743–49.

65. Clayton, P. J. (1982). Bereavement. In E. S. Paykel (Ed.), *Handbook of affective disorders* (pp. 403–15). New York: Guilford.

66. Cleckley, H. (1976 / 1941). *The mask of sanity.* St. Louis: Mosby.

67. Cloninger, C. R., Sigvardsson, S., Bohman, M., & von Knorring, A. (1982). Predisposition to petty criminality in Swedish adoptees. II. Cross-fostering analysis of gene-environment interaction. *Archives of General Psychiatry, 39,* 1242–47.

68. Cohen, D. B. (1979). *Sleep and dreaming: Origins, nature, and functions.* Oxford, England: Pergamon.

69. Cole, D. (1989). Psychopathology of adolescent suicide: Hopelessness, coping beliefs, and depression. *Journal of Abnormal Psychology, 98,* 248–55.

70. Cole, L. E. (1970). *Understanding abnormal behavior.* Scranton, PA: Chandler.

71. Coleman, R. M. (1986). *Wide awake at 3:00 A.M.: By choice or by chance?* New York: Freeman.

72. Coons, P. M. (1988). Psychophysiological aspects of multiple personality. *Dissociation, 1,* 47–53.

73. Coppen, A. (1965). The prevalence of menstrual disorders in psychiatric patients. *British Journal of Psychiatry, 111,* 165–67.

74. Coryell, W. (1980). A blind family history study of Briquet's syndrome. *Archives of General Psychiatry, 37,* 1266–69.

75. Coryell, W., & Winokur, G. (1982). Course and outcome. In E. S. Paykel (Ed.), *Handbook of affective disorders* (pp. 93–106). New York: Guilford.

76. Coyne, J. C. (1976). Toward an interactional description of depression. *Psychiatry, 39,* 28–40.

77. Coyne, J. C., & Gotlib, I. (1986). Studying the role of cognition in depression: Well-trodden paths and cul-de-sacs. *Cognitive Therapy, 10,* 695–705.

78. Critchley, M. (1979). Modes of reaction to central blindness. In M. Critchley (Ed.), *The divine banquet of the brain and other essays* (pp. 156–62). New York: Raven Press.

79. Crowe, R. R. (1974). An adoption study of antisocial personality. *Archives of General Psychiatry, 31,* 785–91.

80. Curran, D. K. (1987). *Adolescent suicidal behavior.* New York: Hemisphere Publishing.

81. Cushman, P. (1990). Why the self is empty: Toward a historically situated psychology. *American Psychologist, 45,* 599–611.

82. Dabrowski, K. (1964). *Positive disintegration.* Boston: Little, Brown.

83. Danion, J.-M., Willard-Schroeder, D., Zimmerman, M.-A.,

Gragné, D., Schlienger, J.-L., & Singer, L. (1991). Explicit memory and repetition priming in depression: Preliminary findings. *Archives of General Psychiatry, 48,* 707–11.

84. Davidson, L. E., Rosenberg, M. L., Mercy, J. A., Franklin, J., & Simmons, J. T. (1989). An epidemiologic study of risk factors in two teenage suicide clusters. *Journal of the American Medical Association, 262,* 2687–92.

85. deCatanzaro, D. (1981). *Suicide and self-damaging behavior: A sociobiological perspective.* New York: Academic Press.

86. Deese, J. (1972). *Psychology as science and art.* New York: Harcourt Brace Jovanovich.

87. Delgado, P. L., Charney, D. S., Price, L. H., Aghajanian, G. K., Landis, H., & Heninger, G. R. (1990). Serotonin function and the mechanisms of antidepressant action: Reversal of antidepressant-induced remission by rapid depletion of plasma tryptophan. *Archives of General Psychiatry, 47,* 411–18.

88. Derry, P. A., & Kuiper, N. A. (1981). Schematic processing and self-reference in clinical depression. *Journal of Abnormal Psychology, 90,* 286–97.

89. Durant, W. (1935). *The story of civilization: Part I. Our Oriental heritage.* New York: Simon & Schuster.

90. Durant, W., & Durant, A. (1968). *The lessons of history.* New York: Simon & Schuster.

91. Durkheim, E. (1955 / 1897). Suicide: A study in sociology. In C. C. Contemporary Civilization Staff (Eds.), *Man in contemporary society* (pp. 384–402). New York: Columbia University Press.

92. Dusky, L. (1990). A cure for PMS? *Parade,* February 25, 1990, pp. 16–17.

93. Egeland, J. A., Blumenthal, R. L., Nee, J., Sharpe, L., & Endicott, J. (1987). Reliability and relationship of various ages of onset criteria for major affective disorder. *Journal of Affective Disorder, 12,* 159–65.

94. Egeland, J. A., & Sussex, J. N. (1985). Suicide and family loading for affective disorders. *Journal of the American Medical Association, 254,* 915–18.

95. Ekman, P., & O'Sullivan, M. O. (1991). Who can catch a liar? *American Psychologist, 46,* 913–20.

96. Endler, N. S. (1982). *Holiday of darkness: A psychologist's personal journey out of his depression.* New York: Wiley-Interscience.

97. Engel, G. L. (1971). Sudden and rapid death during psychological stress, folklore or folkwisdom? *Annals of Internal Medicine, 74,* 771–82.

98. Engelsmann, F. (1982). Culture and depression. In I. Al-Issa (Ed.), *Culture and psychopathology* (pp. 251–74). Baltimore: University Park Press.

99. Enoch, M. D., & Trethowan, W. H. (1979). *Uncommon psychiatric syndromes*. Bristol, England: John Wright and Sons.
100. Faber, M. D. (1967). Shakespeare's suicides: Some historic, dramatic and psychological reflections. In E. S. Shneidman (Ed.), *Essays in self-destruction* (pp. 30–58). New York: Science House.
101. Fabrega, H., Jr. (1975). The position of psychiatry in the understanding of human disease. *Archives of General Psychiatry, 32,* 1500–1512.
102. Fenichel, O. (1945). *The psychoanalytic theory of neurosis.* New York: Norton.
103. Fieve, R. R. (1975). *Moodswing: The third revolution in psychiatry.* New York: William Morrow.
104. Filer, R. (1990). What we really know about the homeless. *The Wall Street Journal,* April 10, 1990, p. A18.
105. Fischer, M. (1971). Psychoses in the offspring of schizophrenic monozygotic twins and their normal co-twins. *British Journal of Psychiatry, 118,* 43–52.
106. Fogel, B. S., & Slaby, A. E. (1986). Neurological screening of psychiatric patients. In I. Extein & M. S. Gold (Eds.), *Medical mimics of psychiatric disorders* (pp. 15–32). Washington, DC: American Psychiatric Press.
107. Foreman, J. (1991). Suicide attempt uses AIDS-infected blood. *Austin American-Statesman,* April 12, 1991, p. A3.
108. Forrest, M. S., & Hokanson, J. E. (1975). Depression and autonomic arousal reduction accompanying self-punitive behavior. *Journal of Abnormal Psychology, 84,* 346–57.
109. Foulkes, D. (1966). *The psychology of sleep.* New York: Scribner's.
110. Fox, J. (1984). The brain's dynamic way of keeping in touch. *Science,* August 24, 1984, pp. 820–21.
111. Fraiberg, S. H. (1959). *The magic years.* New York: Charles Scribner's Sons.
112. Frankl, V. (1985). Logos, paradox, and the search for meaning. In M. J. Mahoney & A. Freeman (Eds.), *Cognition and psychotherapy* (pp. 259–75). New York: Plenum.
113. Frankl, V. E. (1984). *Man's search for meaning.* New York: Washington Square Press (Pocket Books).
114. Freeman, N. B. (1991). The wasteland. *National Review,* October 7, 1991, pp. 40–42.
115. Freud, A. (1946). *The ego and the mechanisms of defence* (Baines, C., Trans.). New York: International Universities Press.
116. Fuchs, V. R., & Reklis, D. M. (1992). America's children: Economic perspectives and policy options. *Science, 255,* 41–46.
117. Fuller, J. L., & Thompson, W. R. (1978). *Foundations of behavior genetics.* Saint Louis: C. V. Mosby.

118. Gainotti, G. (1989). Disorders of emotions and affect in patients with unilateral brain damage. In F. Boller & J. Grafman (Eds.), *Handbook of neuropsychology* (pp. 345–61). Amsterdam, The Netherlands: Elseview.

119. Garcia, J., & Koelling, R. A. (1966). Relation of cue to consequence in avoidance learning. *Psychonomic Science, 4,* 123–24.

120. Gawin, F. H. (1991). Cocaine addiction: Psychology and neurophysiology. *Science, 251,* 1580–86.

121. Gazzaniga, M. S., & LeDoux, J. E. (1978). *The integrated mind.* New York: Plenum.

122. Gelinas, D. J. (1983). The persisting negative effects of incest. *Psychiatry, 46,* 312–32.

123. Gershon, E. S. (1990). Genetics. In F. K. Goodwin & K. Jamison (Eds.), *Manic-depressive illness* (pp. 373–401). New York: Oxford University Press.

124. Gershon, E. S., Hamovit, J. H., Guroff, J. J., & Nurnberger, J. I. (1987). Birth-cohort changes in manic and depressive disorders in relatives of bipolar and schizoaffective patients. *Archives of General Psychiatry, 44,* 314–19.

125. Gitlin, M. J., & Pasnau, R. O. (1989). Psychiatric syndromes linked to reproductive function in women: A review of current knowledge. *American Journal of Psychiatry, 146,* 1413–22.

126. Glassman, A. H. (1993). Cigarette smoking: Implications for psychiatric illness. *American Journal of Psychiatry, 150,* 546–53.

127. Goggans, F. C., Allen, R. M., & Gold, M. S. (1986). Primary hypothyroidism and its relationship to affective disorders. In I. Extein & M. S. Gold (Eds.), *Medical mimics of psychiatric disorder* (pp. 95–109). Washington, DC: American Psychiatric Press.

128. Goldfarb, A. I. (1974). Masked depression in the elderly. In S. Lesse (Ed.), *Masked depression* (pp. 236–49). New York: Jason Aronson.

129. Goldstein, R. B., Black, D. W., Nasrallah, A., & Winokur, G. (1991). The prediction of suicide: Sensitivity, specificity, and predictive value of a multivariate model applied to suicide among 1906 patients with affective disorder. *Archives of General Psychiatry, 48,* 418–22.

130. Goleman, D. (1988). Probing the enigma of multiple personality. *New York Times,* June 28, 1988, pp. 23, 26.

131. Goleman, D. (1992). Family rituals may promote better emotional adjustment. *Austin American-Statesman,* March 15, 1992, pp. D1, D6.

132. Goleman, D. (1992). New storm brews on whether crime has roots in genes. *The Wall Street Journal,* September 15, 1992, pp. C1, C7.

133. Goodall, J. (1986). *The chimpanzees of Gombe: Patterns of behavior.* Cambridge, MA: Belknap (Harvard University Press).

134. Goodwin, F. K., & Jamison, K. (1990). *Manic-depressive illness.* New York: Oxford University Press.

135. Gorenstein, E. E. (1984). Debating mental illness: Implications for science, medicine, and social policy. *American Psychologist, 39,* 50–56.

136. Gottesman, I. I. (1991). *Schizophrenia genesis: The origins of madness.* New York: Freeman.

137. Gottfredson, M. R., & Hirschi, T. (1990). *A general theory of crime.* Stanford: Stanford University Press.

138. Gould, M. S. (1990). Suicide clusters and media exposure. In S. J. Blumenthal & D. J. Kupfer (Eds.), *Suicide over the life cycle* (pp. 517–32). Washington, DC: American Psychiatric Press.

139. Gould, R., Miller, B. L., Goldberg, M. A., & Benson, D. F. (1986). The validity of hysterical signs and symptoms. *Journal of Nervous and Mental Disease, 174,* 593–97.

140. Gould, S. J. (1989). George Canning's left buttock and the origin of the species: Why do we revel in the details of history? *Natural History,* May 1989, pp. 18–23.

141. Gould, S. J. (1992). Dinosaurs in the haystack. *Natural History,* March 1992, pp. 2–13.

142. Greenwald, A. G. (1980). The totalitarian ego: Fabrication and revision of personal history. *American Psychlogist, 35,* 603–18.

143. Halbreich, U., Bakhai, Y., Bacon, K. B., Goldstein, S., Asnis, G. M., Endicott, J., & Lesser, J. (1989). The normalcy of self-proclaimed "normal volunteers." *American Journal of Psychiatry, 146,* 1052–55.

144. Halbreich, U., & Endicott, J. (1985). Relationship of dysphoric premenstrual changes to depressive disorders. *Acta Psychiatrica Scandinavica, 71,* 331–38.

145. Hall, R. C. W. (Ed.). (1980). *Psychiatric presentations of medical illnesses: Somatopsychic disorders.* New York: SP Medical Scientific Books.

146. Hanson, G. (1993). Total recall versus tricks of the mind. *Insight,* pp. 6–10, 34–35.

147. Harpur, T. J., Hare, R. D., & Hakstian, A. R. (1989). Two-factor conceptualization of psychopathy: Construct validity and assessment implications. *Psychological Assessment: A Journal of Consulting and Clinical Psychology, 1,* 6–17.

148. Harrison, W. M., Endicott, J., & Nee, J. (1990). Treatment of premenstrual dysphoria with Alprazolam: A controlled study. *Archives of General Psychiatry, 47,* 270–75.

149. Hartmann, E., Baekeland, F., & Zwilling, G. R. (1972). Psychological differences between long and short sleepers. *Archives of General Psychiatry, 26*, 463–68.

150. Hauri, P. (1976). Dreams in patients remitted from reactive depression. *Archives of General Psychiatry, 85*, 1–10.

151. Healy, D., & Williams, J. M. G. (1988). Dysrhythmia, dysphoria, and depression: The interaction of learned helplessness and circadian dysrhythmia in the pathogenesis of depression. *Psychological Bulletin, 103*, 163–68.

152. Helgason, T. (1979). Epidemiological investigations concerning affective disorders. In M. Schou & E. Strömgren (Eds.), *Origin, prevention and treatment of affective disorders* (pp. 241–55). London: Academic Press.

153. Henriques, J. B., & Davidson, R. J. (1990). Regional brain electrical asymmetries discriminate between previously depressed and healthy control subjects. *Journal of Abnormal Psychology, 99*, 22–31.

154. Heston, L. L. (1966). Psychiatric disorders in foster home reared children of schizophrenic mothers. *British Journal of Psychiatry, 112*, 819–25.

155. Hilgard, E. R. (1977). *Divided consciousness: Multiple controls in human thought and action.* New York: Wiley-Interscience.

156. Holt, J. (1990). Science and literature reconciled. *The Wall Street Journal,* August 17, 1990, p. A9.

157. Holt, R. R. (1968). Editor's forward. In D. Rapoport, M. M. Gill, & R. Schafer (Eds.), *Diagnostic psychological testing* (pp. 1–44). New York: International Universities Press.

158. Holzman, D. (1991). Coincidences may not be so odd. *Insight,* April 15, 1991, pp. 46–48.

159. Horgan, J. (1992). Quantum philosophy. *Scientific American,* July 1992, pp. 94–104.

160. Irving, J. (1989). *A prayer for Owen Meany.* New York: William Morrow & Company.

161. Isaac, R. J. (1992). A detour around crazy mental health laws. *Wall Street Journal,* April 26, 1992, p. A24.

162. Jacobs, W. J., & Nadel, L. (1985). Stress-induced recovery of fears and phobias. *Psychological Review, 92*, 512–31.

163. Janoff-Bulman, R., & Hecker, B. (1988). Depression, vulnerability, and world assumptions. In L. B. Alloy (Ed.), *Cognitive processes in depression* (pp. 177–92). New York: Guilford.

164. Jefferson, J. W., & Marshall, J. R. (1981). *Neuropsychiatric features of medical disorders.* New York: Plenum Medical.

165. Jeste, D. V., Gillin, J. C., & Wyatt, J. (1979). Serendipidy in biological psychiatry—A myth? *Archives of General Psychiatry, 36*, 1173–1178.

166. Jones, J. S., Stanley, B., Mann, J. J., Frances, A. J., Guido, J. R., Traskman-Bendz, L., Winchel, R., Brown, R. P., & Stanley, M. (1990). CSF-5HIAA and HVA concentrations in elderly depressed patients who attempted suicide. *American Journal of Psychiatry, 147,* 1225–27.

167. Jones, L. (1988). Motor illusions: What do they reveal about proprioception? *Psychological Bulletin, 103,* 72–86.

168. Juel-Nielson, N. (1979). Suicide risk in manic-depressive disorders. In M. Schou & E. Strömgren (Eds.), *Origin, prevention and treatment of affective disorders* (pp. 269–76). London: Academic Press.

169. Kagan, J. (1989). Temperamental contributions to social behavior. *American Psychologist, 44,* 668–74.

170. Kahn, R. (1971). *The boys of summer.* New York: Signet (New American Library).

171. Katz, R. J. (1990). Neurobiology of obsessive compulsive disorder—A serotonergic basis of Freudian repression. *Neuroscience and Biobehavioral Reviews, 15,* 375–81.

172. Kendell, R. E. (1975). *The role of diagnosis in psychiatry.* Oxford, England: Blackwell Scientific.

173. Kendler, K. S. (1991). Mood-incongruent psychotic affective illness. *Archives of General Psychiatry, 48,* 362–69.

174. Kendler, K. S., Neale, M. C., Kessler, R. C., Heath, A. C., & Eaves, L. J. (1992). Childhood parental loss and adult psychopathology in women: A twin study perspective. *Archives of General Psychiatry, 49,* 109–16.

175. Kendler, K. S., Neale, M. C., Kessler, R. C., Heath, A. C., & Eaves, L. J. (1992). A population-based twin study of major depression in women: The impact of varying definitions of illness. *Archives of General Psychiatry, 49,* 257–66.

176. Kendler, K. S., Neale, M. C., Kessler, R. C., Heath, A. C., & Eaves, L. J. (1993). A test of the equal-environment assumption in twin studies of psychiatric illness. *Behavior Genetics, 23,* 21–27.

177. Kendler, K. S., Neale, M. C., MacLean, C. J., Heath, A. C., Eaves, L. J., & Kessler, R. C. (1993). Smoking and major depression. *Archives of General Psychiatry, 50,* 36–43.

178. Kerr, P. (1992). Mental care study finds many abuses at private hospitals. *Austin American-Statesman,* April 29, 1992, p. A2.

179. Kety, S. S. (1974). From rationalization to reason. *American Journal of Psychiatry, 131,* 957–63.

180. Kinsbourne, M. (1990). Hemisphere interactions in depression. In M. Kinsbourne (Ed.), *Hemisphere function in depression.* Washington, DC: American Psychiatric Association.

181. Kirmayer, L., Robbins, J. M., Dworkind, M., & Yaffe, M. J. (1993).

Somatization and the recognition of depression and anxiety in primary care. *American Journal of Psychiatry, 150,* 734–41.

182. Klerman, G., & Weissman, M. M. (1989). Increasing rates of depression. *Journal of the American Medical Association (JAMA), 261,* 2229–35.

183. Klerman, G. L. (1988). Depression and related disorders of mood (affective disorders). In A. M. Nicholi, Jr. (Ed.), *The new Harvard guide to psychiatry* (pp. 309–36). Cambridge, MA: Belknap Press (Harvard University Press).

184. Klerman, G. L. (1989). Depressive disorders: Further evidence for increased medical morbidity and impairment of social functioning. *Archives of General Psychiatry, 46,* 856–58.

185. Koestler, A. (1976). *The act of creation* (Danube ed.). London: Hutchinson.

186. Kohut, H. (1977). *The restoration of the self.* New York: International Universities Press.

187. Koluchová, J. (1976). A report on the further development of twins after severe and prolonged deprivation. In A. M. Clarke & A. D. B. Clarke (Eds.), *Early experience: Myth and evidence* (pp. 56–66). New York: The Free Press (Macmillan).

188. Koluchová, J. (1976). Severe deprivation in twins: A case study. In A. M. Clarke & A. D. B. Clarke (Eds.), *Early experience: Myth and evidence* (pp. 45–55). New York: The Free Press (Macmillan).

189. Koshland, D. E., Jr. (1990). The addictive personality. *Science, 250,* 1193.

190. Kraepelin, E. (1921). *Manic-depressive insanity and paranoia* (R. M. Barclay, Trans.). Edinburgh, Scotland: E. & S. Livingston.

191. Kunst-Wilson, W. R., & Zajonc, R. B. (1980). Affective discrimination of stimuli that cannot be recognized. *Science, 207,* 557–58.

192. Kupfer, D. J., & Reynolds, C. F. I. (1992). Sleep and affective disorders. In E. S. Paykel (Ed.), *Handbook of affective disorders* (pp. 311–23). New York: Guilford.

193. Laing, R. D. (1960). *The divided self: An existential study in sanity and madness.* Baltimore: Penguin.

194. Laing, R. D. (1967). *The politics of experience.* New York: Pantheon Books (Random House).

195. Landers, A. (1976). Parents can't absorb total blame. *Austin American-Statesman,* July 27, 1976, p. C2.

196. Landers, A. (1987). Thoughts of a better tomorrow may deter suicidal. *Austin American-Statesman,* April 18, 1987, p. E6.

197. Langer, E. J. (1975). The illusion of control. *Journal of Personality and Social Psychology, 32,* 311–28.

198. Lesse, S. (1974). *Masked depression.* New York: Jason Aronson.

199. LeVay, S. (1991). A difference in hypothalamic structure between

heterosexual and homosexual men. *Science, 253*, 1034–37.

200. Lewin, R. (1980). Is your brain really necessary? *Science*, December 12, 1980, pp. 1232–34.

201. Llosa, M. V. (1992). The importance of Karl Popper. *Academic Questions*, Winter 1991–1992, pp. 16–27.

202. Loehlin, J. C., & Nichols, R. C. (1976). *Heredity, environment, & personality: A study of 850 sets of twins.* Austin, TX: University of Texas Press.

203. Loehlin, J. C., Willerman, L., & Horn, J. (1988). Human behavior genetics. *Annual Review of Psychology, 39*, 101–33.

204. Lorenz, K. (1963/1966). *On aggression.* New York: Bantam.

205. Luce, G. G. (1971). *Body time: Physiological rhythms and social stress.* New York: Pantheon.

206. Lykken, D. T. (1982). Research with twins: The concept of emergenesis. *Psychophysiology, 19*, 361–73.

207. Lykken, D. T., McGue, M., Tellegen, A., & Bouchard, T. J. (1993). Emergenesis: Genetic traits that may not run in families. *American Psychologist, 47*, 1565–77.

208. Mahoney, M. J. (1985). Psychotherapy and human change processes. In M. J. Mahoney & A. Freeman (Eds.), *Cognition and psychotherapy* (pp. 3–48). New York: Plenum.

209. Majeski, T. (1991). Gay teens at risk for suicide, study says. *Austin American-Statesman*, May 31, 1991, p. A7.

210. Malcolm, A. H. (1990). Doctor's act may force confrontation on suicide. *Austin American-Statesman*, June 10, 1990, pp. D1, D4.

211. Mann, J. J., & Kapur, S. (1991). The emergence of suicidal ideation and behavior during antidepressant pharmacotherapy. *Archives of General Psychiatry, 48*, 1027–33.

212. Mann, J. J., Stanley, M., McBride, P. A., & McEwen, B. S. (1986). Increased serotonin$_2$ and ß-adrenergic receptor binding in the frontal cortices of suicide victims. *Archives of General Psychiatry, 43*, 954–59.

213. Marcus, A. D. (1990). Mists of memory cloud some legal proceedings. *The Wall Street Journal*, December 3, 1990, pp. B1, B6.

214. Martinot, J.-L., Hardy, P., Felline, A., Huret, J.-D., Mazoyer, B., Attar-Levy, D., Pappate, S., & Syrota, A. (1990). Left prefrontal glucose hypometabolism in the depressed state: A confirmation. *American Journal of Psychiatry, 147*, 1313–17.

215. Mason, A. A., & Black, S. (1958). Allergic skin response abolished under treatment of asthma and hay fever by hypnosis. *Lancet*, April 26, 1958, pp. 877–80.

216. Mason, J. W. (1975). Clinical psychophysiology: Psychoendocrine mechanisms. In S. Arieti (Ed.), *American handbook of psychiatry* (pp. 553–82). New York: Basic Books.

217. Matarazzo, J. D. (1993). Psychological testing and assessment in the 21st century. *American Psychologist, 47,* 1007–18.
218. Mathews, A., & MacLeod, C. (1986). Discrimination of threat cues without awareness in anxiety states. *Journal of Abnormal Psychology, 95,* 131–38.
219. McCloskey, M. (1983). Intuitive physics. *Scientific American, 248,* 122–30.
220. McClure, J. N., Reich, T., & Wetzel, R. D. (1971). Premenstrual symptoms as indicators of bipolar affective disorder. *British Journal of Psychiatry, 119,* 527–28.
221. McElroy, S. L., Pope, H. G., Jr., Hudson, J. I., Keck, P. E., & White, K. L. (1991). Kleptomania: A report of 20 cases. *American Journal of Psychiatry, 148,* 652–57.
222. McKinney, W. T., & Moran, E. C. (1982). Animal models. In E. S. Paykel (Ed.), *Handbook of affective disorders* (pp. 202–11). New York: Guilford.
223. Medawar, P. B. (1984). *The limits of science.* New York: Harper & Row.
224. Meddis, R. (1977). *The sleep instinct.* London: Routledge & Kegan Paul.
225. Melzack, R. (1992). Phantom limbs. *Scientific American,* April 1992, pp. 120–26.
226. Mendlewicz, J., & Rainer, J. D. (1977). Adoption study supporting genetic transmission in manic-depressive illness. *Nature, 268,* 327–29.
227. Menninger, K., A. (1930). *The human mind.* New York: The Literary Guild.
228. Michell, G. F., Mebane, A. H., & Billings, C. K. (1989). Effect of bupropion on chocolate craving. *American Journal of Psychiatry, 146,* 119–20.
229. Milner, B. (1970). Memory and the medial temporal regions of the brain. In K. H. Pribram & D. E. Broadbent (Eds.), *Biology of memory* (pp. 29–50). New York: Academic Press.
230. Monahan, J., & Shah, S. A. (1989). Dangerousness and commitment of the mentally disordered in the United States. *Schizophrenia Bulletin, 15,* 541–53.
231. Montaigne (1958). We taste nothing pure (Book II, Essay #20). In D. M. Frame (Ed.), *The complete works of Montaigne* (pp. 510–12). Stanford: Stanford University Press.
232. Montgomery, S. A. (1991). Recurrent brief depression. In J. P. Feighner & W. F. Boyer (Eds.), *Diagnosis of depression* (pp. 119–34). Chichester, England: Wiley.
233. Moore, M. S. (1975). Some myths about "mental illness." *Archives of General Psychiatry, 32,* 1483–97.

234. Moscicki, E. K., O'Carroll, P., Rae, D. S., Locke, B. Z., Roy, A., & Regier, D. A. (1988). Suicide attempts in the epidemiologic catchment area study. *The Yale Journal of Biology and Medicine, 61,* 259–68.

235. Murray, H. A. (1940). What should psychologists do about psychoanalysis. *Journal of Abnormal and Social Psychology, 35,* 150–75.

236. Muse, K. N., Cetel, N. S., Futterman, L. A., & Yen, S. S. (1984). The premenstrual syndrome: Effects of medical "ovariectomy." *The New England Journal of Medicine, 311,* 1345–49.

237. Nabokov, V. (1978). Signs and symbols (from *Nabokov's dozen*). In R. V. Cassill (Ed.), *The Norton anthology of short fiction* (pp. 985–90). New York: Norton.

238. Neilson, W. A., & Hill, C. J. (Ed.). (1942). *The complete plays and poems of William Shakespeare.* Cambridge, MA: The Riverside Press.

239. Nisbett, R. E., & Wilson, T. D. (1977). Telling more than we can know: Verbal reports on mental processes. *Psychological Review, 84,* 231–59.

240. Oltmanns, T. F., Neale, J. M., & Davison, G. C. (1986). *Case studies in abnormal psychology* (2nd ed.). New York: Wiley.

241. Oren, D. A., & Rosenthal, N. E. (1992). Seasonal affective disorders. In E. S. Paykel (Ed.), *Handbook of affective disorders* (pp. 551–67). New York: Guilford.

242. Otto, M. W., Yeo, R. A., & Dougher, M. J. (1987). Right hemisphere involvement in depression: Toward a neuropsychological theory of negative affective experiences. *Biological Psychiatry, 22,* 1201–15.

243. Parrington, V. L. (1930). *Main currents in American thought: An interpretation of American literature from the beginnings to 1920: Vol. 2. 1800–1920, The romantic revolution in America.* New York: Harcourt, Brace.

244. Parry, B. L., Berga, S. L., Kripke, D. F., Klauber, M. R., Laughlin, G. A., Yen, S. C., & Gillin, J. C. (1990). Altered waveform of plasma nocturnal melatonin secretion in premenstrual depression. *Archives of General Psychiatry, 47,* 1139–46.

245. Parry, B. L., Berga, S. L., Mostofi, N., Sependa, P. A., Kripke, D. F., & Gillin, J. C. (1989). Morning versus evening bright light treatment of late luteal phase dysphoric disorder. *American Journal of Psychiatry, 146,* 1215–17.

246. Paulos, J. A. (1988). *Innumeracy: Mathematical illiteracy and its consequences.* New York: Hill & Wang (Farrar, Strauss & Giroux).

247. Perutz, M. (1989). *Is science necessary? Essays on science and scientists.* New York: Oxford University Press.

248. Peterson, D. (Ed.). (1982). *A mad people's history of madness.* Pittsburgh: University of Pittsburgh Press.

249. Pincus, J. (1982). Hysteria presenting to the neurologist. In A. Roy (Ed.), *Hysteria* (pp. 131–43). Chichester, England: John Wiley & Sons.

250. Pitt, B. (1982). Depression and childbirth. In E. S. Paykel (Ed.), *Handbook of affective disorders* (pp. 361–78). New York: Guilford.

251. Pool, R. (1990). Closing in on Einstein's special relativity theory. *Science,* November 30, 1990, pp. 1207–1208.

252. Popper, K. R. (1959). *The logic of scientific discovery.* London: Hutchinson.

253. Post, F. (1975). Dementia, depression, and pseudodementia. In D. F. Benson & D. Blumer (Eds.), *Psychiatric aspects of neurological disease* (pp. 99–120). New York: Grune & Stratton.

254. Price, J. (1968). The genetics of depressive disorder. In A. Coppen & A. Walk (Eds.), *British Journal of Psychiatry: Special Publication No. 2. Recent developments in affective disorder* (pp. 37–54). Ashford, England: Headley Brothers.

255. Raine, A., Venables, P. H., & Williams, M. (1990). Relationships between central and autonomic measures of arousal at age 15 and criminality at age 24 years. *Archives of General Psychiatry, 47,* 1003–1007.

256. Ralph, M. R., Foster, R. G., Davis, F. C., & Menaker, M. (1990). Transplanted suprachiasmatic nucleus determines circadian period. *Science, 247,* 975–78.

257. Regier, D. A., Boyd, J. H., Burke, J. D., Rae, D. S., Myers, J. K., Kramer, M., Robins, L. N., George, L. K., Karno, M., & Locke, B. Z. (1988). One-month prevalence of mental disorders in the United States. *Archives of General Psychiatry, 45,* 977–86.

258. Reich, W. (1949). *Character analysis* (T. P. Wolfe, Trans.). (3rd ed.). New York: Noonday (Farrar, Straus, & Cudahy).

259. Robins, C. J., & Luten, A. G. (1991). Sociotropy and autonomy: Differential patterns of clinical presentation in unipolar depression. *Journal of Abnormal Psychology, 100,* 74–77.

260. Robins, E. (1981). *The final months: Study of the lives of 134 persons who committed suicide.* New York: Oxford University Press.

261. Rogers, R. (1987). APA's position on the insanity defense: Empiricism versus emotionalism. *American Psychologist, 42,* 840–48.

262. Root-Bernstein, R. S. (1989). How scientists really think. *Perspectives in Biology and Medicine, 32,* 473–88.

263. Rosch, P. J. (1979). Stress and cancer: A disease of adaption? In J. Taché, H. Selye, & S. B. Day (Eds.), *Cancer stress, and death* (pp. 187–212). New York: Plenum.

264. Rosen, R. (1987). Review of Emily Listfield's *Variations in the night. New York Times,* September 6, 1987, p. 12.

265. Rosenhan, D. L. (1973). On being sane in insane places. *Science, 179,* 250–58.
266. Rosenthal, N. E., Sack, D. A., Skwerer, R. G., Jacobsen, F. M., & Wehr, T. A. (1988). Phototherapy for seasonal affective disorder. *Journal of Biological Rhythms, 3,* 101–20.
267. Ross, C. (1989). *Multiple personality disorder: Diagnosis, clinical features, and treatment.* New York: Wiley.
268. Roy, A. (1989). Pseudoseizures: A psychiatric perspective. *Journal of Neuropsychiatry, 1,* 69–72.
269. Roy, A., Segal, N. L., Centerwall, B. S., & Robinette, D. (1991). Suicide in twins. *Archives of General Psychiatry, 48,* 29–32.
270. Rubinow, D. R., Roy-Byrne, P., Hoban, M. C., Gold, P. W., & Post, R. M. (1984). Prospective assessment of menstrually related mood disorders. *American Journal of Psychiatry, 141,* 684–86.
271. Sack, R., Lewy, A. J., White, D. M., Singer, C. M., Fireman, M. J., & Vandiver, R. (1990). Morning vs. evening light treatment for winter depression. *Archives of General Psychiatry, 47,* 343–51.
272. Sackeim, H. A., & Gur, R. C. (1978). Self-deception, self-confrontation, and consciousness. In G. E. Schwartz & D. Shapiro (Eds.), *Consciousness and self-regulation: Advances in research and theory* (pp. 139–97). New York: Plenum.
273. Sacks, O. (1976). *Awakenings.* New York: Vintage Books.
274. Sacks, O. (1984). *A leg to stand on.* New York: Summit.
275. Sacks, O. (1985). *The man who mistook his wife for a hat: And other clinical tales.* New York: Summit Books (Simon & Schuster).
276. Salzman, C., & Shader, R. I. (1979). Clinical evaluation of depression in the elderly. In A. Raskin & L. F. Jarvik (Eds.), *Psychiatric symptoms and cognitive loss in the elderly* (pp. 39–72). New York: Halsted Press (Wiley).
277. Samenow, S. E. (1984). *Inside the criminal mind.* New York: Times Books (Random House).
278. Sargent, J. K., Bruce, M. L., Florio, L. P., & Weissman, M. M. (1990). Factors associated with 1-year outcome of major depression in the community. *Archives of General Psychiatry, 47,* 519–26.
279. Scarr, S. (1992). Developmental theories for the 1990s: Development and individual differences. *Child Development, 63,* 1–19.
280. Schafer, R. (1954). *Psychoanalytic interpretation in Rorschach testing: Theory and application.* New York: Grune & Stratton.
281. Schallert, T. (1983). Sensorimotor impairment and recovery of function in brain-damaged rats: Reappearance of symptoms during old age. *Behavioral Neuroscience, 97,* 159–64.
282. Schatzman, M. (1973). Paranoia or persecution: The case of Schreber. *History of Childhood Quarterly, 1,* 62–88.

283. Scheier, M. F., Buss, A. H., & Buss, D. M. (1978). Self-consciousness, self-report of aggressiveness, and aggression. *Journal of Research in Personality, 12,* 133–40.

284. Schulsinger, F., Kety, S., Rosenthal, D., & et al. (1981). A family study of suicide. In *Third World Congress of Biological Psychiatry.* Stockholm, Sweden, July 1981.

285. Schulsinger, F., Kety, S. S., Rosenthal, D., & Wender, P. H. (1979). A family study of suicide. In M. Schou & E. Stromgren (Eds.), *Origin, prevention and treatment of affective disorders* (pp. 277–87). London: Academic Press.

286. Seligman, M. E. P. (1975). *Helplessness: On depression, development, and death.* San Francisco: Freeman.

287. Shagass, C. (1976). The medical model in psychiatry. In E. J. Sachar (Ed.), *Hormones, behavior, and psychopathology* (pp. 291–300). New York: Raven.

288. Shneidman, E. (1985). *The definition of suicide.* New York: Wiley.

289. Shneidman, E. S. (1972). Classifications of suicidal phenomena. In B. Q. Hafen & E. J. Faux (Eds.), *Self destructive behavior: A national crisis* (pp. 10–22). Minneapolis: Burgess.

290. Sifneos, P. E. (1972). *Short-term psychotherapy and emotional crisis.* Cambridge, MA: Harvard University Press.

291. Sims, A. (1988). *Symptoms in the mind: An introduction to descriptive psychopathology.* London: Baillière Tindall.

292. Singer, S. F. (1989). Machines won't end air terrorism. *The Wall Street Journal,* June 20, 1989, p. A18.

293. Slater, E., & Glithero, E. (1965). A follow-up of patients diagnosed as suffering from "hysteria." *Journal of Psychosomatic Research, 9,* 9–13.

294. Sommerschield, H., & Reyher, J. (1973). Posthypnotic conflict, repression, and psychopathology. *Journal of Abnormal Psychology, 82,* 278–90.

295. Spitzer, R. L., Skodol, A. E., Gibbon, M., & Williams, J. B. (1983). *Psychopathology: A casebook.* New York: McGraw-Hill.

296. Stanovich, K. (1989). *How to think straight about psychology* (2nd ed.). Glenview, IL: Scott, Foresman.

297. Steele, C. M., & Josephs, R. A. (1990). Alcohol myopia: Its prized and dangerous effects. *American Psychologist, 45,* 921–33.

298. Stone, J. (1988). Sex and the single gorilla. *Discover,* August 1988, pp. 78–81.

299. Stoudemire, A., Frank, R., Hedemark, N., Kamlet, M., & Blazer, D. (1986). The economic burden of depression. *General Hospital Psychiatry, 8,* 387–94.

300. Strauss, J. S. (1989). Subjective experiences of schizophrenia:

Toward a new dynamic psychiatry–II. *Schizophrenia Bulletin,* 15(2), 179–87.

301. Suddath, R. L., Christison, G. W., Torrey, E. F., Casanova, M. F., & Weinberger, D. R. (1990). Anatomical abnormalities in the brains of monozygotic twins discordant for schizophrenia. *The New England Journal of Medicine, 322,* 789–94.

302. Suzuki, D. T. (1956). *Zen Buddhism—Selected Writings of D. T. Suzuki.* New York: Doubleday (Anchor Books).

303. Swann, W. B. (1990). To be adored or known? The interplay of self-enhancement and self-verification. In R. M. Sorrentino & E. T. Higgins (Eds.), *Motivation and cognition* (pp. 408–48). New York: Guilford.

304. Swann, W. B., Jr., Wenzlaff, R. M., & Tafarodi, R. W. (1992). Depression and the search for negative evaluations: More evidence of the role of self-verification strivings. *Journal of Abnormal Psychology, 101,* 314–17.

305. Symons, D. (1979). *The evolution of human sexuality.* New York: Oxford University Press.

306. Szasz (1976). Interview with *The New Physician,* June 1969. In F. W. Miller, R. O. Dawson, G. E. Dix, & R. I. Parnas (Eds.), *The mental health process.* Mineola, NY: The Foundation Press.

307. Szasz, T. (1960). The myth of mental illness. *American Psychologist, 15,* 113–18.

308. Tabachnick, N., & Faberow, N. L. (1974). Accidents as depressive equivalents. In S. Lesse (Eds.), *Masked depression* (pp. 273–301). New York: Jason Aronson.

309. Tagore, R. (1958). *Collected poems and plays of Rabindranath Tagore.* New York: Macmillan.

310. Taylor, G. J. (1990). Alexithymia: Concept, measurement, and implications for treatment. *American Journal of Psychiatry, 141,* 725–32.

311. Taylor, S. E. (1983). Adjustment to threatening events: A theory of cognitive adaptation. *American Psychologist, 38,* 1161–73.

312. Taylor, S. E., & Brown, J. D. (1988). Illusion and well-being: A social psychological perspective on mental health. *Psychological Bulletin, 103,* 193–210.

313. Terr, L. C. (1991). Childhood traumas: An outline and overview. *American Journal of Psychiatry, 148,* 10–20.

314. Thomas, H., Jamison, W., & Hummel, D. D. (1973). Observation is insufficient for discovering that the surface of still water is invariantly horizontal. *Science, 181,* 173–74.

315. Tigay, J. H. (1985 / 1986). The book of Jonah and the days of awe. *Conservative Judaism, 38(2),* 67–78.

316. Tiger, L. (1979). *Optimism: The biology of hope*. New York: Simon & Schuster (Touchstone Books).

317. Toynbee, A. J. (1947). *A study of history*. New York: Oxford University Press.

318. Tsuang, M. T., Lyons, M. J., & Farone, S. V. (1987). Problems of diagnosis in family studies. *Journal of Psychiatric Research, 21,* 391–99.

319. Tversky, A., & Kahneman, D. (1974). Judgment under uncertainty: Heuristics and biases. *Science, 185,* 1124–31.

320. van Lawick-Goodall, J. (1971). *In the shadow of man*. Boston: Houghton Mifflin.

321. Weinberg, S. (1992). *Dreams of a final theory*. New York: Pantheon.

322. Weinstein, N. D. (1989). Optimistic biases about personal risks. *Science, 246,* 246–47.

323. Weissman, M. M., Leaf, P. J., Tischler, G. L., Blazer, D. G., Karno, M., Bruce, M. L., & Florio, L. P. (1988). Affective disorders in five United States communities. *Psychological Medicine, 18,* 141–53.

324. Weissman, M. M., Wickramaratne, P., Merikangas, K. R., Leckman, J. F., Prusoff, B. A., Caruso, K. A., Kidd, K. K., & Gammon, G. D. (1984). Onset of major depression in early childhood: Increased familial loading and specificity. *Archives of General Psychiatry, 41,* 1136–43.

325. Wells, K. B., Golding, J. M., & Burnam, M. A. (1989). Chronic medical conditions in a sample of the general population with anxiety, affective and substance use disorders. *American Journal of Pyschiatry, 146,* 1440–46.

326. Wells, K. B., Hays, R. D., Burnam, M. A., Rogers, W., Greenfield, J., & Ware, J. E., Jr. (1989). Detection of depressive disorder for patients receiving prepaid or fee-for-service care: Results from the Medical Outcomes Study. *Journal of the American Medical Association, 262,* 3298–3302.

327. Wender, P. H., Kety, S. S., Rosenthal, D., Schulsinger, F., Ortmann, J., & Lunde, I. (1986). Psychiatric disorders in the biological and adoptive families of adopted individuals with affective disorders. *Archives of General Psychiatry, 43,* 923–29.

328. Wender, P. H., Rosenthal, D., Kety, S. S., Schulsinger, F., & Welner, J. (1974). Crossfostering: A research strategy for clarifying the role of genetic and experiential factors in the etiology of schizophrenia. *Archives of General Psychiatry, 30,* 121–28.

329. Wigdor, A. K., & Garner, W. R. (Ed.). (1982). *Ability testing: Uses, consequences, and controversies: Volume 1. Report of the committee. Volume 2. Documentation section*. Washington DC: National Academy Press.

330. Willerman, L., & Cohen, D. B. (1990). *Psychopathology*. New York: McGraw-Hill.

331. Willerman, L., Loehlin, J. C., & Horn, J. M. (1992). An adoption and a cross-fostering study of the Minnesota Multiphasic Personality Inventory (MMPI) Psychopathic Deviate Scale. *Behavior Genetics, 22,* 515–29.

332. Willner, P. (1985). *Depression: A psychobiological synthesis.* New York: Wiley-Interscience.

333. Wilson, E. O. (1978). *On human nature.* Cambridge, MA: Harvard University Press.

334. Wilson, J. Q., & Herrnstein, R. J. (1985). *Crime and human nature.* New York: Simon & Schuster.

335. Wilson, R. S. (1978). Synchronies in mental development: An epigenetic perspective. *Science, 202,* 939–48.

336. Witkin, H. A., Mednick, S. A., Shulsinger, F., Bakkestrom, E., Christiansen, K. O., Goodenough, D. R., Hirschorn, K., et al. (1977). Criminality, aggression, and intelligence among XYY and XXY men. In S. A. Mednick & K. O. Christiansen (Eds.), *Biosocial bases of criminal behavior.* New York: Gardner Press.

337. Wolpert, E. A. (1990). Rapid cycling in unipolar and bipolar affective disorders. *American Journal of Psychiatry, 147,* 725–28.

338. Wragg, R. E., & Jeste, D. V. (1989). Overview of depression and psychosis in Alzheimer's disease. *American Journal of Psychiatry, 146,* 577–87.

339. Wu, J. C., & Bunney, W. E. (1990). The biological basis of an antidepressant response to sleep deprivation and relapse: Review and hypothesis. *American Journal of Psychiatry, 147,* 14–21.

340. Wurtman, R. J., & Wurtman, J. J. (1989). Carbohydrates and depression. *Scientific American, 260* (January 1989), 68–75.

341. Yochelson, S., & Samenow, S. E. (1976). *The criminal personality: A profile for change* (Vol. 1). New York: Jason Aronson.

342. Zajonc, R. B. (1980). On the primacy of affect. *American Psychologist, 39,* 117–23.

343. Zilboorg, G. (1941). *A history of medical psychology.* New York: Norton.

ADDITIONAL SOURCES

Adams, F. (1886). *The genuine works of Hippocrates* (Vol. 2). New York: William Wood and Company.

Alison, A. (1859). *Lives of Lord Castlereagh and Sir Charles Stewart* (Vol. 3). Edinburgh: William Blackwood & Sons.

American Psychiatric Association (1987). *Diagnostic and statistical manual of mental disorders* (3rd ed., rev.—*DSM-III-R*). Washington, DC: American Psychiatric Association.

Bell, Q. (1972). *Virginia Woolf: A Biography*. New York: Harcourt Brace Jovanovich.

Beveridge, W. I. B. (1950). *The art of scientific investigation*. New York: Vintage (Random House).

Brunner, H. G., Nelen, M. R., van Zandvoort, P., et al. X-linked borderline mental retardation with prominent behavioral disturbance: Phenotype, genetic location, and evidence for disturbed monoamine metabolism. *American Journal of Human Genetics, 52*, 1032–39.

Burton, R. (1927/1620). *The anatomy of melancholy*. New York: Tudor.

Camus, A. (1955). *The myth of Sisyphus* (J. O'Brien, Trans.). New York: Vintage Books (Random House).

Darwin, C. (1871). *The descent of man*. New York: The Modern Library.

Darwin, C. (1956). *The autobiography of Charles Darwin, 1809–1882*. New York: Harcourt, Brace.

Doubleday, H. A., & de Walden, L. H. (Ed.). (1932). *The complete peerage*. London: St. Catherine Press.

FitzGerald, E. (1947). *Rubáiyát of Omar Khayyám*. New York: Random House.

Fitzgerald, F. S. (1962). The crack-up. In C. Shrodes, C. Josephson, & J. R. Wilson (Eds.), *Readings for rhetoric: Applications to writing* (pp. 52–56). New York: Macmillan.

Goethe, J. W. v. (1962). *The sorrows of young Werther* (C. Hutter, Trans.). New York: New American Library of World Literature (Signet).

Hinde, W. (1981). *Castlereagh.* London: William Collins Sons.

Hyde, H. M. (1959). *The strange death of Lord Castlereagh.* London: Heinemann.

James, W. (1958). *The varieties of religious experience: A study in human nature.* New York: New American Library.

Jelliffe, S. E. (1911). Cyclothymia—The mild forms of manic-depressive psychoses and manic-depressive constitution. *American Journal of Insanity, 67,* 661–76.

Koestler, A. (1963). *Darkness at noon.* New York: Macmillan.

Lewis, C. S. (1947). *The abolition of man.* New York: Macmillan.

Lewis, C. S. (1962). *The problem of pain.* New York: Collier Books (Macmillan).

Mann, T. (1969/1924). The making of *The magic mountain.* In T. Mann, *The magic mountain* (pp. 717–27). New York: Vintage (Random House).

Melville, H. (1970). Billy Budd, Sailor. In H. Beaver (Ed.), *Billy Budd, sailor and other stories.* New York: Penguin Books.

Milosz, C. (1953). *The captive mind* (J. Zielonko, Trans.). New York: Vintage Books (Random House).

Mullahy, P. (1948). *Oedipus: Myth and complex.* New York: Hermitage Press.

Shelley, M. (1818/1984). *Frankenstein; or, the modern Prometheus.* Berkeley: The Pennyroyal Press/University of California Press.

Shrodes, C., Josephson, C., & Wilson, J. R. (Eds.). (1962). *Readings for rhetoric: Applications to writing.* New York: Macmillan.

Tolstoi, L. (1964). My life has come to a sudden stop (excerpt from "My Confession," 1887). In B. Kaplan (Ed.), *The inner world of mental illness* (pp. 405–11). New York: Harper & Row.

Wolf-Man (1971). *The Wolf-Man.* New York: Basic Books.

INDEX